MORE THAN THE EYE CAN SEE

MORE THAN THE EYE CAN SEE

Memoirs of Gopinath Pillai

Gopinath Pillai with John Vater

World Scientific

NEW JERSEY • LONDON • SINGAPORE • BEIJING • SHANGHAI • HONG KONG • TAIPEI • CHENNAI • TOKYO

Published by

World Scientific Publishing Co. Pte. Ltd.

5 Toh Tuck Link, Singapore 596224

USA office: 27 Warren Street, Suite 401-402, Hackensack, NJ 07601

UK office: 57 Shelton Street, Covent Garden, London WC2H 9HE

Library of Congress Cataloging-in-Publication Data
Names: Pillai, Gopinath, author. | Vater, John, author.
Title: More than the eye can see: memoirs of Gopinath Pillai / Gopinath Pillai; with John Vater.
Other titles: Memoirs of Gopinath Pillai
Description: New Jersey: World Scientific, [2022] | Includes bibliographical references and index.
Identifiers: LCCN 2022011167 (print) | LCCN 2022011168 (ebook) |
ISBN 9789811255670 (hardcover) | ISBN 9789811256370 (paperback) |
ISBN 9789811255748 (ebook)
Subjects: LCSH: Diplomats--Singapore--Biography. | Businessmen--Singapore--Biography. |
Singapore--History--20th century. | East Indians--Singapore--Biography.
Classification: LCC DS610.63.P55 A3 2022 (print) | LCC DS610.63.P55 (ebook) |
DDC 959.57/04092 [B]--dc23/eng/20220308
LC record available at https://lccn.loc.gov/2022011167
LC ebook record available at https://lccn.loc.gov/2022011168

British Library Cataloguing-in-Publication Data
A catalogue record for this book is available from the British Library.

For any available supplementary material, please visit
https://www.worldscientific.com/worldscibooks/10.1142/12816#t=suppl

Printed in Singapore

"The ultimate measure of a man is not where he stands in moments of comfort and convenience, but where he stands at times of challenge and controversy."

— Martin Luther King, 1963

"The fault, dear Brutus, is not in our stars,
But in ourselves, that we are underlings."

— William Shakespeare, *Julius Caesar*, 1599

Contents

Foreword by Emeritus Senior Minister Goh Chok Tong ix

Preface xiii

Acknowledgements xvii

Part I: Early Life

1. Birth in Singapore and Childhood in India 3
2. The Communist Movement in Kerala 16
3. A Strange New Home 24
4. School Days (Or, Learning the Language of a New Country) 40
5. University Life 54
6. A Young Lady 70
7. Journalism and Teaching 77
8. Happy Thailand (*Sawadikrab*) 88
9. A "Homecoming" to Malaysia 99
10. An Unexpected Return 109

Part II: Professional Career

11. Raya Mills: The Internationalisation of My Outlook 117
12. Transitioning to a High-Value Economy 126
13. United Industrial Corporation: My Engagement with Taiwan 133
14. Intraco: Forum for the Unheard of and Unexpected 141
15. Inno-Pacific: American Franchises and the High Court 152
16. Breaking into India: A New Era for Entrepreneurs 159
17. Observations and Lessons from Entrepreneurship 168

Part III: Public Service and Extracurricular Activities

18. Non-Resident Ambassador to Iran (1989–2008) 183
19. Friends from Far Places: Ministerial Visits to Iran 197
20. Non-Resident High Commissioner to Pakistan (1994–2001) 211
21. Paying It Forward: A Guild House and Supermarket 218
22. Tradition and the Hindu Endowments Board 231
23. Community Contributions and the Indian Heritage Centre 243
24. ISAS and the South Asian Diaspora in Singapore 257

Part IV: Conclusion

25. A "Medical Diary" 267
26. Parting Observations 275

Notes 281

Index 299

About the Authors 305

Foreword

If I had to summarise Gopinath Pillai in one sentence, it would be, "No matter what task he undertakes, he drives it with passion." He describes himself as a "Jack of all trades" but actually is a versatile man of many talents.

First, Gopi is a member of that special pioneer generation of Singaporeans who laid the bricks of independent Singapore. Call him a bricklayer. Second, he ventured into business during the early years of Singapore's independence, instead of choosing the security of the Public Service. Third, following my remarks on injecting Singapore with a "mild India fever" after my visit to India as Prime Minister, he invested there, showing his entrepreneurial side. Fourth, Gopi was part of the founding batch of Non-Resident Ambassadors (NRAs). He served as Singapore's NRA to Iran as well as Non-Resident High Commissioner to Pakistan. He served a total of eighteen years, the longest serving NRA outside the Ministry of Foreign Affairs. Fifth, he shouldered other public duties when called upon. Lastly, he is a writer!

I interacted with Gopi occasionally as Prime Minister and more frequently thereafter. He convinced me that both Iran and Pakistan were friends worth making. I got to know him up close when he accompanied me on my two visits to Iran in 2004 and 2007 as well as one to Pakistan in 2004. He understood their politics and took a deep interest in their culture.

On our visit to a grand mosque in the historical city of Esfahan, the accompanying Iranian official recited a verse by Omar Khayyam to extol its beauty. "Are you able to do it?" I teased Gopi. "I will try," he replied, and went on to recite several verses. Later, over dinner, he said to the governor-general in Farsi, "Esfahan nesf-e-jahan", meaning "Esfahan is half the world". A good diplomat indeed!

In the 1990s, Gopi had established his own companies in India and built up a strong network of connections. In fact, Gopi was the one who suggested that I visit Gujarat in 2006, when Narendra Modi was its Chief Minister. I am glad I did.

As India grew in geopolitical and economic importance, I thought Singapore should have its own research institute to understand India and South Asia better. I turned to Gopi. He took up my challenge and set up the Institute of South Asian Studies (ISAS) within a few months with Professor Tan Tai Yong as Interim Director. Gopi has been its Founding Chairman since 2004. He raised funds for ISAS and helped ISAS build up good links with India. Today, ISAS is well established and well regarded. Its research gives Singaporeans useful insight into developments in South Asia. It has strengthened ties between Singapore and our South Asian partners.

Gopi has also contributed to Singapore's Indian and South Asian heritage as the Chairman of the Hindu Advisory Board.

Gopi's life journey parallels the many decades of Singapore's growth from a fledgling and vulnerable nation to a prosperous and advanced country. *More Than the Eye Can See* is an appropriate title for a book whose sweep encompasses notable milestones in Singapore's history, beyond the average Singaporean reader's memory. Beyond his own stories, the book also captures the zeitgeist of the times and how the Singapore Spirit evolved with each passing decade. He offers us a glimpse into the social, political and economic life of Singapore and the region through experiences that are not found in textbooks.

His is a wonderful example of the Singapore Story — one of humble beginnings, choosing to settle down in Singapore, managing businesses before establishing one of his own and dedicating himself to public service. It is through the contributions of the pioneer generation like Gopi that Singapore became the successful, meritocratic and harmonious multi-racial society it is today.

Gopi and I are now in our eighties. We have both done our part for Singapore. I hope that reading Gopi's memoir will inspire you to do what you can to keep Singapore glowing.

GOH CHOK TONG
Emeritus Senior Minister
Prime Minister of Singapore (1990–2004)

Preface

I first got the idea to write my memoirs after encouragement from friends, and then talking it over with my family. We are a private family in the sense that we do not believe there is too much to crow about. However, several years ago, I began to get offers from well-wishers to transcribe my interviews and research my life. Ambassador K. Kesavapany, who has himself authored an autobiography, offered to lend a hand, saying, "If you want to write, I will get you a publisher." Many who encouraged me thought I had a story to tell. But I had my reservations, because I felt that such a book would be preaching to the already converted — I did not want my memoirs to imply that what I had achieved was necessarily impressive or remarkable.

Firstly, in preparing to author my story, I wanted to partner with someone who could view my life neutrally and objectively — someone careful and not too partisan. I met my co-author, Mr. John Vater, at the Institute of South Asian Studies, where he worked as a researcher. After hearing his views on contemporary political events, I began to think about how we might work together. I was pleased when he agreed to work on this book. Secondly, as regards the book's contents, I wanted my family to be comfortable with what I had written and to produce a record that would be worthwhile for my descendants.

The stories I have decided to narrate, I should probably explain, emerged in a roughshod manner: I did not curate them or intend them for larger messaging. I wanted to share tales that I felt honestly reflected my journey through life as well as my forays into different countries and occupational fields. The chapters correspondingly have fallen into a sequence, which, maybe indirectly, reflects something about the country's economic, social and political evolution over the past eighty-odd years.

I have always been an enthusiastic storyteller. When recounting certain more "lighthearted" incidents, I often found something humorous to add. The reader, therefore, might not be wrong in wondering whether I am always being straightforward with my accounts. I have always had this habit, you see, of narrating little vignettes, to see how people react. The purpose has not been to "test them out" on anybody. Rather, some anecdotes simply flit across one's mind, which the storyteller builds on with amusement. This layering, in my opinion, adds colour and vibrancy to the text. Readability is also important, and I want my readers to be entertained.

Having said that, readability should not compromise on the facts, and John and I have tried our best to verify them wherever possible. Some memories extend further back than written records allowed us to trace, while others were sometimes far from John's own experience. Where veracity was unclear, we have added caveats like "to the best of my knowledge" or "as far as I can recall".

Several episodes were especially formative in the evolution of my character. These may be worth briefly highlighting here. Shortly before World War II, my mother decided to take my sister and me to visit my grandparents in India. My father and two uncles, meanwhile, had remained in Singapore throughout the war. I spent my childhood in a fairly well-off atmosphere at my grandfather's home village, isolated in the idyllic countryside in Kerala. My grandfather belonged to a now non-existent class of landowner, and we got by with enough from the land.

A memorable incident from this period was when my favourite uncle left home and joined the Communist Youth Movement. This shaped my early political leanings. My mother's legacy — as perhaps the single-most important influence of my life — impressed itself on me through the various stories she told during this sojourn. These stories taught me how to act correctly and associate myself with different environments.

After spending nearly seven years in India, we returned to Singapore in 1946. I was nine years old when our ship drew into the Penang harbour. My father kept his job at the Adelphi Hotel during the Japanese

Occupation (1942–45), and after my arrival was doing well running a printing business. This business later expanded to include one of Singapore's first newspapers in Malayalam, my mother tongue and the language of Kerala. Its success made settling down in an unfamiliar country for a young boy like me easier. Compared to my uncle, my father was not attracted to Marxism; he believed that just because certain social sections had it rough, their hardship did not mean the communists were automatically guilt-free in the type of lifestyles they led — or that by virtue of being communist, they were bound to treat others kindly.

My family's relatively comfortable situation changed after my father encouraged my mother to run as a candidate in Singapore's 1948 Legislative Council Election. He regrettably underestimated the costs required to win, which took a toll on his business. What impacted me as a boy was discovering how people change their attitudes towards you depending on how well you do in life. My father had performed well previously with his printing business and position at the hotel. His only mistake was in believing he would be equally as successful in managing an election campaign. When his electoral hopes for my mother were dashed, it commenced a downward trend. We had a nice house that was later sold off, and we moved to rented premises.

Like most setbacks, our circumstances improved gradually. But I realised how, for good or for ill, success shines a light on all the other things one stands for. For instance, people might ask for your views, but if you are not excelling in your field, they might not take you as seriously. This is why, when I began work, I ensured that in whatever field I occupied, I gave it all that I had, and carried out my work in earnest. This applied to my first job at *Reuters* and later Raffles Institution and Bangkok Bank in Thailand. Later on, I worked in Singapore's emerging corporate sector, broke into new markets in India and met foreign leaders as a Singaporean diplomat.

I did not set out, sword in hand, to conquer the world. Rather, opportunities just presented themselves that allowed me to work hard at it and produce results, which, fortunately, my employers appreciated. If I am able to express the feeling correctly, my desire was never to look for rewards. Rather, I strove to feel satisfied with the work I have done, according to my estimation, and to belong fully to those worlds in which I exist. Professionally speaking, this meant blending what the country was doing with the work that I found interesting and useful. I felt I should play my part, so that I could say at the end of the day I did justice to myself and those around me.

My story thus reflects my multifaceted experiences and some of the unconventional paths that I have tread. While there may be diplomats and politicians who reflect in memoirs on their official responsibilities, fewer perhaps tell the story of what it was like integrating as an Indian boy into Chinese culture. Or who took risks as a trader in India. Or who built up his community heritage. Or saw, from the eyes of a businessman, how Singapore evolved into an international hub for trade and commerce.

I did sometimes have the worry whether all these engagements might make me a "jack of all trades but a master of none". However, I have balanced this concern by gaining as much knowledge from whatever professional framework I was working in as possible — what you might call an experience-based or insider's knowledge. I sincerely hope that these stories will interest readers curious about Singapore's history and economic development; how a certain section of India's diaspora came to reside and thrive in Singapore; and how business and diplomacy opened paths for opportunity and friendship.

GOPINATH PILLAI
Former Ambassador-at-Large
Ministry of Foreign Affairs, Singapore (2008–2021)

October 2021

Acknowledgements

Writing a book is an investment and, in making its dream a reality, there are several people whom John and I would like to thank. Readers often imagine the writing of a book as a solitary exercise, with a writer alone at his desk. But often there is a whole team silently toiling behind the scenes, providing substantive comments and helping to enhance the book's accuracy and quality. John and I are truly indebted to them and wish to express our appreciation and gratitude.

Firstly, we wish to thank those friends and colleagues who sat down with me in the past for various interviews on my life. These published interviews allowed John and I to cross-reference my experiences and prompted many of the topics we discussed in our innumerable meetings together. While a few such interviews appear in the references, there are a couple of interviewers whom we wish to thank in particular. Mr. Santanu Gupta's comprehensive interview with me for the Oral History Centre in 2013 became a palimpsest around which John and I structured notable episodes in this book. We expanded upon several stories that I had shared there by fleshing them out with added context and sharper details, including those thoughts and feelings that arose during pivotal personal life junctures.

I also want to thank Professor Robin Jeffrey for the interview he did with me in 2017 on my early life in Kerala; and Ms. Sithara Doriasamy, for sharing that interview with us for reference. That conversation helped to concretise some details from my faraway childhood reminiscences. Facts from my life as a businessman — often involving the byzantine twists and turns of companies' mergers and acquisitions — could at times be difficult to recall. We are grateful to my secretary, Ms. Judy Choo, for helping to retrieve such details and, more broadly, for her logistical assistance throughout the entire writing process. I also must thank those who assisted in producing *Gateway Distriparks: The Story of a Successful Singapore–India Joint Venture*, a publication of Gateway Distriparks Ltd. We adapted material from two prefatory pieces I had written there for my chapter on learning experiences and observations from doing business in India.

Every book needs a good editor. We thank Mr. Hernaikh Singh for his views on an earlier draft and introducing us to World Scientific; and Mr. Muhammad Yusuf Bin Yacob, for assisting us in formatting the photographs provided in the book for print. Mr. Anirudh Srivathsan assisted us with the index. We appreciate our editor at World Scientific, Ms. Kim Tan, for her patience as we undertook revisions amidst a few concerning health setbacks that I had. We also commend Mr. Jimmy Low for producing a cover that captures the book's spirit, and are grateful to the Indian Heritage Centre and Indira Iswaran, particularly, for granting permission to use two photographs of historic importance.

My younger daughter, Priya, and I had written several draft chapters when I first attempted to start my memoirs some years ago; these were later discovered and have worked their way into the final version of this book. Finally, the debts John and I accrued to my wife and my elder daughter, Preetha, for their indefatigable efforts cannot be repaid — theirs was the true labour of love. They reviewed drafts of the book chapters, offered creative line edits and corrected facts. They also assisted in selecting photographs and scheduled my meetings with John so that we were able to convene safely during the pandemic.

With a thrill of excitement and tremor of trepidation, John and I set down our pens and now pronounce the work "done". We are immensely grateful to Emeritus Senior Minister Goh Chok Tong for his glowing and encouraging 'Foreword', which has given the book a boost. In addition, I extend my humble thanks to all my colleagues in Singapore with whom I have worked closely, as well as those impressive individuals I met abroad, who furnished me with opportunities and experiences that have enriched this book. Their influences have been "More Than the Eye Can See".

Like Mr. Goh mentioned in his 'Foreword', I have also now entered my eighties. Due to problems with my eyesight, I could not scour through the final text, as it is my habit to do. But John has read the final version and earlier iterations aloud to me; and my family picked through the text and proofs with a fine-toothed comb. Any remaining errors are the fault of the authors. I have been involved with many investments in my time. However, writing this book has been a unique venture, for — through the process of re-living and re-examining my memories — part of my investment has already been returned. Momentarily, a Singapore of old was magically restored.

Part I

Early Life

With my mother at four months, 1937.

1

Birth in Singapore and Childhood in India

"Our life in Singapore thus began as a family affair, and the family supported one another... We had a small community that found it reassuring to spend time together: it alleviated pangs for home, and the elder generation spoke to one another in Malayalam, which was a comfort."

Birth in Singapore

In Charles Dickens' classic novel *David Copperfield*, the protagonist opens his biography by declaring, "Whether I shall turn out to be the hero of my own life, or whether that station will be held by somebody else, these pages must show." It is not my intention to come across as some sort of hero. These are my memories, my life as I have lived it, seen through my eyes. If a reader is able to gain something, however minute, from reading my story, that is a plus.

I have always had a good, long-term memory. And so, like our friend Mr. Copperfield, I would like to "begin my life with the beginning of my life". I was born in Singapore on September 18th on the second floor of a shophouse on Rangoon Road, delivered with the help of a midwife and two elderly aunties. The year was 1937. It was the year when the world was swept away by romance — the Duke of Windsor, Edward VIII, had married an American divorcee by the name of Wallis Simpson after abdicating the throne in 1936. On a more sobering note, it was also the year many were still reeling from the effects of the Great Depression. Hitler's power and influence were growing in Europe; and it was reported that during November of that year, he would have a secret meeting at the Reich Chancellery to state his plans to acquire "living space" for the German people. Closer to home several months earlier, Japan had attacked China. Some saw this as the start of World War II in Asia.

My arrival into the world came after the death of my older brother, also named Gopinath, of meningitis. He was only about a year old. My anxious parents called on an astrologer to guide them through the trial of their son's illness. (Such consultations are not uncommon in Hindu families, who may call on astrologers during unintelligible life moments such as this one.) The astrologer predicted that my brother was unlikely to live for long, as he was supposedly a "saintly" person who had been through many cycles of rebirth already — he was meant to only tarry a short while with the family.

"You will have another son," the astrologer nevertheless consoled my mother, "who will live a full life and will look after you in your old age." True to the astrologer's words, about ten to eleven months after my brother's death, I entered the world with much expected of me. According to my parents, it was an easy birth.

My father arrived in Singapore from the southern Indian state of Kerala in the mid-1920s, where he got a job as an accounts clerk at the Adelphi Hotel. Malayalees, as the people of Kerala are known, had been arriving in Singapore and Malaya since the start of the 20th century to find jobs and embark on a new life for themselves. In general, they worked as clerks, teachers and junior assistants to the British in the plantations and in the government. For instance, there were many Malayalees working at the British naval base and British establishments in administrative positions in the Seletar area.[1]

My father proved to be quite adept with numbers, and his friends recommended that he pay a visit to the Adelphi Hotel, connected to the Sarkies family through a Swiss-Jewish group called Messers Sarkies, Johannes and Co. He was not a qualified accountant, but at the time the hotel did not have skilled accountants of any kind in their employ, and he was taken on. He was entrusted with the practical duty of handling accounts with the other junior clerks.

My father's position was not uncommon for Indians coming to Singapore at the turn of the century. Young people with at least a basic education and a fair knowledge of English, especially from South India, arrived in sizeable numbers on the lookout for jobs. Many would go back to India to get married and then return with fresh brides; some needed cash, while others wanted to escape from their stifling family atmospheres.

I never spoke in depth with my father about his reasons for leaving India for Singapore. But as far as I know, he sought greater independence for himself. Several of my mother's family members had also by this time already married and settled down on the island. My mother was a medical student at Madras Medical College but was persuaded to wrap up her studies after her second year when her uncle, Mr. M. R. Menon, the principal of a successful commercial school at the Young Men's Christian Association (Y.M.C.A) on Stamford Road, arranged a good "match" for her with my father.

My mother's family at that time were in the midst of some financial constraints and were struggling to pay her education fees. They said, "What's the point in having a girl study medicine, if she gets married and forgets everything once she becomes busy with children?"

It was when M. R. Menon was visiting Kerala to marry one of my mother's aunts that he promised to fix up her marriage. My father, he told her family, was doing well in his job and would make a suitable groom. My mother was an obedient daughter and did not protest giving up her studies, knowing full well it would be futile. But when I was old enough to understand a little better, I could tell from her tale that she was not fully satisfied with the arrangement. Luckily, she found my father's personality pleasant enough, not least because he was not your run-of-the-mill Indian businessman. Indeed, he was a bit of an intellectual, what we call *Bad'dhika* in Malayalam, with an interest in journalism.

My mother migrated to Singapore and married my father in May 1933. Their first child, my older sister, Sree Kumari, was born about a year after in June 1934 in my grandfather's house in Kerala, as it was our custom for women to return to their parents' house to give birth. My sister's birth was greeted with jubilation, as she was the first girl to be born in the extended family in several decades. (The birth of a girl is important to matriarchal societies like ours.)

A bouncing little girl, she became known for chatting away gaily in Malay to our Chinese domestic helper, Ah Kiew. On my father's insistence,

My parents, Malathi Pillai and K. Sukumaran Pillai.

though contrary to custom, my brother and I were born in Singapore. (He believed the medical facilities in Singapore to be superior.) Nonetheless, my mother practised the various customary rituals carried out by Malayalee women in Kerala for both herself and the baby in the new country.

From early on, I always had the impression (perhaps owing to the circumstances surrounding my brother's death) that my mother considered me a special child. To propitiate the gods and ensure no one cast an evil eye on me, my mother carried out a ritual in a temple when I was an infant. The ritual specified that a mother should "give" her child to a deity. She does this by placing the child on the floor in front of the deity and walking away. Another lady, usually a beggar-woman, then comes along to pick up the baby. At that point, the mother has to literally "buy" her baby back from the woman. This story left an indelible mark on me, not least because my sister never let me forget it. She used to tease me by saying I was actually bought from a beggar!

Our life in Singapore thus began as a family affair, and the family supported one another. My mother's cousin, Mr. C. G. Menon, was employed by her uncle, M. R. Menon, at the Y.M.C.A.* My father also lent a hand in fixing up his two brothers-in-law with jobs by bringing them for interviews at Adelphi Hotel's branch, Sea View Hotel in Katong. We

* The Y.M.C.A. also employed another gentleman by the name of Mr. David Marshall to teach French. He went on to become the chief minister (1955–1956) of Singapore's first elected government. In addition, he was a famous criminal lawyer and had served as Singapore's Ambassador to France (1978–1993).

had a small community that found it reassuring to spend time together: it alleviated pangs for home, and the elder generation spoke to one another in Malayalam, which was a comfort.

Accident at the Adelphi

My father's living quarters at the time were located at the hotel near the junction of Coleman Street and St. Andrew's Road, not far from where the Europe Hotel was torn down and the now old Supreme Court was to be built. The room had a four-poster bed, with a mosquito net — although I cannot remember now if smaller beds were also available for my sister and me.

We could order room service, which was quite the treat. Most of the staff who brought us our meals were also of Indian origin and treated my father respectfully. I believe he was considered one of the senior-most Asians at the hotel. (The Europeans held the top-most positions.) Whenever I got restless and out of hand (which was often) my parents let me run wild on the grounds of St. Andrew's Cathedral under the supervision of our domestic help.

People may not believe me when I say this, but I recall one accident that befell me at the Adelphi when I was around three years old, which for me has assumed some historic significance. To this day, I can still remember the circumstances quite vividly. A wooden counter had separated my father's office from the general lobby where the hotel guests would mill about. The clerks sat behind it when they answered queries. On one occasion when they let me loiter outside my father's office, I decided to experiment with the counter door, as I had never seen a contraption like it in my life — a door that opened upwards, rather than sideways!

Amazed, I went to take a closer look. While playing with it, I failed to remove my hand in time, and the door dropped painfully onto my left thumb, causing me to accidentally sustain a fracture. This is the oldest and physically most agonising memory of my life. My thumb remains disfigured to this day. It was the first of many accidents in my

Me as a three-year-old with my sister, Sree Kumari (possibly at the Adelphi Hotel), December 1940.

childhood, and perhaps augured more painful things to come. Not long after, in 1941, World War II descended upon Singapore.

Caught in the Countryside

One year before the war, my mother decided it was time to introduce my sister and me to her parents in Kerala. My mother's decision was not because of the war (in 1940, it was unclear whether there would be any war). Customarily, Malayalee Hindu women return to their parents' home to give birth. My elder brother and I had been noticeable exceptions to this rule — the first family members to be born outside of India.

My mother had been waiting to go until I was old enough to travel. It was sheer serendipity, therefore, that before the war even started, my mother, sister and I were safely delivered into the arms of my grandparents in the village of Engandiyoor, twenty-three kilometers from Thrissur, sheltered to a large extent from the unfortunate events soon to surround Singapore.

We travelled by ship to Madras, then by train to Thrissur; by car to the river crossing, by boat to Engandiyoor and then on foot to my maternal grandfather's house. It must have taken about ten or eleven days in all. One thing I remember distinctly is my tricycle being unloaded from the boat at Engandiyoor and how, after we reached my grandfather's house, I was passed around and carried by everybody present. When my mother's younger sister held me, I was supposed to have said "*macam Ah Kiew*" ("like Ah Kiew" in Malay). Ah Kiew, as I have mentioned earlier, was our domestic helper in Singapore to whom I was fondly attached.

For a small boy like me — whose experience then was limited to only a few years in Singapore — my grandfather's home in the countryside was a whole new world. My grandfather had a large house with an abundance of coconut, mango and gooseberry trees. There was a gatehouse (*padipura*) beyond which strangers were not permitted entry. In front of the gate, the paddy fields stretched as far as my young and keen eyes could see. Those fields which were in front of the house belonged to my grandfather. The size of my grandfather's land was totally incomprehensible to me.

Usually in such corners of Kerala, homes had their own ponds. Ours had two, which were full of frogs and fish, and a wooded area teeming with snakes. These wooded areas were called *pambumkavu* — "snake gardens" or "snake sanctuaries" — where snakes dwelled undisturbed and it was forbidden to harm them.

Snakes are revered in Hinduism; some are even considered deities. To this day, many houses maintain shrines to them. Although origin stories about snake worship abound in Kerala, a German gentleman who had been operating a hilltop resort in the state (many Europeans visit during the monsoon season) once shared a colourful tale with me. According to this legend, Kerala was created from the Arabian Sea. The virgin land was flooded with snakes, and so the local residents began to worship them, offering milk and sometimes rice in return for protection. Today, lamps are lit on auspicious occasions, and, on special days, *pujas* are performed. These prayers were well attended by the neighbours and paddy field workers who lived across the fence.

When my sister, the neighbouring children and I swam in the nearby ponds, one of the workers would keep an eye out for water snakes. Extracting them from the pond had its own ritual. The worker would trap the snake in an earthen pot by placing food inside. After the snake slithered in, he would cover the pot and release it into a grove a short distance away. We treated the snakes reverentially. As children, it was also quite fun to watch the snake peek its head out from the pot and flick out its tongue!

~

Within only a short period after arriving at my grandfather's house, the rest of the world started to move in a different direction; and what was supposed to have been a short family visit of about five to six months turned into a nearly seven-year stay! In 1941, Japan invaded Malaya. While my mother's youngest brother and younger sister were safe with us, my father and two uncles were stranded in Singapore. Nobody had ever imagined that the supposedly "invincible" British would be defeated.

History shows that the British turned their sights to the sea, ready to give the Japanese a bloody nose when they landed. But an invasion by bicycle from the northeast caught them completely by surprise: the British forces were utterly routed. Britain's Prime Minister Winston Churchill called the fall of Singapore "the worst disaster and the largest capitulation in British history."[2] It was a poorly managed war. The family decided that we should not return to Singapore after the sinking of the HMS Prince of Wales and the HMS Repulse by the Japanese off the east coast of Malaya in December 1941. Singapore fell to the Japanese on February 15th, 1942. Singapore was no longer; for the next three years or so, she was to be known as Syonan-to.

World War II lasted longer than anyone in the family could have expected. My mother (being an excellent student, and maybe better equipped than most housewives to understand the severity of the global situation) was totally unprepared for being caught in India with her children for nearly seven years. Where my childhood was therefore full of new wonders, my mother lived in a perpetual anxiety, fretting over the safety of her husband and two brothers.

When news of Singapore's fall had reached us in Kerala, it sparked pandemonium. My grandfather Narayana Nair held steady and asked everyone not to speculate until we got more news. My grandfather, perhaps accustomed to leadership as a local landowner, seemed always to hold the answers to life's difficult questions. A hot-tempered, physically strong man, he was looked up to in the village. He advised my mother not to weep and dwell on negative thoughts.

He was a great believer in the power of prayer, and suggested that she pray and continue to hope for the best, accepting whatever life might throw at us. Partly due to Hindu teachings of worldly detachment, he was often stoic; one could not always tell from his expression what he was feeling. But I suspect he must have felt deeply for my mother's predicament, and was as concerned as everyone else about the fate of those left in Singapore, including his sons, who were unable to return.

Isolated with no electricity and poor radio signals, updates were intermittent. The English language newspaper *The Hindu* was not delivered regularly. Although we had the Malayalam newspaper *Mathrubhumi*, the news was often outdated. Frustrated at being left in the dark, my mother would perk up on discovering that a Japanese vessel had been sunk or a plane shot down somewhere — but just as soon worried, "What if my brothers and husband were caught in that raid?" If there was any unfortunate development anywhere, there was much handwringing in the house.

My mother rarely threw a tantrum. She was instead more of the reflective sort; when she cried, she would seek the privacy of her room. As a child, I often ran after her and, as parents do, she comforted me while comforting herself. I remember her trying to explain to me the reasons behind the war and Japanese cruelty.

After the war, one of the first letters we received from my father, in fact, expressed his views on the cruelty of the occupying forces. He said that when the Japanese first came to Singapore, he found them, as a people, to be very polite — friendly and pleasant to be around. However, over the course of the occupation, he described their transformation — into devils, nasty and uncompromising in their treatment of the local population, especially the Chinese.

~

During these seven years in India, I too began to develop my own moral compass. One day, a beggar had visited the house while I was enjoying a meal by the window. He stood before it, but, being an outsider, did not enter. I remember him gesturing for food, stretching out his hand. I devoured my food with relish, while the hungry man gazed imploringly at me. I could almost hear him moaning. But being young and immature, I found the situation comical. I took what I was eating and started dancing, showing off what I had.

I then heard my mother scream, "What are you doing?" I spun around, utterly shocked to find her towering over me. "Go to your room!" She called the house help and ordered some food to be brought for the beggar. I was stunned, because moments before I had found the situation entertaining. The plate of food was given to the man. My mother took me to the side (she never smacked me) and clearly explained the concept of sin.

"It is called *paap*," she said (the Sanskrit word and its equivalent in Malayalam). "You have committed the biggest sin and now you will pay for it. That man was hungry and you mocked him. You have food, but you did not alleviate his hunger — you just danced around. That sort of response is the worst thing a person can do. If you hit a person, the pain eventually will fade. But if you humiliate him..."

The concept of sin after that became a subject I have long pondered on. If you do something that cannot be justified, you get nothing out of it, just pleasure and misguidance. This was a major lesson she taught me — a set of rules a family also learns to adhere to and live by. I realised that this sin is actually something that a person must always be sensitive to. A person may get angry and scold somebody else but should never humiliate him. This is not just for the religious reason that sin affects your next life but also because it does real damage in this one. My mother's outrage left a lasting impression on me.

A Mysterious Ritual and News of My Father

We continued to live in a haze of uncertainty. It so happened that after some weeks had passed, our family's situation became known in the village, and a most fascinating incident occurred when I was around five years old. An intermediary introduced two mysterious persons to my grandfather, who told him they had supernatural ways of establishing contact with people far away. They volunteered to help "trace" his son-in-law, my father.

"It may be right, it may not be right, but in either case, it will not cost you very much," they said.

Like in Indonesia and Malaysia, where bomohs practise black magic in the villages, there was a widespread practice of *Manthravadam* in rural parts of Kerala through which a practitioner undergoing rigorous training can attain supernatural powers. This was the same practice that the two visitors proposed; they wanted to perform a ritual called "*Mashi*". For these "mediums" (as I call them), I suppose their help to my grandfather was a bit of publicity, as he was an important figure.

My family felt a good deal of trepidation regarding this "black magic". However, eager for more news and lacking better options, my grandfather decided to go ahead with the plan. My mother's sole wish was to find out whether her husband and two brothers were alive and unhurt.

The mediums came dressed in ordinary *veshti* (like sarongs) and brought along a container of tar-black oily ink which they said had to be rubbed on the palm of a child who had not yet reached puberty. The child, they explained, could then see the faces of people far away and communicate with them, if they were still alive.

My sister, who was three years older than me (and therefore had a clearer memory of my father and two uncles), was chosen to "contact" them. The ink, or *mashi*, was applied on her palm. One of the mediums instructed, "Whoever you wish to see will appear there," and told her to direct her questions to that image on her palm. With folded hands, Kumari faced the east and whispered for my father's image to appear.

Within minutes, my sister's face broke into a gleeful smile. Then I heard her scream, "*Achan* is here! *Achan* is here!" She claimed she could see my father. I was standing some distance away. "He has a little black dot on his front tooth!" She glanced at us, utterly convinced.

"He has very nice teeth," my mother corrected. "There shouldn't be a dot."

"But I can see the dot," she insisted.

The medium prodded her onwards, directing her to ask my father to clap his hands if he was happy. The image (according to my sister) clapped without hesitation. Everyone was encouraged and greatly relieved. Then they moved to my elder uncle, Unni. Unnimama, as we called him, also clapped after being posed the same question. But when it came my younger uncle Rameshan's turn, he refused to clap. The family members huddling around my grandfather murmured, "Maybe something is wrong. Ask Rameshamama to clap his hands if he is unhappy."

"*If you are unhappy, clap*," the medium told my sister to repeat. The image of Rameshamama clapped, to show he was not happy.

The instructor concluded the session and said that all three were still alive. "Two are happy. One is alive but may not remain so. This is all we can say."

The whole incident made a tremendous impression on my family. It was a great comfort to my mother that my father, especially, was alive and well. My grandfather asked the mediums whether we could follow up with them after a few weeks, but they said "no" quite emphatically. Minor practitioners would have pitched all kinds of odd jobs to earn a few extra bucks if given the chance. But these men were honest: they had a dignified approach to their work and genuinely voiced their limitations.

~

When we later returned to Singapore after the war, the first thing my sister noticed was that my father did, in fact, have a cavity on his front tooth. We also got news that Rameshamama had argued with a senior Japanese officer and for a short time been jailed. (As it was not a political crime, the punishment was not severe.) My father, meanwhile, as one of the senior-most Asians at the Adelphi, was put in charge. Unnimama joined him. We discovered the two had been safely working at the hotel through the end of the war.

For a time, I used to visit Kerala about once a year, and recently tried to find out if the practice of *Manthravadan* still exists. In ancient times, there were wise men, they say, who would sit and meditate for hours to ascertain who was moving from where to where. Apparently, they had alternative methods for tracking down missing people and objects in those days. I cannot speak on the accuracy of it, but it is a matter of curiosity.

Incidentally, I learned that this practice *does* still exist in some of the remoter parts of Kerala. But the few families who possess this "tracing" art keep it a secret. For instance, if you were to lose a piece of jewellery, they could find it; if a man disappears, they would be able to locate his whereabouts. Often, people go troubling them for news about this or that person or object; and, in some cases, they reveal information that is not necessarily in the interests of others. Quite naturally, the mediums fear for their lives, and do not go about performing their work publicly for fear of retribution by those who could have been exposed. I believe there are some families out there still practising this art.

2

The Communist Movement in Kerala

"[O]ne incident that caused major upheaval in my family was when my youngest uncle, C. Janardhanan ('Kochapamama'), abandoned his university education to join the Communist Youth Movement... Certainly, my uncle's beliefs influenced my own political values that were to surface later on."

Growing Up on the Family's Land

The war seriously affected the family, due to the separation from my father and two uncles, but I was spared for the most part. During my stay at my grandparents' house in India, I became the focus of a lot of attention. My grandfather was very fond of me, and he was known to spoil me: for example, if I fell sick, my favourite foods would not be cooked in the house to prevent anyone else from enjoying them. My grandmother Parukuttyamma (a sickly person who suffered from chronic asthma) also doted on me. As far as she was concerned, I could do no wrong. I was also looked after by my mother's younger sister, Indira: although we used to have regular fights, she was always very caring. Young and then unmarried, she treated me like a younger brother.

Rural India in my childhood felt indulgent, almost like a holiday. I had an easy, idyllic life, surrounded by rice fields and coconut trees; animals like cows, dogs and goats; and so on. I was untouched by the war in that I lived my life not fully aware of the calamities all around, but was deeply affected in another sense, as my mother's worry hovered over us like a dark cloud.

My grandfather exerted a strong influence over me during these childhood years. He was a strict person — kind and fair, and could be

With my family in Thrissur, Kerala in the 1940s. First row: me (bottom right) with my grandfather Narayana Nair (sitting, centre), my grandmother Parukuttyamma (beside him), my grandmother's uncle, and my sister, Sree Kumari (left). Second row (from left): my mother, Malathi Pillai; her youngest brother, C. Janardhanan; her younger brother, Unni; and her younger sister, Indira.

very particular about your prayers. He was fairly well off, with cultivatable land, and was especially solicitous of our livestock. If there was a heavy rain, and the animals had not been properly cared for, it would anger him. He would launch out of the door with his cane to berate the workers.

My grandfather, as I said, could be hot-tempered, and was quick to use his hand. But he was also incredibly generous. If he saw some young fellow running through the fields or on the road, he would ask why the lad was not in school. The young fellow might reply to his questioning, "I have no money," to which my grandfather would say, "Here, I will give you the fees," and send him on his way.

Despite being a landowner, my grandfather dressed simply. When he swung his walking stick, one tended to stay out of his path. During the rainy season, he carried an umbrella. Earthen mounds rose in a path through the fields, and when the workers from the farming families spotted him approaching from afar, they stepped aside. This sometimes required stepping back into the damp paddy fields and getting their feet muddy and wet; the path was narrow. Although my grandfather wore nothing distinguishing, he expected to be, and was, recognised and respected.

My family was not necessarily religious, but we observed the traditional Hindu beliefs and customs that had been passed down through the generations. This included observing certain ritual practices at home and, on special occasions, visiting the village temple. For example, I remember my grandfather requesting me to wake up very early in the morning as there were verses from devotional *bhajans* which he enjoyed listening to me sing. He never demanded a performance, but simply explained that listening to them made him happy.

Being young and energetic, it was not difficult to rise at daybreak. Upon rising, I would rush to my grandfather's bedside and plead, "Come on, listen to me sing." That was the time before the day's duties, when he was calmest. My grandfather was also quite good at Indian chess, *Chaturangam*; he travelled around various parts of the state to identify good players with whom to compete. Chess is also something I much later shared with my son; when he was six or seven years old, I used to take him to chess competitions to watch him play.

I cannot recall my grandfather's winning record now, but I have always had the impression he was a formidable player: whenever he was in the middle of a game at the house, he demanded absolute silence. My grandfather was quite proud of the fact that chess was invented in India before it spread to other countries through the conquest of the Arabs. He tried to teach my sister and me how to play. In my case, this was without too much success. But my sister soon became adept at the game.

~

My sister kept busy with her studies and did not make for the best playmate; as one consequence, I was somewhat of a lonely child. Still, she was my closest companion and, to me, a strong, fearsome person who would not hesitate to give me a good whacking. She was a bit of a tomboy — not lady-like in the least. I loved her dearly.

I was less fond of school, however, which required my grandfather to call a teacher to the house for my lessons (private tutoring was one of the perks of growing up in India). He came in the morning and, if free, a couple hours in the evening. My mother assisted with my studies as well.

My mother never gave up on her interest in education, even though her uncle and relatives had decided she should quit her studies to marry. At bedtime, she read me poems, Hindu classics and stories from all across the globe — from Iran, China and the biblical tales of Israel. For instance, I became quite familiar with the famous Persian story 'Rustam and Sohrab'. I was also told about Jesus, and was fond of the episode in John 2:1–11 where he converts water into wine.

In 1945, by the time I was about eight years old, the war ended and preparations commenced for our return to Singapore. As we made ready, my mother began reading the full *Mahabharata* to us. With around 130,000 verses, this Hindu epic is supposedly the longest poem ever composed by man. My grandfather translated it for us from Sanskrit into colloquial Malayalam (the local version had parts in Sanskrit, which only he could understand). It is interesting to note that in those days of no television or radio, people had to create their own entertainment.

I still remember distinctly his elaborations on aspects of the epic. While translating into the Malayalam for us, he linked the deities from one epic to another, explaining why certain characters behaved as they did, and what other engrossing story lay behind it. We finished reading the entire *Mahabharata* before our departure. This was an invigorating experience — and no mean feat!

Youngest Uncle Joins the Communist Youth Movement

Before we left India, one incident that caused major upheaval in my family was when my youngest uncle, C. Janardhanan ("Kochapamama"), abandoned his university education to join the Communist Youth Movement. The independence movement in India was gaining political momentum. Although the Congress was somewhat divided about how to pursue independence during the war, the majority under Mahatma

Gandhi's leadership felt that India should support Britain first. "We do not seek independence out of Britain's ruin," he is supposed to have said.[1]

Separately, communism began rising to prominence in Kerala in the 1930s. It is not exactly clear why its popularity was unique to Kerala. According to Thomas Nossiter in *Communism in Kerala*, "Politics is the national sport of the Malayalees," and the language "lends itself to political rhetoric."[2] A large number of young, middle-class men from mainly Nair families were apparently being drawn to Marxist ideology. My own family was also not left untouched.

My grandfather was furious when he found out about his youngest son's decision to join the communists, although he himself was responsible for instilling political consciousness in his children. (He was a nationalist, and had got them a *charkha*, or spinning wheel, to make yarn out of cotton to reduce dependency on imported British fabric.) He practically disowned Kochapamama and refused to speak with him for a long time after his departure. Even Kochapamama's own friends were unhappy with his decision. One of his classmates candidly told my grandfather that he would break his legs should my grandfather permit him to do so! Of course, nothing of the sort was done, but all this made a huge impression on my childish mind.

I must have been around five years old then and recall it being a big event. My uncle had thrived in university and was looked upon as the family's future. To me personally, he was a hero: I felt empathy listening to him talk about the ills of society where many had no proper food or income, and caste discrimination was rife. My mother was in tears, while I recall my grandfather stood speechless. My uncle would not be swayed by their hopes for his life, however, and left the house.

One reason my grandfather disapproved of Kochapamama's decision was perhaps due to his social standing. In Kerala in the early 20th century, agricultural land was owned by the landlords and tilled by the farmers. The farmers paid a levy and, in return, were given a fee and part of the produce.[3] But those from my grandfather's age group and class status had around this time entered into a social decline. The locals had long ago gone to my grandfather with their disagreements; and my grandfather, acting as something of a patriarch, would call them together to sort out their disputes. I recall visitors regularly coming to the house to see him. Very often, he would be reading his newspaper or a book when they entered the room. Sometimes (though he knew they sought a meeting) he would carry on reading his paper. The visitors would wait patiently for him to finish, not daring to interrupt him.

He was not the only strong character in the village; several other families also oversaw the nearby groups of cultivating tenants and tillers of the soil in a similar fashion. However, by the time we left for Singapore, Indian society was already transforming rapidly, and more frequently people were beginning to ask the police or civil service to mediate in their disputes.

Given the super-charged political climate around independence, such social change was inevitable. In various places, the struggle to dislodge the British was on. The communists felt that the Congress was maybe not as committed to social change as they perhaps claimed to be, since they made side deals with the British. They saw the *Communist Manifesto* as much more revolutionary, since it asserted abolishing the system of absentee landlords. Kochapamama also, even after independence, persisted in fighting for land reform and proper compensation for the workers. He went underground after the government of Jawaharlal Nehru issued a warrant for his arrest. He was an excellent orator and organiser of the peasants. The first communist government in the world, interestingly, was elected in my home state of Kerala, which came to power in 1957.[4]

On the surface, my grandfather always wore an expression of composure; but I suspect that he too must have been preoccupied with the tumultuous political events emerging. His landholdings were not flourishing; and in the 1940s, the arrival of my mother, sister and I would have added to household expenses. The assumption then was that when the daughter of the family marries, her family is self-sufficient, as her husband will work and pay for their children's upbringing. But our separation from my father had upended these expectations. My grandfather, being a thoughtful person, probably therefore fretted over how he would care for all these people who had come to live in his house. Maybe he thought it was impossible in Engandiyoor. "Maybe I will have to buy a house in the city," he mused, "to look after them all! But where will I get the resources? And who will help me?"

Kochapamama later rose to a position of prominence in the Kerala communist party in independent India and became a member of parliament (MP) in Delhi from 1967 to 1970.[5] I visited him in New Delhi many years later around this time at the MP's quarters. Certainly, my uncle's beliefs influenced my own political values that were to surface later on. One inadvertent effect of Kochapamama's influence was that I did, for a short time, ignorantly begin to admire the communists, although these sympathies were course-corrected by my father after we returned to Singapore later on.

My uncle for a period had a very tough life underground, being hunted by the police and so on. But occasionally he would return to enjoy the taste of his mother's cooking. This proper meal was important for him, because he was not well fed. During his visits, he sometimes told me stories of Joseph Stalin and Benito Mussolini as well as about local revolutionaries such as Bhagat Singh and the famous armory raid at Chittagong. I was in awe of his high ideals and sat in rapt attention as he narrated the many acts of heroism by the freedom fighters. In a humourous episode, my grandfather one day between his visits had gotten me a puppy. In an effort to please my uncle, I named him Stalin.

Rather than being pleased, he became very annoyed. "How can you name a little dog after this great man!" Kochapamama actually suggested that I change the name.

But my grandmother Parukuttyamma, who usually did not intervene or kick up a fuss, put her foot down. "You should appreciate his intent. You were not here when the puppy came and should allow him to keep the name as Stalin."

Later, after settling into my new home in Singapore, I would request my mother to write to my grandfather at every chance I got to ask how Stalin was getting on!

~

With our departure for Singapore, my grandfather was no longer interested in country life. After the communist government was elected in Kerala, new limitations were placed on how much land for the paddy fields and coconut plantations one could own — what was not cultivated in person had to be sold to the tillers of the soil. My grandfather lost a sizeable chunk of his property. Land holdings, in general, were diminishing, and so he decided to move to the city. The first time I saw him again was in the late 1960s after my uncle became an MP. The change was palpable. He took me back to the old house in Engandiyoor, where I was shocked that the villagers acted as if they hardly knew him. Some of the older people showed respect, but the younger generation's attitude suggested, "We no longer have anything to do with you."

From a personal point of view, I think what happened in Kerala was a welcome change: the transition from a feudal society to a more egalitarian one. The transformation started while the British were still in power. However, after India gained independence, around the time Kochapamama was underground, the new government went on to arrest my uncle and tortured him. His captors broke his legs by hitting them with iron rods. He was then admitted to the prison hospital. Although his wounds were festering, a nurse told him that she had overheard a conversation in which the police had informed the doctors not to properly treat his wounds. They wanted his legs to be amputated to render him immobile.

Upon learning this, Kochapamama launched a personal hunger strike and petitioned the court for proper external medical treatment. In true dramatic fashion, he crawled from the entrance of the court to the judges' bench to plead his case. This had the desired effect: the whole courtroom was electrified! The judges ordered that he be transferred to another hospital and granted the necessary medical attention.

3

A Strange New Home

"My father was ... very watchful about my immature attraction towards the communists... I suppose he was a Gandhian, concerned with moral questions of right and wrong... Over time, Kochapamama's influence on me waned, while my father's grew."

New Life Adjustments

In 1945, the Japanese surrendered and in 1946, when I was nine years old, we boarded the ship for Singapore. An air of sadness seemed to descend upon the house on the day of our departure. But I was excited by the prospect of travelling to a new place that, strangely enough, was to be my home. I remember our last night, when my grandmother Parukuttyamma came to my bed and gave me a hug and a tearful kiss. The next day, in December 1946, we left on the SS Jalagopal. I never saw Parukuttyamma again, as I did not return to India until around 1967. She had died about ten years before that.

When we originally departed from Singapore to India in 1940, we had bought three return tickets from the British travel agency Thomas Cook. My mother was rather pleased to discover that she could use these same tickets many years later. Thomas Cook honoured their pledge of travel by welcoming us aboard.

There were several ocean routes from India to Singapore in the 1940s. Some shipping vessels held a course to Singapore from Madras and Visakhapatnam. Another shipping line put into Penang, from which one took the train south to Singapore. We took the route to Penang, where at the port my father was waiting to receive us. He was eager to be around at the first point of contact. He was practically a stranger to me after these many years apart.

We spent one night at the E & O Hotel in Penang before taking the train. At the Singapore railway station, my uncles, relatives and friends greeted us. Our reunion in Singapore was full of joy, as my mother had endlessly speculated about the safety of her husband and two brothers. My sister and I gleefully participated in their celebration, although our memory of our father and uncles had by that time grown hazy.

However, I remember two things vividly from this encounter. One was Unnimama unbuttoning the top button of my shirt and chastising me because he thought I looked too much like a country bumpkin (though I was exactly that). The second was that I had my first taste of chocolate — a dark chocolate bar, given to me by one of the peons from Adelphi Hotel. My transformation from a small-town boy to a city-slicker had begun, along with my lifelong love of chocolate!

Upon reaching Singapore, we unpacked at our father's house on Haig Road. My father appeared to have become fairly prosperous, as he now had a car and a driver named Zaman. Compared to my grandfather's property, the house in Singapore was quite modest. It had been partially damaged during the war. But I liked it, for two reasons: because of the car parked inside the garage — a second-hand Austin 10, a fairly large

My house on Haig Road.

car which was considered high quality back then; and the calf that my father had bought for us to play with. He must have got one thinking it would be fun for the children.

Although I missed my old life in Kerala, I was enchanted by this strange new city that was to become my permanent home. Thanks to my father's car, we were quite mobile, and, on the weekends, we drove to a nearby beach where I swam and rowed a boat to an island with Unnimama. At the beach, my father regaled us with stories of the Japanese Occupation and its aftermath.

Just after the war, cases of petty theft and robbery were rising. My father told us that shortly before our return from India, three or four robbers armed with knives had actually broken into the house! They had tied up my father and stole practically everything of value. Understandably, he became preoccupied with keeping the house safe.

He also described in harrowing detail the circumstances of the Japanese Occupation and the heinous acts they committed. These stories sounded exciting to a young boy like me. My father was a quiet man; he usually did not talk much. But when he took us out on one of his adventures, he really opened up. My mother complained that he was not a very good driver, as his attention continually drifted from the road whenever he got absorbed in one of his yarns. He also had a habit of eating peanuts when driving, which annoyed her.

"You better concentrate! Don't eat and don't talk!"

Over time, the calf matured into a cow, and in full circle birthed a baby calf. I was naturally thrilled! But the municipal authorities warned my father that he had to get rid of the animals because they were not household pets and could not be kept in our premises. Opposite our house were also some government gardens and godowns, where the cow liked to wander and graze (she left the evidence of her intrusions behind). So the animals had to be sold off. My sister unwittingly revealed that male calves were generally put to slaughter while female calves were kept for their milk. I tried to avoid thinking about the newborn that was a male, as it gave me a sad, sinking feeling.

We lived in a friendly multi-ethnic neighbourhood. On the left of our house lived a Chinese family of contractors — the father and children were all in the family business. They built small carpentry pieces such as cabinetry that were used in construction. They must have worked from home, because I observed trunks loaded with work materials being trundled up and down the stairs at all times of the day. Their North Indian watchman held the door for them. Sometimes, the father would walk over to the fence to share how happy he was that we were staying there as his neighbours. He kindly offered to let us use their driver whenever we wanted, since my father's driver, Mr. Zaman, had resigned shortly after our arrival.

On the right of our house was a Eurasian family by the name of D'Silva — Portuguese Eurasian. They were a little more aloof, but they had three or four children, and soon, we all became great friends across the fence.

Me (left) with my sister and Unnimama at our new house on Haig Road.

Starting the Printing Business and Newspaper

By the time I arrived, the economic scene in Singapore was changing, and my father had left his job at the Adelphi Hotel to start a printing business full-time. He had invested in printing equipment and was doing jobs for other clients. Unnimama, who had worked with him at the hotel, also left the hotel business and was considering taking on contracting jobs for the British army. Rameshamama was meanwhile considering a return to India. After the war, many Indians had decided to return home. This included my mother's uncle M. R. Menon who, having built the school at the Y.M.C.A. into a fairly reputable organisation, decided to hand the school over to my mother's cousin C. G. Menon.

The exit of the Japanese and return of the British significantly impacted employment for the resident Indian community. The background to this is of some historical interest. Many Indians in Singapore during the war had thrown in their support with the Japanese as sympathisers or recruits of the Indian National Army (INA). "Netaji" Subhas Chandra Bose, a respected nationalist leader from the Bengal province of British India, had formed the INA through the support of the Japanese and recruited Indian troops throughout Southeast Asia to liberate the country from the "imperialists".

The INA alongside Japanese forces marched on the British across the India Burma border in March 1944. The invasion was thwarted, however, and they were "defeated and forced to retreat".[1]

My father had a friend, Mr. K. P. Menon, one of several lawyers of Indian origin who had settled in Singapore for work. He was an influential figure who opposed Bose's violent methods. The Japanese were not very happy with him for rebuffing their efforts to win his support for Bose (which would have legitimised their authority). Allegedly, K. P. Menon said that by joining with the imperial Japanese and cavorting with the Germans, Bose himself had become a conspirator of fascists.[*]

The Japanese responded to K. P. Menon's intransigence by throwing him into jail and interrogating both him and his son. The Japanese had repurposed the Y.M.C.A. building into prison accommodations where he was kept. Later, when the British returned to the island and learned this, they put Menon on a pedestal as a "loyal British citizen". But in the same forthright manner, he maintained that he was not a British citizen but rather an Indian who, although ardently seeking his country's independence, would not deal with the devil to gain it. He was very much a Gandhian. (Even among the Indians in Singapore, many opposed

[*] From the post-war discussions his relatives had with my father, I gathered that K. P. Menon had a deep aversion to Bose. Indeed, Bose had already gone once to Germany to tie up an alliance in 1942.

the INA-Japanese alliance and worried that it would merely replace one unacceptable master with another. I believe the Indian community, if given the choice, would have actually preferred British rule.)

After the war, K. P. Menon and his son were some of the first friends my father visited. Under the new British system, they were welcomed back into society with open arms. K. P. Menon's profession as a trial lawyer furnished him with many opportunities; later, like others, he returned to India, where he was made a high commissioner under the new government to Sri Lanka (then known as Ceylon). He eventually returned to Kerala and became the publisher of the *Mathrubhumi*, the same paper which had provided my family with valuable nuggets of information during the war.

Those who collaborated with the Japanese, meanwhile, had a tough time of it adjusting to the post-war scene. While some Indians living in Singapore returned to India, other retired INA soldiers migrated to Singapore to look for jobs. Some succeeded while others scrambled. My father's cooperation with the Japanese at the Adelphi Hotel — and his need to adjust to the post-war environment — was one reason he decided to go into printing.

~

To briefly recap, the hotel business in the period leading up to World War II (when my father was employed as an accounts clerk) had been faring well. The Adelphi Hotel and the Sea View Hotel were considered the two dominant hotels on the island. But the war had soured the economy, and many lost their jobs. Staying alive became their paramount concern, and keeping the family safe from bombing raids. As stated in a placard at Singapore's Indian Heritage Centre, "World War II and the subsequent Japanese Occupation (1942–1945) were turbulent periods for Indians in Singapore and Malaya with many experiencing economic hardships, hunger, poor sanitation and illness."[2]

As the "mediums" who visited my grandfather's home in Kerala had divined, my father, compared to many, had been quite fortunate in keeping his job under the Japanese and in receiving a promotion by them. The Japanese employed Indians due to their perceived association with the INA. The Swiss and other Europeans who had not fled the island were conversely maltreated or thrown in jail.

According to my father's account, the traffic of visitors to the Adelphi kept up throughout the war. My father had even picked up a smattering of Japanese on his own. During one of our family outings to the beach, I recall my father recounting a particular meeting he had with one prominent guest whom the Japanese had hosted: President Sukarno from Indonesia.

While many of the Japanese could not speak English, my father could communicate with the little Japanese that he knew. He was therefore asked to act as an interpreter for the Indonesian delegation members. When the European management returned to Singapore, it appears that they were slightly unhappy with him for cooperating with the Japanese. He knew such "collaboration" did not look good, so he stepped down of his own volition. He had by this time already started on his idea for a newspaper.

~

My father, as my mother discovered, was a bit of an intellectual, and always had an interest in Malayalam literature. He had gotten the idea to start a newspaper even before the war broke out after being told about the availability of a Malayalam press in Malacca. He bought this press with Malayalam types from Mr. I. V. K. Nair. (I later discovered he was the father of Mr. Devan Nair, who in 1981 became the third president of Singapore.) My father then got a group of young Malayalee writers together — including Mr. V. P. Abdullah, Mr. Siva Raman Nair and others — to constitute the nucleus of the paper's management. The Malayalam-speaking population in Singapore was growing, as the British naval forces were employing many from the community as clerks, providing him with a viable commercial readership.

He started the paper part-time, but it slowly gained traction and allowed him to work full-time. He not only printed and managed his own newspaper but also did printing jobs for other customers. For instance, he later printed the *Naujawan*, a Punjabi newspaper started by Mr. Dewan

Singh Randhawa. Many Indians migrating to Singapore were hungry for commentaries on recent political developments in their home country. My father thus spent a lot of time reading through Indian news reports and adapting them for local consumption.

I recall him being especially active in propagating news on activities and events associated with the independence movement, the most important being the day India acquired its freedom with the blessings of the British. One report he read to me (despite my limited understanding) was of a speech by Nehru, widely known then, called India's "Tryst with Destiny".

As a publisher he worked quite hard, often getting up at the crack of dawn to leave home by 6.30am or 7.00am. The staff handled the management while he reviewed the articles, to ensure everything that was printed in the newspaper was correct. The newspaper carried separate sections in both Malayalam and English. The paper's name was the *Kerala Bandhu*. "Bandhu" in Malayalam means "relation". "Kerala Bandhu" in translation means "Relative of Kerala".

Influences of My Father

As I started adjusting to my new home, I came to learn that my father's temperament differed in some significant aspects from my grandfather's. Where my grandfather could be quite strict, my father was more liberal and lenient in his attitude towards me. He did not overly upset himself over trifles — for instance, he would not scold you if you fell, whereas my grandfather could really "smite" you. My father's personality was such that he never greatly cared.

However, there was one exception. While under my father's tutelage as a boy, I remained greatly enthused by how much Kochapamama had sacrificed to join the Communist Youth Movement. From his stories, I was very much in the thrall of the heroic communists. My father was therefore very watchful about my immature attraction towards communism, and he made efforts to ensure that I did not blindly accept the Soviet propaganda that the communists would become the saviours of the world. He would

My father, and publisher of the Malayalam newspaper *Kerala Bandhu*, K. Sukumaran Pillai.

intervene to influence my views if I ever showed too much sympathy for the communist cause.

Like many other Indian families at this time, mine was very inclined towards tracking political developments. My father, too, had very definite ideas about politics and politicians. He was not moved by the communist philosophy or the communists' zealous approach to revolution. With socialism, he was more sympathetic. I suppose he was a Gandhian, concerned with moral questions of right and wrong. He felt that the communists treated their enemies too harshly; for instance, he saw Stalin as thug-like in how he eliminated political opponents by force. He stressed that although the capitalists also exploited you, they at least were probably gentler with their opponents in how they went about it. He also argued that there was no room for democracy in the communist movement, where the common man had no choice but to toe the party line.

One memory I have of my father perhaps best exemplifies his values. In the late 1940s, Singapore did not yet have a modern sanitation system — it had a system of buckets, which the municipal workers cleared out once a day. Every building had a service lane at the back, through which the trucks collected the night soil.

One day, the municipal workers were on strike due to some pay dispute. This precipitated a crisis: if they were striking, who would clear the buckets? The government assigned the task to the Japanese prisoners-of-war. My father and I watched them clean from outside. Their faces were covered with masks to ward off the stench. Before being captured, some of them were probably high-ranking officers.

When my father saw them being assigned to such tasks, he became agitated and asked them what they were doing. He was up-to-date on the recent literature of how prisoners-of-war should be treated and felt such assignments were beneath them. "If you punish a person for a crime, you can dispense a commensurate punishment," he explained to us at home, "but if a person is fighting for his country and is captured, such prisoners should be treated differently." He was quite civically conscious. Although he did not go making noise on the streets, he made his views clear to us.

His arguments concerned my mother. "Why are you raising all this fuss? The British are our rulers now. They will decide what they want to do, just like the Japanese before them. There is no need for us to make trouble." My father responded to this practical reasoning by asserting that we should all have some principles to live by. The strike ended after a few days, and fortunately all was sorted out.

~

Over time, Kochapamama's influence on me waned, while my father's grew. He brought to my attention the atrocities in the Soviet Union. This made a difference, because the more I read and analysed, the more I too agreed that I was not a great fan of the Soviets. My schoolboy enchantment with communism gradually began to fade.

Much later, one incident left a particularly disagreeable impression. The then Soviet minister of intelligence, Lavrentiy Beria, known to be a close friend of Stalin, was executed on December 23rd, 1953. I must have been sixteen years old at the time. The circumstances surrounding the killing were murky, but I recall plenty of stories being printed about it in the papers. The ruthlessness of the Kremlin in purging its political enemies galled me. I determined this was a party whose philosophy I could not share and moved away.

However, before my father's wisdom had meaningfully sunk in, I childishly insisted on taking a photograph while holding the communist flag with the recognisable hammer and sickle. My father grew angry when he heard about my wish. My mother mediated and whispered to me in private not to worry: we would take the photograph in secret. She permitted me to hide it beneath my pillow.

I suspect that I still have that photograph somewhere. I was proud of it and would pull it out from under my pillow quite regularly to hold it up in my hands and admire it. When I wrote to my uncle, I boasted of the time I spent gazing on the photo, a confession to which I received no reply. To his credit, Kochapamama never tried to overtly influence my political views. Merely because he was a favourite of the children, what he thought was good we also held in high esteem.

The 1948 Legislative Council Elections

The late 1940s were heady political times around the world and, politically, much was going on that made an impact on me and my family. Self-determination movements were increasing, and the call to end British rule intensified in strength in many colonies. That same year, politics came closer to home with Singapore's first-ever elections for the 1948 Legislative Council. The Singapore Indian community had started becoming more politically conscious, following India's independence. Many had also wanted a say in the running of Singapore, although through peaceful means rather than agitation.

My father was always bringing in the news with the latest updates. His paper, as I mentioned earlier, had a special edition on the momentous occasion of Nehru's speech "Tryst with Destiny", which was translated into Malayalam. I remember accompanying him and my mother to a big function with the Commissioner for Southeast Asia on Bras Basah Road, in front of St. Joseph's Institution (now the Singapore Art Museum). We then walked to the Esplanade, where a memorial to Bose had been dynamited by the British. A contingent of ex-INA officers, led by Mr. John Jacob, a close friend of my father, did a march past. The Indian representative, Mr. John Thivy, took the salute and laid a wreath at the site.

My parents' joy at India's independence, however, turned to sorrow when, several months later, a Hindu fanatic named Nathuram Godse assassinated Gandhi on January 30th, 1948. As Nehru put it, "The light has gone out of our lives."[3] My father left the house early that same morning to get the paper out as early as possible. My parents, like many Indians all over, were greatly disturbed by Gandhi's death. They attended several condolence sessions. At ten years old, I too felt I was a player in this drama that was unfolding.

One of the most important contributions Indians made to politics in Singapore was in raising their fellow Singaporeans' political awareness. The Indians as a community participated most enthusiastically in Singapore's early elections; I believe if one had taken stock of the different candidates at that time, Indians would have proven to be over-represented (relative to the community's size).

John Thivy at Indian Independence celebrations in Singapore, August 15th, 1947. (Gift of Ambassador Gopinath Pillai. Collection of Indian Heritage Centre.)

Me on a bicycle in 1947.

The Chinese, by contrast, were more apathetic towards the election process (although this was not the case later on). Major events were unfolding in China in the late 1940s, like Mao Zedong establishing the People's Republic of China; but they did not appear to be affected to the same extent. Many were probably less interested in politics than getting by from day to day. The average Chinese shopowner, for instance, was most likely unsure about the direction of the Chinese communist movement — indeed, in the late 1940s, it would have been impossible to guess how China's economy would transform. The Chinese students, to compare, were politically active in protesting against capitalism and the British imperial presence.

Low-levels of electoral involvement amongst the Chinese community convinced Mr. Lee Kuan Yew in the 1950s, who was then Secretary General of the People's Action Party (PAP), to work with Chief Minister Lim Yew Hock of the Singapore People's Alliance (SPA) to make voting compulsory.[4] Part of this drive was also to eliminate corruption from politics. Calls for universal suffrage were steadily growing louder; indeed, the 1959 Legislative Assembly Election would be Singapore's first after achieving self-government.

The Legislative Assembly passed the Citizenship Ordinance in 1957, which along with making all residents born in Singapore or the Federation of Malaya eligible for citizenship also offered foreign-born Chinese a pathway through naturalisation.[5] The Legislative Assembly Election Ordinance was later amended in January 1959 to require all on the electoral roll to vote. The voter turnout in the election was a stunning 92.9 percent.[6] The Indian participation in the subsequent elections declined proportionately to the increase by the other communities. But compulsory voting was a good decision and, as my father had argued, a necessary one — if the majority did not participate, democracy lost its meaning.

~

The 1948 Legislative Council Election, held only one year after India's independence, hinted at decolonisation when the British introduced limited elections to positions on the Legislative Council. My mother became an independent candidate at my father's behest — the first woman to ever stand for elections in Singapore.[†] The contest happened in Seletar district, where the Malayalee population resided as employees of the British naval base.

My father, who ran the campaign, thought that my mother would win easily, as Seletar was very much an Indian stronghold and he believed ethnic loyalties would translate into votes. Why did my father himself not stand? He was not inclined to public life. He did not believe that he was articulate enough to be a politician. My mother, on the other hand, was an eloquent speaker and a forceful personality, along with being an ardent admirer of the Indian freedom fighter, Sarojini Naidu.

The other two competing candidates in the election were Mr. A. P. Rajah, who represented the Progressive Party and later became a judge of the Supreme Court; and Mr. S. C. Goho, an independent candidate and Bengali lawyer, who had links to Bose as his former secretary. My father

† This is true, as far as I am aware. The Singapore Elections Archive indicates she participated in the 1948 Legislative Council Elections. As a boy in the thick of things, I have strong memories of her political participation.

underestimated the degree to which Goho was revered in the Indian community, and it thus came as no surprise (except perhaps to my father) when Goho won 50 percent of the votes (the combined votes garnered by my mother and Rajah were less than the votes Goho received alone).[7] My mother obtained the second largest share of the votes. I recall my sister weaving a garland of flowers in excited anticipation of our mother's victory. After the results were announced, she threw it away in a huff.

After the election, droves of Indians from around the Seletar area visited us and apologised to my mother for not voting for her. "We have to remember how much Goho supported the Indian independence movement. We must show our gratitude. Forgive us. If you stand again, we will vote for you." Goho, as later reported to me by my parents, also admitted to my mother that she would have won the election. However, because of his association with "Netaji", the "Respected Leader", they gave him the votes.

~

Not long after the election, Goho fell seriously ill. Before he died, he requested my mother and father to see him. One of the first things he reportedly told my mother who was at his bedside was, "We need to settle a few things, because I am not going to be around for much longer." A by-election was on the way, and he wanted her to stand. But my mother, being stubborn, refused. She could be slightly overbearing, and take a trifle seriously. She had taken her loss to heart.

"No, the electorate rejected me, and so I will not stand again," she declared, and true to her word, she withdrew from politics. She went on to work for the Welfare Department, where she gave free lessons in English. I thought this was appropriate work for her. But my father took her loss badly. It also negatively affected our material well-being.

A lot of money had been spent on the election, partially because in those days candidates were expected to transport voters to the polling booths at their own expense, such as by hiring cars. Moreover, the campaign had caused my father to neglect his printing business. He once received a lot of government printing jobs (I think one of the first electoral registers had been printed by him, since there were very few printing presses in Singapore). But all this came to an end, and in the mid-1950s we went into a very difficult period financially.

Our spacious house in Haig Road was heavily mortgaged. The house was eventually sold, as was the car sometime earlier. My sister was sent to college in Madras, as my father could not afford to send her to the University of Malaya; and my mother went to live with her parents in Kerala. The election had taken a toll on my mother's health. My father and I, meanwhile, moved to a single rented room in a house in Mulberry Avenue in Sennet Estate. This was during my secondary school years, around when I was preparing to enter pre-university.[‡]

My father had other magazines published; and others also came to him with their publication ideas. But he was not sure if he would make money from these ventures, and was not too enthusiastic. When my father found that he could not handle the paper anymore, he handed it over to Mr. V. P. Abdullah, who was its editor at one time. He worked with another gentleman, Mr. V. M. Mathews. The paper's print-run reportedly continued until 1988.[8] However, they also struggled to make ends meet.

‡ The Malayalam readership, I believe, would also enter into a decline over the following years with the withdrawal of the British naval bases as part of the East of Suez Policy in 1971. The Malayalee population had started to return to India after the closure of the bases due to a policy of the British Labour Government under Prime Minister Harold Wilson. When the bases were pulled out, the Malayalees left their jobs. Some were given British passports and settled in London while others returned to India, as they found London's cost of living too high.

4

School Days (Or, Learning the Language of a New Country)

"My father also thought it would benefit me to attend a school with mainly Chinese students ... as time would tell, it put me at an advantage in getting to know the real Singapore. Our home was located on Koon Seng Road, near to East Coast Road — Joo Chiat — where many lower-income Chinese stayed. I got along well with the Chinese students and made many close friends."

Choosing the Right School

When I first came back to Singapore from India in 1946, I knew very little English. My parents decided that I needed to improve my understanding of the language as I progressed with my schooling.

The English language, in Singapore and in many other countries on the verge of gaining their independence, was seen as a language of aspiration. Although the majority of the population conversed in Malay, various Chinese dialects or different Indian languages, most desired to learn English to secure a good job and improve their fortunes. I was enrolled in St. Hilda's School in 1947 on Ceylon Road, just walking distance from our house. Having no knowledge of English, I was almost immediately demoted to Standard One and then further demoted to Primary Two after a couple of weeks.

But I had a good teacher, a Eurasian lady, who realised that actually in subjects such as mathematics I was quite advanced for my years. It was only in the English language that I struggled. She took the initiative to ask whether my mother could perhaps find me a good English language tutor. Another Eurasian lady, partly Keralite, who lived on Dunman Road, was thus hired to tutor me. By the end of that term, I was back in

Standard One and was promoted to Standard Two by the end of the year.

My father also thought it would benefit me to attend a school with mainly Chinese students, since Singapore was our home. So after studying at St. Hilda's for one and a half years, he arranged for my transfer to another nearby school, Choon Guan English School (later renamed Presbyterian Boys' School), which started out primarily as a Chinese school but was later converted for English education.[1] The rest of my family almost suffered a heart attack on hearing of my potential enrolment there, and debated vociferously whether I should study at a seemingly "political" Chinese school or instead find a place at a "proper" and "decent" English one.

Education in Singapore was very much bifurcated in those days. Chinese middle schools tended to be more politically active than their English counterparts, while the English schools were viewed as having greater discipline (at least from my family's perspective).[2] As I explained in my last chapter, the Chinese were divided into two camps. The first was the business community which, while proud of China, seemed to be politically apathetic and mainly concerned with keeping their families happy and fed. Second were the Chinese students who participated in the labour-oriented politics of the day by drawing up workers' programmes for unions and advocating for the end of colonial rule. From time to time, the Chinese student demonstrations turned violent, which required the police to haul the protesters away.

Raffles Institution, St. Joseph's Institution, Anglo Chinese School (ACS) and so on, tended to receive the cream of the crop amongst student enrolments. These high-performers concentrated mostly on their exams, which my family approved of. Several relatives teaching at ACS and St. Joseph's saw English schools as better for my advancement. But my father stressed that if I was going to live in Singapore, I should befriend the Chinese. My sister, meanwhile, joined Methodist Girls' School.

Language Learning

By the time I reached Standard Three, I had already spent a couple of years in Singapore and had acclimatised to the local environment. The school offered the Chinese language at Standard Three (from what I recall, Choon Guan was one of Singapore's first to do so). I studied Mandarin at my father's insistence. I did not appreciate the complexity of Singapore's colourful linguistic landscape in the 1940s and 1950s; but its vibrancy later became apparent to me from the stories I heard of others' time in National Service (NS).

As a slight digression, I recall the army leaders during NS in the late 1960s struggled to communicate their instructions to the cadets (who spoke various dialects such as Hokkien, Teochew and Cantonese). To overcome language difficulties, they were forced to relay their orders in English. The government began to view such barriers to communication as a social problem and, shortly earlier in 1966, had initiated a bilingual policy which was adopted into the national curriculum, requiring the study of two languages, including the formal study of Mandarin by the Chinese. In 1965, Education Minister Ong Pang Boon stated, "The breaking down of the language barrier, inimical to racial unity, must be further intensified to strengthen the foundations of a multi-racial nation."[3] By 1980, Mandarin language study was compulsory at government schools, increasing its usage in Chinese homes.[4]

This same strategy was not possible for the Singapore Indian community, as the linguistic gap between the Indian mother tongues was too great to bridge. While one could not teach all Indians the same language, one could nevertheless extend educational opportunities to facilitate communication among the communities, especially in Singapore's official languages. As one plank of its bilingual policy, the government schools instituted courses in Chinese, Malay and Tamil as well as English as the common working language: "the state permitted Indian students whose 'mother tongue' was not Tamil to study any of the three second languages on offer."[5]

Given prevailing linguistic complexities, my father had his own pragmatic philosophy on my language learning. Firstly, one must know one's mother tongue: in my case, Malayalam. (Despite having no formal schooling in the language, I made personal efforts to master it since my father ran a Malayalam newspaper. I am proud to say I became quite proficient — even to the point of impressing my relatives in Kerala!)

Of course, having a strong command over English would also be a prerequisite for success. Next, he said that one must learn Mandarin, because he foresaw it emerging as an important language in the future. Finally, he wanted me to learn Hindi, because he had another theory: "Everywhere in the world, Indians are getting kicked out of foreign countries. From Africa, Burma, wherever — so if you ever get kicked out too, the only place you will have left to go is India."

All of this to say, if anything were to go wrong in Singapore, the Indians had only one sanctuary to turn to in exile.

My father had been exaggerating, as it was not entirely true that Indians were being chased out of the former colonies. The British Empire needed administrative staff, which led them to employ an educated class of Indian clerks. Their employment sparked animosity with the local population, which, in seeking its independence, was reluctant to share jobs with the foreigners. In Burma, quite a bit of anti-Indian sentiment was stirred up because the Indian communities excelled there commercially, while Indians in Singapore, Malaysia and Indonesia had no such problems.

For this practical reason, my father insisted that I learn Hindi and enrolled me for private tuition at Netaji Hindi High School to learn the "Indian national language".[6] The classes offered at the high school followed the same exam system conducted by Hindi organisations in India like the *Dakshina Bharat Hindi Prachar Sabha* (the South India Hindi Promotion Society), which, along with teaching Hindi at various levels, held examinations and granted "degrees, diplomas and certificates for proficiency in the Hindi."[7] The prospect of Hindi's elevation as India's "national language" was controversial and widely debated in India, but my father believed Hindi would rise in prominence and prove useful for me to know in future.*

Then, when I was in Standard Six, around thirteen or fourteen years old, I made a mistake that upset my father: I switched subjects from Mandarin to Latin. Our class teacher had explained that for those

* Hindi was campaigned for as a national language during the Indian Independence Movement of the 1920s through the 1940s, but it was not made an official language of the new union until 1950 following mass agitations, most notably by South Indian communities in the 1930s.

of us doing higher studies, Latin would be useful. (In those days, Latin was seen as a language of prestige — the language of lawyers, doctors and better-off students. I also personally did not think that they quite had the numbers to fill the class.) My father gave me an earful when I got home. He said I should go back to studying Mandarin and saw no value in a "dead language". But to his credit, he never stopped my Latin studies, which I took up to Cambridge "O" Level. As a parent, he mostly gave me latitude to reap the consequences of my actions, which stood me in good stead.

Adjusting to School Life

My father was vindicated in his decision to enroll me in Choon Guan. Indeed, as time would tell, it put me at an advantage in getting to know the real Singapore. Our home was located on Koon Seng Road, near to East Coast Road — Joo Chiat — where many lower-income Chinese stayed. I got along well with the Chinese students and made many close friends.

While my family was debating which school I should attend, my father consulted an acquaintance of his, Reverend Charles B. Paul, who had taught at ACS, for his advice on whether I should stay at Choon Guan or be moved elsewhere. "Let's watch him for a bit and see how he does," the reverend had counseled.

After attending Choon Guan for some time, the reverend advised my father that, as I was as happy as a lark, "You should not move him anywhere." While my father was pleased with the answer (as the school was only a short walking distance from our house) my mother was crestfallen: she would have much preferred for me to go to a well-known English school.

I was quite active and often at the forefront of organising various school events at Choon Guan. For a small neighbourhood school, there were plenty of activities to become a part of — inter-class debates, poetry contests and so on. Music lessons and choir practice were mostly limited to the big, well-established schools. Still, our teacher Mr. Tan Keng Kang fostered an interest in music in a modest school like ours. He tested the voices of upper primary students like me who were keen to participate.

I also discovered that I was fairly good at reciting poetry and did well in the school poetry contests.

In addition, students were elected to official administrative positions, which they held for a year — class monitor, school prefect, civics club president, school librarian, house captain and so on. I was elected to all five posts. This vibrant, democratic atmosphere amongst the student body was suitable for a boy like me whose family had a background interest in politics. Although I was one of the very few non-Chinese in the class, I somehow managed to frequently come up for re-election.

~

Two specific events come to mind regarding my involvement in the school's Civics Club. These interestingly intersected with some of the broader political trends of the day. During the lead up to the 1955 Legislative Assembly General Election (the first time a majority of legislators were elected by popular ballot), the Civics Club in 1953 allowed mock elections to be held following a few days of campaigning. I stood against the PAP as an independent political candidate and won!

Closer to the time of the General Elections, the club also organised a public lecture for the occasion, which several political leaders from the competing parties — Mr. Toh Chin Chye, the chairman of the People's

Mock Election Candidates, 1953 (me on the extreme left).

Action Party (PAP) and an independent journalist from *The Straits Times*, Mr. John Bartlett — came to attend. I was the student assigned to welcome them.

My election to the school's top posts occurred so frequently that our Civics Club teacher grew concerned for the "health of our democracy", and pleaded with the students to stop electing the same person over and over. I recall one student stood up to reply, "But Sir, we must exercise our democratic rights!"

Since my school days, I have privately wondered what it was that allowed me to get along with my Chinese classmates so well. I was not necessarily a great student (I would not get top marks, like my sister). On reflecting on why my classmates continued to vote for me, I concluded that they liked how enthusiastic I was. Indeed, with the distance of years, I feel that the Chinese have a special character — if they think you are capable, then they will respect and support you. No matter whether it was sprinting, mathematics or any other field, if you were good, they were very happy to put you forward; personal effort came first.

"Beware of Colonial Stooges!" Choon Guan Presbyterian School Debate.
(Quotation written on the back of the photo.)

For Indians, caste and family position sometimes complicate one's social interactions. The Chinese focus on the quality of one's work, however, makes it easier to integrate. You just have to work hard and do your best. So between the football matches and inter-class debates, we had a good mix of sportsman-like and semi-intellectual influences and teachers who taught us what was relevant.

A Strong Civics Education

Our principal at Choon Guan Presbyterian School, the "Great Democrat", B. F. Atherton.

As a schoolboy, I kept records of the Singapore elections in a thick accountant's volume, which I stored in a drawer of the desk in my bedroom. My father approved of this style of accounting. Every year when I took out the volume, his chest swelled with pride; he was pleased that a boy of my age was taking such an interest in local politics. Indeed, politics followed me throughout my youth. During the 1948 Legislative Council Elections, I remember going out campaigning with my mother while she made speeches and my father handled the campaign logistics. As a boy (thanks to the influence of my father's newspaper) I could rattle off the names of India's political leaders off the top of my head!

Choon Guan's principal, Mr. Bernar Atherton — a Welshman inspired by the freedom struggles unfolding in Asia and Africa — was the ultimate democrat. Though a staunch Christian, he was open and liberal minded and held abundant respect for all religions. He decided to run the school democratically by emphasising civic education and raising our general political awareness. The quality of education provided at Choon Guan, thus, fell somewhere between the "proper" English and the "political" Chinese schools, which, with our music programme, made it unique. (Of the non-elite Singapore schools, ours was the only one that taught Western music and won music competitions.)

During Standard Six, our class teacher Mr. M. Ignatius, of Sri Lankan origin, tasked us with assembling a small magazine of articles on the 1952 American presidential election. The contest was between Dwight D. Eisenhower and Adlai Stevenson. I wrote an article in favour of Eisenhower. With hindsight, this was probably because he received better publicity than his opponent as a hero of the Second World War. (I admired how he was a gentleman.)

I later sent the article to my youngest uncle in India. Kochapamama would normally never interfere ideologically in anyone's business. But on this occasion he blew his top. He wrote back furiously, "You should have been much more fair and read more widely! Your judgment is totally wrong." My father, however, told me to stick with my beliefs. "One must not keep changing to suit the audience," he advised.

~

Communism, as a political force in Singapore, reared its head in the late 1940s and 1950s. On one occasion, when I must have been in Standard Four (by personal estimation, 1951),[†] a group of young people marched into Choon Guan, demanding that everyone surrender their identity cards (ICs) to them. The colonial government had issued ICs for individuals over twelve years of age (perhaps as a part of the 1948 Emergency Regulations [Registration] legislation, which was implemented by the colonial government to weed out communist infiltrators).[8]

Being young and easily impressed, we appreciated these cards with our photographs on them. But the ICs were considered an outrage by the hardcore communists and nationalists who felt that this was yet another humiliating policy of the British. The situation appeared rather frightening when these goons rounded up the teachers together in a room and tore up the cards right in front of them.

As students, we did not quite know how to react to this intrusion. It happened on the first day of work for poor Bernar Atherton. One teacher told us just to do as they said and not to resist. The police were called once they had gone, and asked us some questions as follow-up. But nobody was caught and the action taken afterward was minimal.

[†] We established the timing according to circumstantial details. Identity papers were introduced in 1938, which were replaced with identity cards in 1948. Bernar Atherton became Choon Guan's principal in 1951. The ICs were perhaps initially issued in 1948, and maybe re-issued separately later; I would have been a student in Standard Four around this time.

From then on, the teachers began patrolling the school during assembly to prevent such break-ins from reoccurring. New ICs were issued.

With political activism gaining increasing visibility, the balanced civics-style education Atherton practised gave the students, I think, a rare degree of autonomy and maturity in their thinking compared to other schools, as the system of democratic elections was still a novel governance concept in Singapore at that time. It served me well, from my perspective, as it gave me many chances to get involved in student life. I believe the other students also benefitted — in my class of forty students, I do not think many would have been exposed to the same manner of political education that I had.

Some of the students were less appreciative, and they complained to the principal that civics should not be offered as an examination subject: they said only proper tests under the Cambridge system should be allowed. Despite their "right to protest", they were nevertheless made to sit for the class civics examination. Still, while Atherton's approach to education provided us with the knowledge and experience of a working democracy, there were probably too many elections, which distracted us from our studies. Most schools only elected prefects; but at Choon Guan, we had five or six elections per year. Compared with primary education today, I venture students have become more education-focused. However, with social media and a more active political climate, this might be changing.

Drama

At this point, I would also like to highlight some notable extracurricular activities, which added to the quality of my life and influenced several non-work related interests later on.

Choon Guan had an excellent literature and drama instructor, Mr. Seow Cheng Fong. He was one of the great actors of the time — a left-wing Teachers' Union activist, a big persona and one of the most divisive voices you could ever get. He produced and acted in a few plays like Shakespeare's *Macbeth*. His part was perhaps a small one, as a tailor or watchman, but he had a resounding voice that carried powerfully throughout the auditorium. He also had a strong stage presence. When the play was over, everyone would be twittering about the character's terrific performance.

Cheng Fong, along with my mother, fuelled my budding interest in poetry. He liked the fact that I was fond of literature. My mother, whenever we argued, had used an adapted quote from Alfred Lord Tennyson's 'Charge of the Light Brigade' to me as a form of reprimand: "Yours is not to reason why." She tactfully left out the rest of the poem, which continues: "Yours is but to do and die."

One memorable play Cheng Fong put on with the students was *Julius Caesar*. I wanted to play the part of Mark Anthony, since he is the one who makes all the great speeches and turns the crowd against the plotters of Caesar's murder. Instead, he cast me as Brutus (the leader of the rival group of conspirators), whom he referred to in class as the "noble man". He explained he picked actors who resembled the character. "Brutus," he pointed out, "is a very sensible man; he does not kill Caesar just because of his politics, but because he was too ambitious." Brutus realised that Caesar's ambition was not for the good of his country. "You have some principles, and are not an opportunist. So I cast you as Brutus."

As one further feather to his cap, Cheng Fong produced a Chinese play in English about the last empress of China, a dowager. The play was called *The Motherly and the Auspicious*. I did not act in this play, as it required 100 percent Chinese actors. But Cheng Fong insisted that there should be one non-Chinese person, if for nothing else than to walk across the stage a few times to move some props. This was to convey to the Singapore audience that this was a Singapore production. Of course, I was the one designated to move around the set pieces.

An interesting and important character in the story was a eunuch. In imperial China, only eunuchs were granted permission to visit the women's quarters — normally, men were forbidden from entry. As I was the one allowed to enter various parts of the set, the actors began to joke and ask me whether I was the eunuch. I did not find this very funny.

My engagement with the arts was mainly motivated by my personal appreciation. Occasionally, I was asked to write snippets of poems. I tried, but I decided I was better off reading good poetry than writing bad poems. Today, I feel that the study of the arts is necessary for our public servants and politicians, as it expands our empathy and cultural understanding. Reading poetry is also worth our while — not just English poetry but also reading in one's own mother tongue, especially if one is from a multi-lingual family. There are some poems from Malayalam, for instance, which I find to be especially poignant.

All across the world, life is moving at a faster pace, and people are becoming increasingly preoccupied with the question of "what can I gain from my endeavours?" With poetry, I feel, people are most likely inclined to think, "This crazy thing is not even going to earn me a penny, and so what worth is there in writing or reading it?" But I find this type of reasoning — to not develop or articulate a passion towards that which one is inclined — to be very unfortunate.

THE STAFF

(From left to right) Sitting: Mrs. Tan Keng Kang, Mrs. Mabel Tan, Mrs. Soh Ghee Soon, Mr. B. F. Atherton (Principal), Mr. Gay Wan Guay, Mrs. Khoo Poh Ann, Miss Yeo Soo Hoon. Second Row: Messrs. Lim Siak Kim, Robert Tully, M. Ignatius, Seow Cheng Fong, Koh Hock Heng, Lee Kong Boon, Hee Ah Nghot. Third Row: Messrs. Lee Fook Leong, Wee Seng Hiok, Tan Chek Sian, C. I. Joseph, Tan Keng Kang.

We had excellent teachers at Choon Guan dedicated to teaching us what was relevant. First row: B. F. Atherton (sitting, centre). Second row: M. Ignatius and Seow Cheng Fong (standing behind Atherton). Third row: Tan Keng Kang (extreme right).

Pre-University

I sat for my Senior Cambridge Examinations (now known as "O" Levels) at Choon Guan. By the early 1950s, I had started to feel great stress seeing my poor father struggle with his printing to make ends meet. I decided to ease his burden by going to work when I finished my exams. My father was not averse to the idea. My mother, however (with whom I regularly communicated while she was in India), exploded at the mention of quitting my studies to work. She wanted me to study at the University of Malaya, and I did not want to break her heart.

Thus, reluctantly, I gave up the idea of getting a job. When I finished Senior Cambridge, I went on instead to study at St. Andrew's Secondary School for my pre-university. Choon Guan did not have the facility for doing the university entrance examination; I had to switch schools if I wanted to progress.

When seeking admission to St. Andrew's Secondary School, the principal, Reverend Canon R. K. S. Adams (an Australian), interviewed me. He asked a few questions about my studies and checked my report card. He pronounced my name very correctly and asked if I was from Kerala. I was shocked by his insight.

The principal of St. Andrew's Secondary School, Rev. Canon R. K. S. Adams.

"How did you know I am from Kerala?"

"Because our students from Kerala are very good at their studies."

I could not help but laugh. "Sir, I am very impressed by your knowledge."

"Of course," he said offhandedly. "It is essential for us to know the backgrounds of the children we teach."

He then offered me a place at St. Andrew's. I did quite well there, and then went on to the University of Malaya. Little did I know I was about to embark on possibly what was the most exhilarating journey of my life.

Me (left) in pre-university debating with classmates on whether "Malaya is Fit for Independence".

5

University Life

"In the 1950s and 1960s, university students were politically active. Today, to some extent, they have become less so. There should be a greater airing of views and freedom in political debate, for a wider presentation of the facts. Not argument for argument's sake, but rather, developing a conversation on how the country should look at important issues."

Debate with My Father: Law or Arts

In 1957, only one university existed: the University of Malaya based in Singapore. The University of Malaya had started a law faculty, and my father, keen that I should do law, thought that I would be a suitable candidate. The Law Faculty then was easy to get into. I could not get a scholarship or bursary to do a law degree; however, I could get a bursary for an arts degree with a bond for three or four years for teaching. I was insistent that I should take up the arts bursary, not because I was against doing legal studies, but because I did not want to strain my father's financial resources, which had just started to stabilise.

My father's finances were improving, as he had given up his publishing business and become a salaried man. He became the superintendent of the newly set up Asian Seamen's Club, which gave him reasonable pay and accommodation for his family. He was confident he could pay for my studies if I did a law degree and stayed in Singapore. Nevertheless, I had one principle that I stuck to, which was that while I might remain dependent on my father for my clothes and books, I was adamant that, at the very least, he would not pay for my fees. This could have been due to manly pride.

Family photo taken during my time at St. Andrew's Secondary School.

I became a member of the university student body on September 18th, 1957. This was also my twentieth birthday. During university, I became quieter and more focused compared to my school days. In terms of my academic and extracurricular pursuits, I learned that tomorrow I could still work at it: not everything needed to be consumed in one sitting. My mother supported my decision to pursue the Arts, hoping that I would specialise in her favourite subject, English literature. I did two subjects at University — economics and history — and took English as a subsidiary degree. I also carried on with those extracurricular activities I had developed a fondness for in primary school: plays, debates, elocution contests and so on. I should also mention that it was during this period I met the young lady who would later become my wife.

~

That year, the University of Malaya tried out an experiment by sending the first-year arts students to Kuala Lumpur to start a second campus. We were housed in the Technical College campus based in rented premises on Gurney Road. Before boarding the train for Kuala Lumpur, the Singapore students were required to attend one week of orientation at Bukit Timah Campus. There, we were called "freshies" — students fresh from school, ready to be ragged.

Indians were the worst raggers, and one "senior gentleman" (whose girlfriend had informed him she had met me at a beach picnic) caught hold of me on the first day. He seemed to have been waiting. He insisted that I get into the Bukit Timah canal and show him how well I could swim! I did not have to swim much, but I got drenched in the filthy water. I escaped by running to the Dunearn Road/Whitley Road junction and caught a Green Bus back to the campus. The Chinese bus conductor who saw me all wet said loudly, "*Lu punya orang selalu mabok!*" (Your people are always drunk!) This was as good an example of racial stereotyping as any!

The Technical College campus in Kuala Lumpur had only basic facilities. I was given a room with a quiet boy from Kedah. This was the first time I had interacted with a Malay student. Quite a few boys and political figures hailed from this state. Prior to this, I did not know many. In university, I found them to be very polite. (I think my roommate maybe found me too robust.)

In our second year, we were brought back to Singapore. Several female undergraduates in the Arts Faculty complained about the spartan facilities at the Technical College, which they had found appalling. The university dispatched the engineering students in our place, who were almost entirely boys (there were hardly any female undergraduates in the Engineering Faculty then). Maybe owing to social perceptions at the time, they thought the boys would be better able to rough it out.

The University Socialist Club

One of the first things I did on returning to the Singapore campus in my second year was to join the University Socialist Club (USC). The USC was seen by some to be a very Leftist group. Gravitating to left-wing politics was only natural for me, given the early influence of Kochapamama.

The wonderful stories my uncle had shared with me while we were in India stoked my skepticism of capitalism's internal contradictions. This left-leaning stridency, as I have recounted earlier, was moderated under the watchful eye of my father during my first few years in Singapore. But I had firmly believed former Premier of the Soviet Union Nikita Khrushchev when he declared to the capitalist West in 1956, "We will bury you"* (though this did not turn out to be the case).

Cheng Fong, my school teacher at Choon Guan, had also constantly spoken to me about the need for an intellectual Left. Several Socialist Club members propounded that socialism was the only philosophy that could end exploitation and discrimination and establish a more egalitarian society. My friends and teachers were maybe understandably concerned when I joined the USC, fearing that I would get involved in some unfortunate business that would jeopardise my future. Similarly,

---

* A more accurate translation would be "we will outlast you".

everyone in security and the government were keeping a close eye on the students.

An idealistic adolescent, I saw too much exploitation in the world, and felt it was one's moral obligation to devote energies towards elevating those who were struggling. I thus boldly entered university with the mindset that a degree was not as important as an education. Education was what was necessary — the opportunity not just to learn, but more specifically, to learn that which would be of value to others.

I also admired the USC's official publication, *Fajar*, for which the club was perhaps most popular. Cheng Fong was the first person to present me with a copy. "Fajar" is an Indonesian/Arabic word that means "The Dawn". The publication had earned the USC a reputation when *Fajar*'s previous editorial committee had been accused of sedition and taken to court in what became a big case.

One remarkable aspect of the 1954 Fajar trial was Mr. Lee Kuan Yew's service as a legal advisor to the USC. Although accounts vary (some state he was first approached by the Chinese middle school students), he

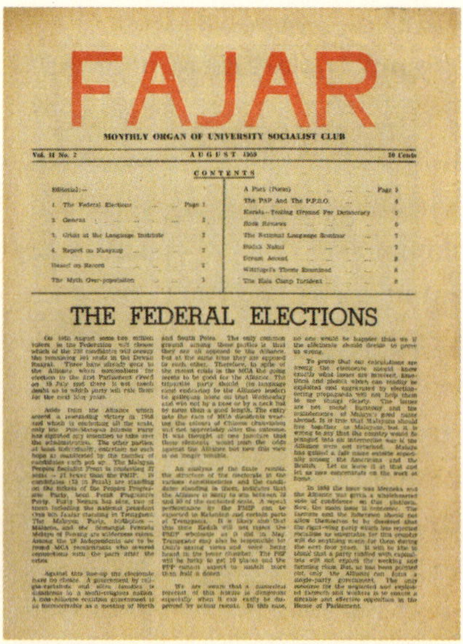

FAJAR

MONTHLY ORGAN OF UNIVERSITY SOCIALIST CLUB

Vol. II No. 2 AUGUST 1959 10 Cents

CONTENTS

THE FEDERAL ELECTIONS

Fajar, Monthly Organ of the University Socialist Club, Vol. II, No. 2, August 1959.
Front page article in 1959, "The Federal Elections" in Malaya.

"arranged the Queen's Counsel", Mr. D. N. Pritt, to defend them, "while he himself acted as junior counsel."[1] Pritt represented the students free of charge and won the case. It was one of the successes of the justice system at that time. The Supreme Court rejected the accusations and acquitted the students. Pritt turned into a hero.

I followed the Fajar trial of 1954 through *The Straits Times* almost daily, and was thrilled when the students were acquitted by the court. The successful conclusion to the trial also made *Fajar* well known and vaulted its popularity; it brought a few students into the university with tendencies towards activism, perhaps exacerbating parental concerns. The USC held public debates and, in the absence of similar politics-based organisations — excluding the Chinese schools and the Singapore Polytechnic Political Society, whose publications had a limited readership — it stole the limelight.

Special Edition of *Fajar*

Having received my first copy of *Fajar* from Cheng Fong, and having closely followed the 1954 Fajar trial in the papers, I felt that I too would be associated with this publication one day. When I became its publication secretary after joining the USC, it was a dream come true.

Membership in the USC was intellectually rewarding. Firstly, it enabled me to understand in a more nuanced manner the fast changing political scene in Singapore and other countries. A simple example was what happened at the City Council when Singapore was given city status in 1951.

The Progressive Party, which considered itself the rightful successors of political power from the British, was discussing how the new City Council would function. Speculation brewed about who the mayor would be. If my memory serves me right, Ms. Amy Laycock, daughter of a well-known lawyer and Legislative Council member, Mr. John Laycock, was asked what she would be wearing when she attended the council meetings. The Progressive Party's scrupulous attention to dress-code became irrelevant after the PAP swept the Council elections and Mr. Ong

Eng Guan became the mayor, with Mr. Ong Pang Boon as his deputy. The men in white came in, and there was no more discussion on the sartorial tastes of the members! All this had a tremendous effect on students like me.

Listening to Mr. S. Woodhull (a founding member of the USC who later became an influential trade union leader)[2] recount for the benefit of newer members his participation as an observer at the Bandung Conference was its own education. The Bandung Conference was an era-defining meeting held in Bandung, Indonesia, where twenty-nine African and Asian countries met to establish third-world solidarity amidst the emerging great power rivalry of the Cold War. Woodhull would drop in on club activities after graduating to offer his advice and views on major global events; I was very impressed with the way he spoke and his great sense of humour.

The third benefit of USC membership was the excitement of being involved in its political activities. Allow me to go into a few of the significant events.

~

This is a short episode from 1961 about *Fajar*, when the licence to print the publication was in my name. We got wind through the international media that the prime minister of the Congo, Patrice Lumumba, was killed on January 17th, 1961 by the Belgian police. Congo had recently become an independent nation, free from Belgian rule, and Mr. Lumumba was its first democratically elected prime minister. The murder was received as a galling affront by nations around the world fighting for their independence.

The club held a protest meeting at the Victoria Theatre, where I spoke on behalf of the students. The USC immediately decided to publish a special edition of *Fajar* to express our outrage and enjoin the United Nations (UN) to take appropriate action against Belgium.

An article I wrote for Fajar entitled "Kerala — Testing Ground for Democracy", July 29th, 1959

KERALA—Testing Ground for Democracy

The Question

"Charge-Sheet"

The Opposition

STOP PRESS

Much attention has been recently focussed on the state of Kerala. This state first came into the limelight 27 months ago when for the first time in history, a Communist Party was elected into office. Today, Kerala has again hit the headlines due to the very questionable tactics employed by the opposition to compel the Central government to establish Presidential rule.

Kerala has shown an inclination towards the left for some time and it came as no surprise when the state elected a Communist government in the first elections held after the three political units of Travancore, Cochin and Malabar were united to form the state of Kerala. If we are to analyse the choice of the electorate we can find some very definitive reasons for the victory of the Communists and the defeat of Nehru's once all powerful Congress Party…

The opposition has hitherto worked on the assumption that as soon as some action of the Government causes discontentment amongst certain sections of the people, however small this particular section might be, the Government is obliged to resign and hold new elections… They seem to forget that there is no democratic government in the world which can claim 100% support of its people. The fact that the people are in a position to show their opposition openly against a government action is itself a sign of a healthy democratic system…

The question that the Central government is facing today concerning Kerala is whether they should intervene to terminate the rule of a constitutionally elected party which has hitherto confined itself within the limits of the constitution. The decision they take will be of vital importance to India and the rest of the world…

Stop The Press

Soon after this article went to print, the Indian Central Government decided to abandon Democracy and install Presidential rule in Kerala. In view of this I feel justified in changing the title of this article to "KERALA-Death-bed of Democracy."

We decided to bring out a special bilingual edition, both in English and Mandarin, to enlarge our audience and reach a wider readership, and had the special edition on newsstands within a few days. We then started elatedly planning the follow-up events that would ensure Singapore would show its indignation at the murder of this respected Congolese independence leader.

However, this euphoria was short-lived, and the sky caved in on us. I remember receiving a letter from the Ministry of Home Affairs asking us to show due cause for why our printing licence should not be revoked (*Fajar* was supposed to be published only in English). Stupid as it may sound, I had no idea that there was any such restriction. I decided to seek help where I could get it.

Communication was slow in those days, and visiting folks with whom you wanted to speak was typically a better option than calling them. So I went to the Middle Road Union Headquarters (considered a somewhat militant, left-wing organisation) and spoke to Mr. S. T. Bhani, a trade unionist, and Mr. Dominic Puthucheary. Dominic, like S. Woodhull, was one of the "Big Six" trade union leaders; from 1956 onwards, he had occupied roles in the Singapore Trades Union Congress, the Singapore's General Employees Union and the Singapore Association of Trade Unions (Satu).[3] With their help, I secured an appointment to see the person in charge of the issuance of permits, Dr. Lee Siew Choh.

My friends took pains to impress upon me that I was to eat humble pie and apologise for my mistake of publishing in Chinese; they said I should clarify that I had no intention of challenging the government. "Assure him that the mistake will not be repeated. Look genuinely remorseful."

Despite my fears, Dr. Lee was forgiving. He gave me a full half an hour lecture on the importance of honouring commitments. I recall him asserting at one point in his monologue, "There is no hope for us all if educated people start to break the law."

He listened to my explanation, looking impatient at times, and said he needed to think it through and consult with his staff. It would take a few days. Meanwhile, he instructed for the publication not to be distributed and for me to write a letter of apology asking the Ministry not to revoke our licence. I was let off the hook.

I pledged that I would not distribute any more copies until they granted the approval. But a good number had been distributed already, particularly to the institutions of higher learning. That same year (1961), Dr. Lee left the PAP and, with the other aforementioned left-wing political figures like S. Woodhull and Dominic Puthucheary, formed the party Barisan Sosialis. He became the party's chairman.[4]

My Altercation with the Vice-Chancellor

Our vice-chancellor, Sir Alexander Oppenheim, struck the students as an intimidating character. During our gathering in a large hall for first-year orientation before we departed to start the new campus in Kuala Lumpur, he imparted a warning that we would never forget. "Look to your left, now look to your right. Of the three of you, only one will leave the university with a degree." This declaration instilled enough fear to doubly motivate us to finish our bachelor's degree!

As time would tell, this was not my last memorable encounter with Oppenheim. Sometime in my third year, I learned that there were some students, mostly of Malay background, whose parents were earning as little as fifty dollars a month as junior clerks at a British company. This came as a shock to me, and so we at the USC decided to take a survey of the salaries of clerical workers at European firms. A group of us went with this information to the Middle Road Union, where I again spoke with Dominic Puthucheary, and asked him if he was aware that people were being paid such low salaries.

He said that he was aware, but explained there was little he could do, as he did not have the statistics to back up the claims. When I asked why the information was lacking, he told me that they did not have the manpower to conduct a study. I proposed to collect the data myself. If he was prepared, I said he could provide me with a detailed questionnaire of the type of information he required. I would organise a small group to collect the data for him at one of the factories.

He spoke to the secretary-general of the National Trades Union Congress (NTUC), Devan Nair, a powerful union member, and Mr. K. M.

Byrne, the minister for labour and law. Both men supported the idea — the latter even came out with a statement complimenting the USC on carrying out such an undertaking. Somehow word got around to the press about the survey (perhaps leaked by the union), which then came to the attention of the International Chamber of Commerce. Oppenheim was furious and summoned me to his office.

As I entered, not knowing why, he barked, "What do you think you are doing?"

"If you can explain, Sir, what the issue is about?" I asked hesitantly.

"Writing articles, and pretending to be an academic!" He stared hard at me with his thick bushy eyebrows. "What makes you think you are qualified to do this?" He was informed that I had been targeting European firms with an investigation into the workers' welfare on behalf of the university.

I replied as calmly as I could that we were simply conducting a survey — a clerical job of collecting answers for a questionnaire by NTUC — not writing a thesis or report. (European firms, in general, were better organised with proper salary structures and records in English. We believed that the information we obtained should be made available to everyone, who could make their own analysis.)

Oppenheim was not convinced; he forbade me from continuing with the survey. Not wanting to give in so easily, I said I would discuss it with my committee. To this, he replied somewhat angrily that it was not up for discussion. "If I asked you to stop this nonsense and not to proceed, would you do it?"

I answered that as a university student I would definitely do as he told me.

The International Chamber of Commerce consisted of representatives from European firms. Its members must have felt alarmed that a Leftist movement was trying to coerce them into providing a more attractive deal for the workers. I think that the business community probably also partly funded the university along with the government, and that this may have been why the Vice-Chancellor had accused us of dragging down the university's good name. The uproar could have also been caused by the perception that the Leftists were instigating students against the British.

I agreed to his request to end the survey. I was about to graduate, and it would not have affected my contemporaries and me in any case. However, I did not want the first-year students who were keen to carry out the survey to land into trouble.

"You may go," Oppenheim said, and I exited the office. But I still managed to publish a small write-up on the matter for *Fajar* before receiving written instructions from the Vice-Chancellor not to do so.

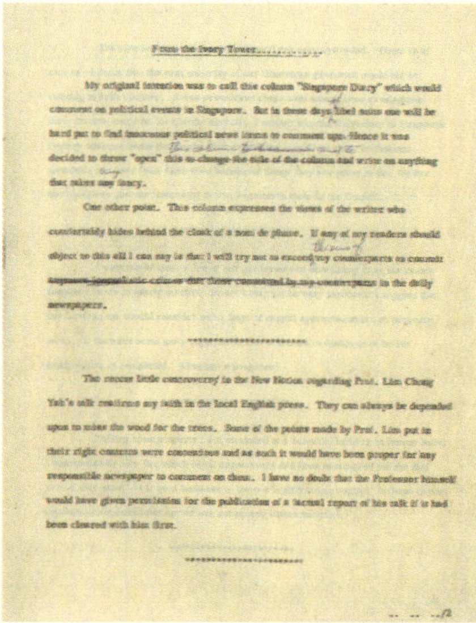

From the Ivory Tower...............

My original intention was to call this column "Singapore Diary" which would comment on political events in Singapore. But in these days libel suits one will be hard put to find innocuous political news items to comment upon. Hence it was decided to throw "open" this to change the title of the column and write on anything that takes any fancy.

One other point. This column expresses the views of the writer who comfortably hides behind the cloak of a nom de plume. If any of my readers should object to this all I can say is that I will try not to exceed my counterparts as columnist [illegible] in the daily newspapers.

****

The recent little controversy in the New Nation regarding Prof. Lim Chong Yah's talk confirms my faith in the local English press. They can always be depended upon to miss the wood for the trees. Some of the points made by Prof. Lim put in their right contexts were contentious and as such it would have been proper for any responsible newspaper to comment on them. I have no doubt that the Professor himself would have given permission for the publication of a factual report of his talk if it had been cleared with him first.

****

-- -- --/2

A separate article draft, perhaps intended for The Straits Times or The Sunday Times

"My original intention was to call this column 'Singapore diary' which would comment on political events in Singapore. But in these days of libel suits one will be hard put to find innocuous political news items to comment upon. Hence, it was decided to throw 'open' this column and to write on anything that takes my fancy."

The USC Community and Presidential Elections

Besides these exciting incidents, perhaps what I cherished most about the USC were the many friendships I made. In the senior batches before me were recognisable figures who continued to attend club functions and participate in its discussions: Mr. James Puthucheary, Mr. S. Woodhull, Mr. Poh Soo Kai, Mr. Lim Hock Siew, Mr. Jeyaraj Rajarao, Mr. P. Arudsothy and a few others. They were more politically assertive than us and became activists and trade unionists. James Puthucheary became famous for writing *Ownership and Control of the Malayan Economy*. Notable juniors in the batch after me included Mr. Ramalingam Joethy, Mr. Wong Kum Poh and Mr. Tan Jing Quee, the last of whom sadly passed away a few years ago.

I would be remiss if I did not mention a few special figures from my cohort, such as Professor Tommy Koh, who I found to be one of the most organised and hard working people I had ever met. He carried cards on which he wrote down the gist of any serious conversation he had and what follow up was needed (these were subsequently indexed). Mr. Tan Guan Heng is another dear friend from that period. Guan Heng was perhaps closest to me, as we shared similar views on people and events. In spite of having lost his eyesight after graduation, his approach to life is always cheerful. Even today, a fortnightly conversation with him perks me up.

In our third year, elections were held at the USC, and everyone was holding their breath in anticipation of Tommy Koh becoming president. The third year was effectively the final year for those of us who were not pursuing an Honours degree — indeed, critical for many starting to contemplate their careers. It thus felt like a bomb had been dropped on us when Tommy announced that he would not be running for president to focus instead on his studies. He wanted to do well in Law and would not have time for other commitments.

All of us were in the same boat. Exams were coming, and most of us were diffident about taking on this time-consuming task. As publications secretary, the senior-most ranking member in the USC after Tommy, everybody looked at me. "You have no choice. You must become the president," they argued.

I became president in Tommy's place and was quite active. We pursued several initiatives under my leadership, such as forming a separate organisation with the students of Nanyang University Political Science Society and the Singapore Polytechnic Political Society, with whom we brought out another magazine.

Lee Kuan Yew Addresses the Student Body

The PAP won a handsome victory in the 1959 Parliamentary Election, and Lee Kuan Yew became the prime minister (although Singapore was at this time still a British colony).[†] The Socialist Club welcomed the PAP to power and became one of the first organisations to invite the prime minister to address the student body after the election was held. As USC president, I chaired the meeting.

Lee Kuan Yew, for some time, had been looked upon as a socialist leader. When Lee Kuan Yew's PAP was formed in 1954 (one year before Singapore achieved limited self-government) the far left wing had pivoted away from radical "revolution" towards an electoral alliance with the PAP. In the preceding years, the government had cracked down against the Communist Party of Malaya (CPM) for its involvement in "bombings, assassinations, ambushes, train derailments [and] fire-fights in the jungle".[5] These violent acts elicited a harsh response from the British; they invoked an "Emergency" with support from the Malayan military, intelligence and police.

To the best of my memory, however, far left-wing politics had nevertheless entered into a decline in the early 1950s. Yeo Kim Wah states, "[w]ith the outbreak of the communist insurrection in Malaya, a strange tranquility descended on the political and labour scene..."; the detention of "thirty-four left-wing, communist-oriented leaders [in 1951]... mark[ed] the end of overt leftwing activity in the colony till 1954".[6] The pro-communists had again later "attempted to attain political power through a united front with the [PAP]"[7] from 1954 to 1961. According to a report by the ISEAS-Yusof Ishak Institute, the PAP's moderate leadership was in an uneasy relationship with the pro-communists to "get the vote of the Chinese masses to win elections to advance their own agenda".[8]

Apart from his political leanings, one reason we at the USC invited Lee Kuan Yew to speak was that he was a fantastic orator; we liked how he never minced his words and always gave a frank and honest assessment of developments. If a referendum had ever been held, Lee Kuan Yew, I am sure, would have at any time still walked away with a majority. People liked his no-nonsense style. The struggle between the

[†] Some politically informed people joked that you had a group of elected members of parliament and a cabinet reporting to the colonial government.

left-wing socialists and the moderate English-educated leaders within the PAP would, of course, come to a head in July 1961, when the left-wing faction split from the PAP. I cannot recall what the levels of membership in the USC were like in the early 1960s — maybe dwindling. The club was not what you would call a rising sun but was holding its own.

~

The Prime Minister's address started at 8pm. Unexpectedly, while he was up on stage, just before 9pm, a group of students had started to walk out of the auditorium. The auditorium could fit around one hundred-and-fifty to two hundred people: their exit was visible.

I sat on the stage next to the Prime Minister. Lee Kuan Yew turned to me and, with shock and disappointment in his voice, asked, "Why are they leaving? Are they bored?" The question made me nervous.

"They have gone to collect red spotted books."

"Red spotted books? What are they?"

"Books which the university are in short supply of," I answered. "They can only be borrowed after 9.00pm. They have to reserve them in advance, and return them the next morning. They probably went to collect their books on reserve."

"Will they come back?" This was difficult to answer, as it required some guesswork.

"I think they will come back," I ventured.

My gamble paid off, and after about twenty to twenty-five minutes the group of students returned. I breathed easily again. Without looking at my face, he said, "Yes, they have come back." It came off as a successful event.

Job Offer from the PAP and a Misunderstanding

Before I left the university, James Puthucheary approached me to gauge whether I would be interested in joining the editorial board of *Petir*, the official publication of the PAP. He might have offered me the job because of my experience writing columns at the university as well as my exposure to political issues. I had to turn down his offer because I was under a teaching bursary from the government. The conversation was held in a public space.

Several months later a by-election was held in Hong Lim Ward in 1961.[9] As the chairman of the joint committee of the Socialist Club, the Nanyang University Political Science Society and the Singapore Polytechnic Political Society, I released a statement in support of the PAP candidate Jek Yuen Thong against his opponent Ong Eng Guan. The opposition candidate won, and, as it turned out, the PAP candidate was defeated.

In one unexpected post-election development, I learned that an anonymous letter had been circulated to the other political societies alleging that I had forced through the statement supporting the PAP because of a job promise by the party. The Polytechnic club members confronted me over the allegations. Refuting the rumours, I confirmed that this was absolutely untrue.

6

A Young Lady

"In thinking back on the various obstacles I faced in my youth, I was fortunate in that I generally did what I enjoyed and did not have to try too hard. Wooing Shyamala was the first major challenge I had to overcome! I started pursuing her as soon as I set eyes on her."

A Significant Meeting

Undoubtedly, the most significant event of my first year was when I met a rather quiet, serious girl from Malaysia. She was tall, elegant and carried herself well. She always seemed to be in deep thought and sometimes wore a sad expression on her face. There was something about her that made me want to make her smile.

I soon discovered that her name was Ms. Shyamala Devi. Shyamala was a Malayalee from Kuala Pilah, a small town near Seremban in Malaysia. She was also a first-year arts student and had plans to major in English. She, like my sister, was a better student than me. In thinking back on the various obstacles I faced in my youth, I was fortunate in that I generally did what I enjoyed and did not have to try too hard. Wooing Shyamala was the first major challenge I had to overcome! I started pursuing her as soon as I set eyes on her.

A short story from my pre-university days is perhaps worth recounting here. After finishing my university entrance examinations, I remember basking in the afterglow of having survived the crucible with my Chinese friends. As young boys do, we chatted about girls and tried to guess what sort of person each of us would marry.

When my turn came, my friends — maybe because they were all Chinese — guessed that I would marry someone who was Chinese also. My class teacher Mr. Chong Hock Hai was listening to our conversation and interjected to offer his views. "You are judging a person based on only one aspect of his character. However, you need to probe Gopi's character more deeply."

Hock Hai used to address me by my abbreviated name, Gopi, as many of my friends continue to do. He was of the opinion that I had inherited Indian values because of my family upbringing and would therefore feel most at home in an Indian environment. I found this observation interesting, although maybe not entirely accurate.

The Courtship

Dating in the mid-twentieth century was not so robust as it is in the twenty-first. The early part of my courtship was thus predominantly confined to the university campus.

In our first year at the Technical College at Kuala Lumpur, Shyamala used to visit the common room during her free time to listen to Hindi music, which I also enjoyed. Soon, I would appear whenever she went there. She had a graceful walk that reminded me of Lord Byron's poem 'She Walked in Beauty'. On one occasion, I even recited the poem to her. (I think she enjoyed it, although it was not in her nature to tell me so.) I pursued her relentlessly that year, which perhaps gradually increased her fondness for me a little.

"To Dear Gopi, All the Best — Shyamala."
(Written on the back of the photograph.)

After the arts students were brought back to Singapore and we entered our second year in 1958, I was given a room in the newly opened Raffles Hall, a stone's throw away from Eusoff College, the girls' hostel, on Evans Road. This was also a newly opened hostel where Shyamala stayed. Again, I took every opportunity to go and see her. As our relationship developed, I found Shyamala to be a gentle and caring person. She was also intelligent, and probably could have gone further in her education had it not been for me constantly distracting her. By nature, I tended to be hotheaded. She was my exact opposite. Even till today, after almost sixty years of marriage, she remains my alter ego, my better half.

Whenever I went to visit her at the girls' hostel, I used to wait for her in the sitting area. One day, an Indian security guard on duty admonished me in Hindi for loitering. "Look, it is not in our culture to visit a girl every evening and spend time like this. If you think you want to marry her, you should seek her parents' approval — otherwise, you'll give yourself a bad name!" He gave me quite a long lecture.

Shyamala's father also came from Kerala and was working in Malaya in the clerical service. Her family was more conservative than mine, and her parents were not keen for their daughter to be dating. Marriages were conventionally arranged, so our courtship was closely watched. While living in the student hostels, contacting each other was easy — we just had to ring on the telephone. But during the holidays, I was discouraged from ringing the house. To contact each other, we had to employ a roundabout method.

Given the obstacles involved, it took some time before I mustered the courage to pay her a visit at her home. The first time I went, I recall the gate was under repair. As I passed through, I remember whispering to myself, "Thank God, at least now they can't shut it on me!"

The Family

There were slight cultural differences between her family and mine. My wife's family was a little more Malaysian in their upbringing, very hard working with strong moral values, whereas mine had a greater interest in political activities and events. We were similar, however, in that, broadly speaking, both were from middle class backgrounds and both sets of parents had prioritised their children's education. Her father's strong ambition was to make sure that his children gained a proper university education, which was a goal he largely achieved.

In terms of educational qualifications, my wife's family performed quite well. She was one of three girls and four boys, four of whom held university degrees. Balan, her eldest brother (now deceased), became a police officer. The second, Rajan, went into medicine and became a dermatologist. Gopan, the third (also now deceased), was a colonel in the Malaysian army, and the fourth, Radhakrishnan (who unexpectedly passed away in October 2020 after a short battle with cancer), became a lawyer. Shyamala also has two sisters: Leela, who was a housewife, and Rani, who studied English and became a teacher, like my wife. My wife is very close to her siblings and tries to see them as often as she can, though this has not been possible in the last two years.

I have related my university background; my sister was also university educated. Kumari went on to become a teacher of chemistry at Cedar Girls' Secondary School. After teaching there for a couple of years, she

Seated from left: Shyamala's younger sister, Rani; her parents, Padmavathi and M. K. Pillai, in the middle; her younger brother, Radhakrishnan, on the right. Back row from left: her eldest brother, Balachandran; Shyamala; her second brother, Rajagopal; her eldest sister, Leela; and her third brother, Gopakumar.

My sister, Kumari, with her husband, Satya N. Nandan, in Fiji.

left for England, where she was trained in law. She married one of her classmates, a bright young Indian man from Fiji, whose family came from the Indian state of Uttar Pradesh.

When Fiji received its independence in 1970, the government recruited my sister and her husband to the diplomatic service. Her husband, Mr. Satya N. Nandan, was Fiji's representative at the United Nations (UN) in New York. She was his deputy. He also contributed to the Third UN Conference on the Law of the Sea, where he was a conference leader who helped draft the negotiation text that went into the United Nations Convention on the Law of the Sea (UNCLOS).[1] He was a close friend of Tommy Koh, President of the Conference and Singapore's Permanent Representative to the UN. Satya was also secretary-general of the International Seabed Authority where Tommy was chairman.[2]

Satya passed away in February 2020; some months later, I attended the virtual launch of his book posthumously, titled *Reflections on the Making of the Modern Law of the Sea*, where he is described as "one of the key personalities behind both the agreement and the subsequent development of Law of the Sea in the decades since UNCLOS was adopted".[3] He was a serious-minded scholar who worked very hard for a small country like Fiji — its interests might have been lost if there were no strong people like him to lead it. The partnership between Singapore and Fiji was constructive, and their international collaboration allowed them to make a mark.

The shared values around education between our two families notwithstanding, my wife's family initially viewed someone like me courting their daughter as an oddity and a situation they were not quite familiar with. My father-in-law did not fully approve of a young man walking up to his house. It would thus not be until several years later, in an entirely different country and context, that I would fully earn his trust.

Early Reflections on Political Activity and Family

Along with my responsibilities at the USC, I continued acting in university. My first play was *Strangers at the Gate*, written by Singapore graduate Dr. Lloyd Fernando. The play was about two left-wing detainees who, after being freed from prison, found it difficult to adjust to life in the outside world. I played Raja Singam, one of the detainees, while my friend Mr. Ernest Wong played the other.

Ernest was two years my senior at university. He was a talented actor and an excellent student — one of my many good friends at university. A non-exhaustive list of other friends would include Mr. Gopal Baratham, Mr. Herman Hochstadt, Mr. Pravin Patel, Mr. Haider Sithawalla, Mr. S. Rajendran and Mr. Kumaraguru, who collectively made sure that my university life never suffered a dull moment.

Just as in school, I became totally immersed in campus life. In addition to *Strangers at the Gate*, I acted in *Six Characters in Search of an Author*, by Luigi Pirandello — a marvelous tale where characters wander around and create their own story. I also represented Raffles Hall in inter-hostel debates for two years.

One thing, however, was becoming increasingly clear: although I enjoyed my extracurricular activities at university, I soon found it harder to balance my time. This was also the period when my political inclinations were coming to the fore. From my uncle, I had witnessed up close how much sacrifice goes into a political life, and privately began to question my ideological commitment. Even earlier, it had weighed on me

University of Malaya Drama Society staging "Strangers at the Gate" by Dr. Lloyd Fernando. Me (standing centre stage) with Ernest Wong and Peggy Leong [Mrs. Herman Hoschstadt] on the right.

how Karl Marx characterises religion in *The Communist Manifesto* as "the opium of the people". As a Hindu, I felt that I was somehow unknowingly guilty of using religion for exploitation. I had a long discussion with P. Arudsothy, another senior club member, on the matter. He assured me that there was no contradiction between belonging to a religion and being a socialist. He said not to worry.

But motivating my introspection was another and more important concern: after some time at University, I had also begun to want to start a family. Family and intense activism, I thought, did not go well together, and I foresaw that it could become a source of hardship later on. Indeed, not long after I left university, the government also began to feel the USC was getting too active in the national political scene. In their view, its club members were supposed to be students focusing on their studies, not throwing themselves into politics.

Then in February 1963, after I had graduated, *Fajar* was banned. I could not fully understand the rationale behind this decision — I did not think they were doing any harm, although I am not in possession of all the facts. The discussions in social media today are much more aggressive, in my opinion, than what the USC used to bring out in those days.

7

Journalism and Teaching

"Then this learned gentleman said something encouraging, which I will never forget. 'You do not need to do an honours or postgraduate degree. You can go out and start working. Don't worry: it doesn't matter if you cannot do history, economics, or political science. I am quite certain that whatever job you undertake, you will perform well and succeed.'"

An Honours Degree in Political Science

Although I decided to put a damper on my activism, I still had a strong academic interest in politics. When I finished my degree, the university had just introduced political science as a new course and brought in a new lecturer to teach it, Professor R. S. Milne. I had spoken to various lecturers about the possibility of pursuing an Honours Degree in Politics for my fourth year, even though I had not studied the subject formally at the intermediate level. Still, I had written a paper for one class which some of the lecturers thought satisfactory.

The Political Science Programme was to be part of the History Department, and Professor Milne had indicated to me that I had a fair chance of gaining admission. He clarified that the decision was not his to make, however, and that I would need to check with the head of the department, which I did. I then went to the Dean of Arts, Lim Tay Boh (who later became the university's vice-chancellor), to confirm the acceptance of my application.

To my astonishment, the head of the department had not put forward my application due to some administrative confusion. Without his approval, my enrolment for the honours programme could not proceed. "Why did you request a new subject like politics?" he asked me. "It is new to the university, and everybody is being a little careful. Why didn't you apply for economics? I am a professor in that department. Granting the approval would have been easy."

"In that case," I said dejectedly, "can I change my application to economics?"

He laughed. Then this learned gentleman said something encouraging which I will never forget. "You do not need to do an honours or postgraduate degree. You can go out and start working. Don't worry: it doesn't matter if you cannot do history, economics or political science. I am quite certain that whatever job you undertake, you will perform well and succeed."

Professor Lim was brave to have said this, and it helped to rally my spirits. But after the discovery, I was still feeling a little empty, knowing that I could not pursue my passion in this area.

Journalism

Since my first year at university, I had thrown myself fully into the student journalistic scene. I became interested through my father's newspaper. I wrote articles for *Fajar* and, for almost a year, a short weekly column called 'Campus Notes' for the *Sunday Mail*. I had inherited 'Campus Notes' from Gopal Baratham, the late writer and neurosurgeon; it focused mainly on reviews of books and plays. Gopal, a brilliant student — and quite witty — was the son of the first vice-chancellor of the university, Dr. B. R. Sreenivasan. If you ever asked him what his father's initials stood for, he would say, "Bloody Rogue!" (though his relationship with his father was strong and loving, as far as I knew).

SUNDAY MAIL, JULY 31, 1960.

CAMPUS NOTES

By Gopinath Pillai

TO err perhaps is human. But to be caught erring is rather humiliating. Last week, I referred to the International Union of Students as a Communist organisation. In fact the Federation Government's White Paper, "Communist Threat to Malaya" had supplied me with this information.

Mr. Abu Gidray, one of the vice-presidents of the I.U.S., laughed when I suggested that his union was a Communist front organisation. "Perhaps, if I tell you the numerical strength of the Communists in the I.U.S., you will get the true picture," he said, rather understandingly.

The I.U.S., had representatives from forty-five national unions and only thirteen of these unions were Red.

He then went on to point out India, Burma, Japan, Nepal, Sudan, and Tunisia as examples of non-Communist countries in the I.U.S.

I.U.S. at the time was also partly to be blamed for the split. "They did not realise," said Mr. Gidray, "that a new generation of students with an entirely new outlook were taking the place of the old one." The leadership did not adjust itself to the changing situation.

Mr. Gidray also saw another reson for the split. This was that the governments in the colonial territories "did not like the idea" of their student organisations attending the I.U.S.

In 1954, many changes were made in the constitution of the I.U.S. Now, according to Mr. Gidray, the

Sunday Mail, July 31st, 1960
"To err perhaps is human. But to be caught erring is rather humiliating. Last week…"

I also did a few interviews, such as with the head of the Chemistry Department, Professor Kiang Ai Kim, whom I recall had carried out some special research in the field. I found writing enjoyable. I had received a bursary with an obligation to teach after graduation, but teaching was not my first preference, and I harboured certain ambitions of becoming a journalist.

A friend of my father with a journalistic background knew the new head of *Reuters* in Singapore. The editor, a gentleman by the name of Mr. David Chipp, offered me a job there. He had a certain halo around him because he had been one of the early journalists to enter China after the communists took over.[1] For those of us who followed the journalistic scene, he was seen as an iconic figure.

When I was interviewed, it struck me how both of us were keen to know what was happening in China. China, then, was generally seen as a land of mystery (for a long time, journalists had been shut out of the country). I was interested in the India–China relationship, especially since relations between the two countries had started to look rosier in the 1950s.

When the Japanese imperial army invaded China in the 1930s–40s to fuel its industrial growth, "the West" had mostly turned a blind eye to Japan's atrocities there. When communist China emerged from the Japanese invasion and its own civil war a reinvented nation, it sought legitimacy from the international community. India was one of the first countries to recognise China. During the second Sino-Japanese War, I believe Nehru supposedly said, "From one fellow slave country to another, my support to you can only be verbal. However, my heart goes out to you. Five doctors have volunteered. I have asked them: will you go serve in China and tend to the wounded?"[2]

One of the five physicians who travelled to China as part of the Indian Medical Mission Team in 1938 was Dr. Dwarkanath Shantaram Kotnis. Almost all the doctors dispatched to China later returned home safely after supporting the injured Chinese soldiers — all except for Dr. Kotnis. He remained in China, performing major operations and lending his expertise to control a plague outbreak. He later married a Chinese nurse.

Dr. Kotnis, regrettably, suffered from epilepsy and died in 1942. According to reports, whenever Chinese premiers or presidents subsequently visited India, they would send flowers to his relatives. Not long ago in 2006, for example, Chinese President Hu Jintao visited his family members in Mumbai, where he said, "Kotnis is still being remembered and loved in China and we shall never forget him for his services."[3] Mao Zedong himself mourned Kotnis' death: "The army has lost a helping hand, the nation has lost a friend. Let us always bear in mind his internationalist spirit."[4] The sacrifice Kotnis made, according to an article in *The Hindu*, was later dramatised in two movies: the 1946 Indian movie *Doctor Kotnis Ki Amar Kahani* (based on the short story 'And One Did Not Come Back' by Khwaja Ahmad Abhas)[5] and another, *Dr. D. S. Kotnis*, released in China in 1982.

Despite Nehru's desire for pan-Asian cooperation, and the popularity of the Indian political slogan "*Hindi-Chini Bhai Bhai*" (India and China are brothers), which was making the rounds in India at that time, some trouble started brewing as early as the 1955 Bandung Conference. Nehru was a driving force of the conference's organisation, and he exuded a sense of leadership among the Asian nations. Some speculated that his confidence irked the Chinese. Such irritation was reflected in an anecdote told about the prime minister when he decided to introduce China and Premier Zhou Enlai to the world. The Indian diplomat V. V. Paranjpe, familiar with the high ideals of these comparable and esteemed post-colonial leaders, writes,

> "Out of sheer goodness of heart, [Nehru] wanted to introduce Zhou to the assembled Asian leaders whom he knew well. The Indian Prime Minister thus virtually chaperoned his Chinese counterpart. But this had the flavour of a 'big brother' attitude. Nehru had probably ignored the fact that China was a bigger and more important country… The Geneva conference of 1954… [had] also brought home to Zhou the importance of China in world affairs… No wonder, Zhou Enlai did not take kindly to Nehru's treating him as a junior partner or a younger brother, and [had] thought Nehru to be a little 'patronising'."[6]

However, others would perhaps counter that Nehru "did his best to let [Zhou] project himself and his country on centre-stage", and that China diplomatically benefited from India's support.[7]

Observing these heady international dynamics, what bothered me slightly was the Chinese leadership's apparent tendency towards greater political control. China in the 1950s and 1960s was still a poor country, but strong and full of nationalism: the Chinese very much felt it their duty to fulfil their destiny. They were building an assertive political construct that I felt less affinity with. India, on the other hand, despite being a bit slow in taking off, had a model of civic engagement that appealed to me. I was curious to see how this relationship would unfold.

I started working at *Reuters* as a sub-editor. I assumed that if I had a regular salary, I could pay back my bond to the Ministry of Education over time for my bursary. I reported to the chief sub-editor, a Singaporean who did not seem to like graduates much. His reaction to me was "Graduate, ah? Big deal!" Perhaps not coincidentally, they started me out on the graveyard shift. I would start work at 11pm and worked till 7am. All the teleprinter operators, maybe seeing that I was a bit wet behind the ears, were very friendly and shared funny stories with me.

As a reporter, I had to report on the news topics that were sent to me, edit the write-ups and then send on the fact-checked reports to my superiors without adding any commentary. A memorable story I worked on was the Bay of Pigs episode, when in 1961 it appeared likely that the Americans would attack Cuba. I had to produce a factual piece to send to my bosses. My sympathies, due to my politics at the time, lay with the Cubans.

Within the first month of working at *Reuters*, the chief sub-editor called me up to have a drink with him. He took me to a bar on Robinson Road. It was my first time at a bar, and I did not drink then. He told me that I had come through well and gave me his best wishes. Then, after having worked at *Reuters* for no more than three months, the Ministry of Education (MOE) caught up with me. MOE sent me a letter reminding me about my bursary and obligation to become a teacher. I would either have to pay back the money I borrowed or start teaching. I got my posting letter for my assigned school — an old and uninspiring place, which in those years was seen as quite rowdy. Some of the teachers complained of boisterous students who would scratch your car if you punished them.

I went to speak with David about my pre-existing financial commitment. He was outraged on my behalf that I would have to resign, and felt that the government should show more understanding (he saw my journalistic work at *Reuters* as part of my commitment to the country). He sat down to write a letter to the Prime Minister, attesting I had demonstrated great talent. I watched as he typed out the letter, but do not know whether he ever posted it. Strangely enough, I later received another letter from MOE re-assigning me to Raffles Institution. The principal maybe saw my background papers and thought he could use me.

Teaching at Raffles Institution

I taught at Raffles Institution for almost two years on subjects like general paper, history and English. I was quite happy, and found the conversations with the mature "A" Level students to be engaging and fulfilling. Normally, teachers who had either acquired extensive teaching experience or postgraduate qualifications were given "A" Level subjects to teach.

Working side-by-side with the mathematics teacher, Mr. Wong Loke Jame, I also became "Master" of the Raffles Players, the school's well-known drama group. We put on *The Merchant of Venice* by Shakespeare. Watching the passion with which I threw myself into the production, friends thought it prudent to take the time to warn me, "Don't get too involved in drama, or you might switch jobs!"

My salary was meagre, so I also taught night classes under the Adult Education Board; these after-hour classes provided a decent income and allowed for a robust exchange of views among the adult students. We were allotted a certain number of hours to teach. I secured the maximum number. What I enjoyed most about the nightly setup was that we could speak freely. Some had jobs and families, so their burden was greater. However, they earned their certificates without any problem.

Several students from this period remain my friends to this day. They look almost as old as I am now. Whenever they introduce me to their acquaintances, I joke, "You don't have to go into detail about who was teacher and who was student. Just say that we were both in school together." This is not technically a lie!

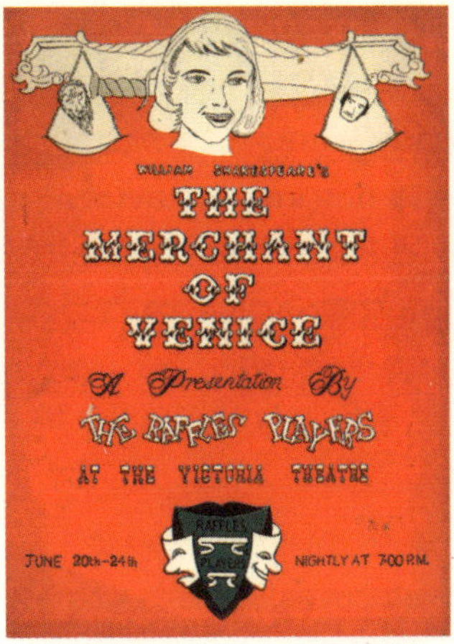

The Raffles Players stage Shakespeare's *The Merchant of Venice* at the Victoria Theatre (June 20th–24th, Nightly at 7:00pm). The Cast and Producers, with President of Raffles Players, Wong Loke Jame.

Nevertheless, though I enjoyed teaching, the longing to write was still with me, and the students had themselves observed that I was not entirely content with my work. After one night class, an Indian student alerted me to an advertisement in *The Straits Times* for a research officer's position at Bangkok Bank in Thailand. I was skeptical at first, but when I went and checked the papers it was absolutely true: an advertisement for a research officer, with the ability to write and analyse! The job, if I got it, would have me posted to Bangkok.

Interview at Bangkok Bank

I applied for the post and was called for an interview at the bank. The bank's chief of research and statistics division, Mr. Paul Sithi-Amnuai, came in person to Singapore to interview the applicants for the job. A large number of people were already waiting at the bank when I arrived. The bank had lowered its standards slightly to cast a wider net. Competition in the 1960s was fierce, and they were only able to select two candidates from the applicants. Indeed, Singapore's economic situation was poor and getting jobs then was a struggle — a teacher's salary was only in the range of a few hundred dollars. It was certainly not a time of milk and honey: one worked hard.

We were given a written test and a face-to-face interview. I handed copies of my newspaper column to Paul, which he flipped through. "Come and see me tomorrow," he said after glancing at them. "I may have a job for you."

To my surprise, I was one of the two candidates selected for the role. Paul, who was Thai-Chinese and educated at the London School of Economics, tried to assure me that I should not worry about moving to Thailand: "You will not be lonely in Bangkok. There are many foreigners there and you will be happy." (The other young gentleman selected to join the bank decided to drop from the running after getting a job with the civil service. He was perhaps not too eager to uproot to a foreign land).

I signalled to Paul that I had one problem, however, which was my bursary. He suggested that I now check with the government, as my two-year teaching bond had been served. The government was fortunately able to work out a solution to my financial obstacle and granted permission to pay back the loan in instalments.

Pre-Journey Preparations

The other main issue I faced was my marriage — I had hoped that after securing a permanent job, Shyamala and I could get married. But now that I was to travel overseas to work in Bangkok, I reckoned with having to possibly postpone the wedding. Foolhardy as I was, I floated the idea to our parents that we get married first. (I was afraid that if I did not marry Shyamala soon, her parents might marry her off to somebody else! Arranged marriages were quite common in those days.) Within a short period, I planned to get accommodation in Bangkok so that she could join me.

My parents visited Shyamala's family in January 1962 to discuss the details of the wedding and when and where it should take place. I think everybody was a little apprehensive about the plan. They worried whether two people could live on the salary of one person. My mother wanted me to continue with my studies abroad (she was not fully satisfied with the degree I got from the University of Malaya). Moreover, my family had a practical concern — how would I manage in a foreign country where I did not speak the language? Shyamala backed me up, however, and said we would go together. Determined to start a new life with my young bride, I married my college sweetheart on July 8th, 1962.

My political consciousness at this time had not entirely dissipated; and, in fact, while working as a teacher, I had joined the Singapore Teachers Union (STU), where I became vice-chairman of the graduate branch and its research secretary. We were active but not aggressive and supported the National Trades Union. STU, meanwhile, was coming under greater scrutiny by the government, which had indicated that they would treat the organisation with severity. I saw that staying on might interfere with my family life. After being accepted for the job at Bangkok Bank, I arranged for someone to take over my position.

While making the arrangements, S. Woodhull, the senior Socialist Club member and Leftist union leader, joked, "Oh, you are going to Bangkok, you are going to convert the Thai generals to socialism!" Thailand was known for its right-wing leaders; he was being sarcastic.

I answered, "And why not? I'm working at a strategic organisation." Bangkok Bank, though private, had strong military support. The chairman was the Minister of Interior, and several other ministers were also serving army officers.

But my political commitments were not as strong as they once were, and my decision to move to Thailand was an inflection point for my involvement in several respects, as it was also when I had consciously resolved to slowly withdraw as an activist from the political scene to focus on my family. Indeed, as my working life progressed and I left teaching for other jobs — particularly in the business world — I became less and less involved in politics.

Although I sympathised with the socialist movement, I could not see myself as a politician, managing a street demonstration or anything that one normally associates with a political party while simultaneously bringing up a family. I felt that if I was going to proceed on the basis of starting a family life with children, I ought to avoid situations in which

I could be at loggerheads with the government. My wife also would not be happy with the trouble such activism might cause. I could not imagine subjecting her or any of my children to hardship because of my views, and opted therefore to retreat and provide what support I could from the sidelines.

Astrological Insights

The day I collected my visa and travel papers, my father brought home a well-known astrologer for a check on the prospects of my new job in Thailand. (As I have explained earlier, it is not uncommon for Hindus to consult astrologers when they undertake major life decisions. This is basically to ensure that one is prepared to handle life's eventualities. I cannot clearly indicate how accurate the science is. But my parents were open-minded, and my experience with astrologers up until that point had been quite good.)

The astrologer astonished us by declaring, "You will travel away from Singapore, and will be working in another country." This came as a shock to us, because my father had not revealed any of the details of my journey to Bangkok. "In fact, you should have bought the tickets by now." That very morning, I had secured my ticket via an agent! He then examined my horoscope and said I would benefit from the transition.

"What happens if I decide not to go to Thailand and stay here instead?"

He gazed at me calmly and answered, "You will go to jail." I could not believe it!

~

I took a Cathay Pacific flight to Bangkok in October 1962. About four months after settling in Thailand, I read in *The Bangkok Post* that a large number of people had been arrested in Singapore as part of Operation Coldstore in February 1963. The Malayan and Singaporean governments, taking approval from the Internal Security Council, had rounded up major

Leftist activists and put them in jail on the basis that they were communist sympathisers who threatened national security. It was a profound event that shaped the early political trajectory of Singapore. Some claimed that it eliminated Singapore's only significant political opposition. A lot of my friends and former Socialist Club members were detained.

While sitting in Bangkok reading the newspaper, I thought back to the astrologer's prediction about my landing into trouble, which I had never taken seriously. The experience was perplexing: how did he know?

There is a story in the Hindu scriptures that attempts to explain why only certain astrological predictions come true. The son of Shiva, Subramaniam, is supposed to be the master of the astrological sciences. One day, his mother, Parvati, told him to check his father's horoscope and read his future. Shiva said, "Yes, let me see if you have a science that other people can believe in!"

The little boy examined his father's horoscope and said, "I am very sorry, but you will become a beggar." Shiva became very cross at hearing this, and spluttered, "Your science has no validity. I reject it. It should not be practised on earth." But after his wife had calmed his temper, he revised his instruction: "If someone with an innocent mind or pure heart interprets another's future to help them, let that be right. But not the charlatans, who use it for money!"

Regardless of the prescience of the astrologer's reading, it was a reconfirmation that my decision about the change in job and location was the right one, and would not lead to something more troublesome later on.

8

Happy Thailand *(Sawadikrab)*

"Thailand means land of the free; it's a land where people are happy. They have a saying 'In the river, there is fish; and in the fields, there is paddy'."

Adjustment to Life in Thailand

I set off for Thailand with trepidation: although I had been chosen for the job at Bangkok Bank on the basis of my English proficiency, I did not know any Thai. My strength in English made me an asset, because Thailand in the 1960s lacked good English speakers. The salary was fair, and I calculated that it would be enough to help me pay off the balance of my bursary instalments. The rent for accommodation was higher than I anticipated; but assimilating to life in Bangkok, on balance, was not hard. The bank was understanding and gave me a housing allowance, such that within a month I found a nice apartment, and in six months my wife came to join me.

My immediate boss and the chief editor of the bank, Paul Sithi-Amnuai, was pleased with the quality of my work, and the managing director, Khun Boonchu Rojanastien, also took a special liking to me, not least because I helped him with his English. The management went the extra mile in making us feel at home.

At Bangkok Bank, I held the formal title of 'Economic Research Officer'. My employers required my assistance in producing a monthly bulletin on the Thai economy for correspondent banks and customers who were finding it difficult to obtain reliable information in English. I was to assist Paul on the publication. In addition, we received frequent requests by correspondent banks to produce brief reports on commodities like rice, maize, jute and so on, which kept my hands full.

Bangkok Bank was the first organisation to come out with analyses like these. The reason they had advertised for a research officer in Singapore was that foreigners, particularly Americans and Europeans, had started to show an increased interest in Thailand's economy. Thailand is a large maize and rice producer, and the country at that time was becoming progressively industrialised, as was tangibly seen in the types of modern buildings that were coming up. English became useful in communicating developments to parties keen to look at the country's economic prospects.

Such interests coincided with wider geopolitical developments in the region during the Cold War. Thailand, in 1954, had become a member of the Southeast Asia Treaty Organization (SEATO) and a staunch ally of the Americans. Together with Thailand, SEATO comprised other Asian countries like Malaysia, Pakistan and the Philippines as well as the United States, Great Britain, France, New Zealand and Australia. India at that time was not a member of any regional organisation, preferring instead to uphold a non-aligned foreign policy.

While my work life was thus progressing well, the world over the next few years started to move in a direction that I found alarming. The Vietnam War was escalating and American presence in the country was intensifying. In 1962, a clash between India and China broke out on their disputed Himalayan border. This was traumatic for India, as it was totally unprepared for war; having looked on China as a friend, it felt betrayed. Nehru was too idealistic a person to face the geopolitical realities, and died in 1964, probably a disillusioned man. (Some of my Thai friends who travelled to India, meanwhile, had problems because they were mistaken for Chinese.) Tunku Abdul Rahman, the prime minister of Malaysia, started a "Save Democracy" fund to help India. Many Chinese in Malaysia resented this; I have no clue how much money was actually raised.

Thailand was quick to grasp the value of foreigners and was keen to make use of its expatriates' connections and knowledge. The Economic Commission for Asia and the Far East (ECAFE), for instance, was full of foreigners — mainly Indians with degrees in economics and engineering. Bangkok Bank wanted to become more involved in the commercial world and found it useful to get people educated in English to answer

A small get-together with my colleagues from Bangkok Bank.
Me (left) with my boss Paul-Sithi Amnuai (extreme right).

questions on whatever topic foreign clients took an interest in.

Paul, who as editor was the bank's professional outward looking face to the English speaking world, was a good boss who encouraged me to write. My first article at the bank was called 'Thailand–EU Trade Prospects', on the Thai–European common market. The bank got it translated into Thai and distributed it our major clients. Afterwards, I had a lot of people calling me up for more information. Paul and I also co-authored a book called *The History of Banking in Thailand*.

One of my most amusing (although also slightly embarrassing) stories during my employment at Bangkok Bank was when a colleague notified me that there was a gentleman who wanted to speak to me about my article. They sent a car to pick me up and took me to the residence of a Thai general, who asked me many intelligent questions. After chatting with him for a time, I could no longer hold back my curiosity. "From your uniform, I gather you are in the army. May I ask what you do there?"

"I am Minister for Finance," he said. He had been taking plenty of notes.

I never expected him to be a minister. "I am very sorry," I said. He told me he would call occasionally, because he was very interested to hear what I found out.

Within a year of joining Bangkok Bank, I saw my responsibilities widen. Paul was appointed as a resident representative to the bank's first U.S. office in New York. Rather than requiring clients to journey all the way to Bangkok, the idea was that they could query Paul directly at the foreign office. I was promoted to take his place as chief of the research and statistics division. As a result, another journalism opportunity fell into my lap.

Paul was the Thai correspondent for the *Far Eastern Economic Review* (*FEER*), and he had a good relationship with the local English papers. He called me one day to say, "I am going to New York, and *Far Eastern* has asked me to introduce you to them. You can replace me as correspondent." I was delighted, and through Paul came to know *FEER*'s editor Dick Wilson and later Derek Davis quite well.

Far Eastern Economic Review, Vol. XLI, No. 4, July 25th, 1963.

Far Eastern Economic Review, Vol. XLI, No. 5, August 1st, 1963.

My journalistic correspondence for *FEER* was separate from my official duties at the bank, and I did a variety of articles for the magazine.

For instance, I was fortunate to meet and interview influential people in Southeast Asia, such as Philippines' former Vice President Emmanuel Pelaez and then Prime Minister of Malaysia Datu Abdul Razak. Although I could not meet him in person, I also did a written interview with President Diosdado Macapagal while in the Philippines.

FEER kept my hands full with writing engagements. No matter what the subject, I was always acknowledged as a staff of Bangkok Bank. My position as *FEER* correspondent and research position at Bangkok Bank had a useful synergy; my bank association conferred legitimacy to what I wrote and helped me to make contacts. Whenever I called to cover a story, I would drop that I was from Bangkok Bank and would be treated respectfully. They could see that I was not a run-of-the-mill reporter but

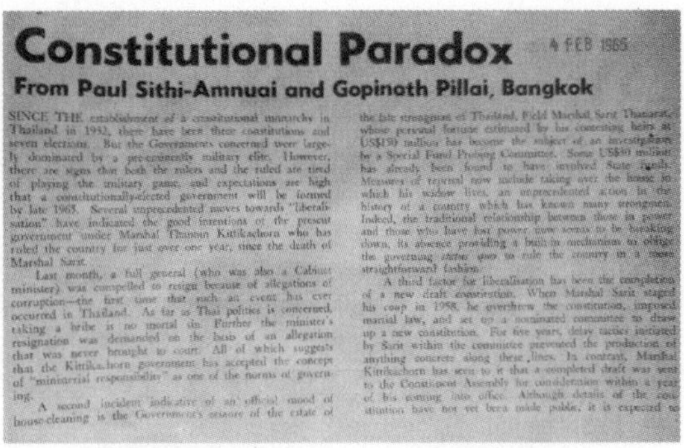

Constitutional Paradox 4 FEB 1965

From Paul Sithi-Amnuai and Gopinath Pillai, Bangkok

SINCE THE establishment of a constitutional monarchy in Thailand in 1932, there have been three constitutions and seven elections. But the Governments concerned were largely dominated by a pre-eminently military elite. However, there are signs that both the rulers and the ruled are tired of playing the military game, and expectations are high that a constitutionally-elected government will be formed by late 1965. Several unprecedented moves towards "liberalisation" have indicated the good intentions of the present government under Marshal Thanom Kittikachorn who has ruled the country for just over one year, since the death of Marshal Sarit.

Last month, a full general (who was also a Cabinet minister) was compelled to resign because of allegations of corruption—the first time that such an event has ever occurred in Thailand. As far as Thai politics is concerned, taking a bribe is no mortal sin. Further the minister's resignation was demanded on the basis of an allegation that was never brought to court. All of which suggests that the Kittikachorn government has accepted the concept of "ministerial responsibility" as one of the norms of governing.

A second incident indicative of an official mood of house-cleaning is the Government's seizure of the estate of the late strongman of Thailand, Field Marshal Sarit Thanarat, whose personal fortune estimated by his contesting heirs at US$150 million has become the subject of an investigation by a Special Fund Probing Committee. Some US$30 million has already been found to have involved State funds. Measures of reprisal now include taking over the house in which his widow lives, an unprecedented action in the history of a country which has known many strongmen. Indeed, the traditional relationship between those in power and those who have lost power now seems to be breaking down, its absence providing a built-in mechanism to oblige the governing status quo to rule the country in a more straightforward fashion.

A third factor for liberalisation has been the completion of a new draft constitution. When Marshal Sarit staged his coup in 1958, he overthrew the constitution, imposed martial law, and set up a nominated committee to draw up a new constitution. For five years, delay tactics initiated by Sarit within the committee prevented the production of anything concrete along these lines. In contrast, Marshal Kittikachorn has seen to it that a completed draft was sent to the Constituent Assembly for consideration within a year of his coming into office. Although details of the constitution have not yet been made public, it is expected to

"Constitutional Paradox". From Paul Sithi-Amnuai and Gopinath Pillai, Bangkok, February 4th, 1965.

Wednesday, July 10, 1963

Pelaez Reported Against ASA Expansion For Time Being

The Association of Southeast Asia should not consider taking in new members until it has been proven effective, Philippine Vice - President Emmanuel Pelaez told the Bangkok Bank late last month.

The Vice President' sentiments were revealed in the June edition of the Bangkok Bank Monthly Review which was released yesterday.

Asked about the admission of Communist or left-leaning neutralist countries into ASA, Mr. Pelaez, who is also Foreign Minister, replied,

"The Communist countries are definitely out. There is no place for them in the ASA. The Philippines herself would object to it.

"We are a free democratic society and we respect the dignity of man. But about 'left-leaning neutralist countries,' it's a rather ambiguous term."

The Bank representative mentioned Indonesia.

"Indonesia by our esteem is a non-Communist country," Mr. Pelaez said. "I would not say that she is leaning either left or right. She is only trying to establish her own Indonesian identity by trying to bring out the best in Indonesian nationalism.

"In due time," he added, "ASA can think of inviting other Asian countries to join. However, I feel that it is too early to talk of bringing in more partners. We have to prove first that ASA is effective."

What possibility, asked the representative, would there be for an Asian Common Market to grow out of ASA?

"No, not from the ASA" said the Vice-President. "A common market is a much larger regional group. ASA is sub-regional; however, it can be considered as a small

"Pelaez Reported Against ASA Expansion for Time Being". From Gopinath Pillai, July 10th, 1963.

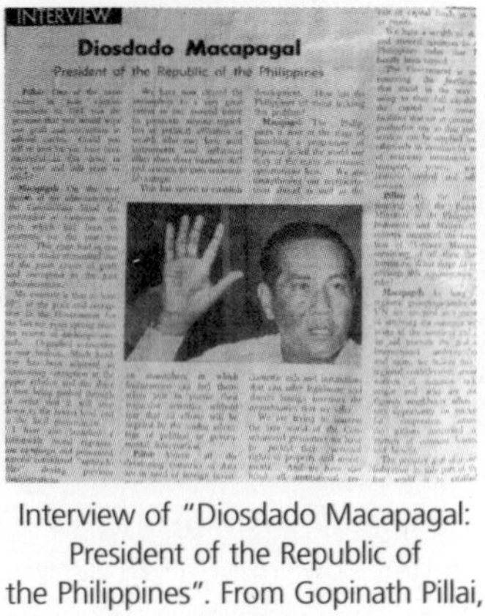

INTERVIEW

Diosdado Macapagal

President of the Republic of the Philippines

Interview of "Diosdado Macapagal: President of the Republic of the Philippines". From Gopinath Pillai, July 1963.

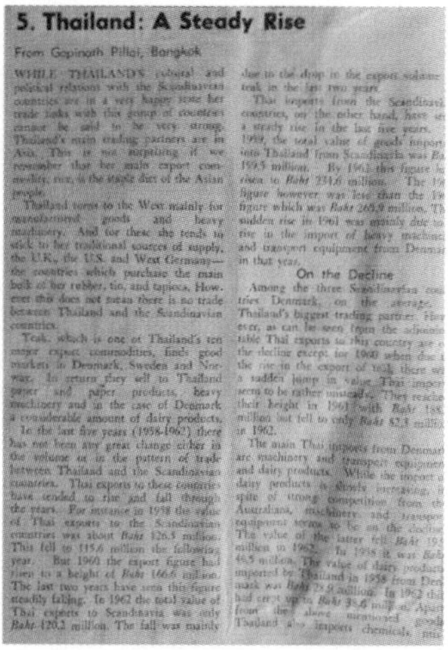

5. Thailand: A Steady Rise

From Gopinath Pillai, Bangkok

Thailand turns to the West mainly for manufactured goods and heavy machinery. And for these she tends to stick to her traditional sources of supply, the U.K., the U.S. and West Germany—the countries which purchase the main bulk of her rubber, tin, and tapioca. However this does not mean there is no trade between Thailand and the Scandinavian countries.

On the Decline

"Thailand: A Steady Rise".
From Gopinath Pillai, Bangkok.

"Thailand turns to the West mainly for manufactured goods and heavy machinery. And for these she tends to stick to her traditional sources of supply, the U.K., the U.S. and West Germany — the countries which purchase the main bulk of her rubber, tin and tapioca. However, this does not mean there is no trade between Thailand and the Scandinavian countries..."

rather a senior bank officer. Whether this respect was deserved or not, I do not know, but they did give me my appointments very promptly!

I also travelled to Singapore to do an article on Jurong Industrial Estate. Land in the early 1960s was just beginning to be reclaimed from the swampy areas, and construction was set to begin. A gentleman in the government, Mr. Lee Ong Pong, a former schoolmate, facilitated my coverage. I had a very good interview, and photographs were taken.

Life in Bangkok was pleasant and, in the professional sense, a formative experience. I had never done a job in the commercial sector like this before, as I had transitioned straight from university into journalism and teaching. I was lucky to have made friends and acquaintances who expedited my meetings and for the opportunity to write what some found to be reasonably readable articles.

Kind and Generous Neighbours

Not long after we had arrived in Thailand, a friend of mine, Mr. V. R. Raghavan (who lived in the same block of flats as us), assisted in introducing Shyamala to the United Nations Educational, Scientific and Cultural Organization (UNESCO) office in Bangkok. Raghavan had spent several years at ECAFE, where he had become a fairly senior figure. He had studied at an American university and was well connected. As a sign of the company he kept, his son later married the daughter of the eighth president of India, Venkataraman. Following his introduction at UNESCO, a kind Indian gentleman, Professor T. K. N. Menon, helped to find Shyamala a job.

Professor Menon was a genuinely nice person from Baroda University in India, and occupied an office that I think was called the Division for Education and Research. He was a professor of education and also head of the department there. We became very close to him and his wife because they had children of our age back in India. He offered Shyamala a job as a research assistant (RA). He had been on the lookout for an English-speaking assistant since the quality of work provided by his assistants thus far had been sub-optimal.

The reason my wife decided to take an RA position rather than go into teaching (for which she was trained) was that local and international schools had a policy which required them to hire only "native speakers" of English. The first eight months she was thus sitting idle, learning how to speak Thai, until the RA position at UNESCO came up. She did the groundwork for Professor Menon's projects. After a few months, he declared her work outstanding and suggested that she pursue a master's degree in the U.S.

Shyamala (sitting, centre) with her UNESCO colleagues, 1964.

Many of those who spent time in Thailand were very much orientated towards America. I had also observed that in those days more and more people in India as well as other countries were travelling to the U.S., rather than Britain, to pursue higher studies: America's understanding of technology was perceived as stronger. Professor Menon got Shyamala a scholarship to a university in New York, the State University of New York (SUNY) at New Paltz. The plan was that after a year or so, when I had saved enough money, I would join her.

A Favourable Impression

After we had spent some time in Bangkok, my wife's older brother passed through the city on his way to London to do his postgraduate degree in medicine. My father-in-law travelled with him. Bangkok differed from Singapore in that communication was a challenge; the inability to speak Thai limited one's mobility. But my father-in-law, after staying with us a few days, saw how well we had adapted to life in Thailand and came away pleased with the life we had made for ourselves.

This was heartening, because, indeed, one of my objectives in coming to Thailand was to make sure that Shyamala and I had a comfortable place to settle down — where my wife would be able to find a decent job, make friends and be happy. During weekends, we toured the country in our car, visiting temples and nurturing our understanding of the country's habits and cuisine. Thailand was a wonderful place to start our married life as well as a career outside of Singapore.

My father-in-law, following his positive experience there, I think realised that he need not be too worried about me. Later, when I went back to Malaysia to visit my wife's family, he was warm and welcoming. He shared family secrets he had not told me before, demonstrating that he accepted me into the family. "It is interesting," I had mused, "how you turn an outlaw into an in-law!"

~

While my wife learned to read and speak Thai colloquially, I started to study Thai from a linguistic, scholarly point of view. As one facet of my fascination with the country, I became curious about how elements of the culture bore traces of Indo-Buddhist influence. In Thai, for example, the Sanskrit and the Sanskrit-based language Pali had been made tonal in keeping with the Chinese language. (The Thais, from what I understand, were a Chinese people who had been driven south into the agricultural land of Southeast Asia.)

I began tracing the etymology of Thai words for fun. Take, for instance, Thammasat University. "*Thammasat*" derives from the Sanskrit "*Dharmashastra*", meaning the science of "righteousness" or "ordinance", extrapolated to the liberal arts. The Thai word "*Kesetsart*" means the science of agriculture (in Sanskrit, *Krishishastra*), while "*Thorsaphth*", the Thai word for "telephone" came from the Sanskrit "*Durbhashanyantram*". I also saw that Indian films with mythological themes dubbed in Thai were popular in rural Thailand.

The Thais were happy to see an outsider taking an avid interest in their culture — and not only taking an interest but displaying a little knowledge too! On one occasion, we visited Ayudhya. (Ayudhya, or "Ayodhya" in Hindu mythology, is the capital where Lord Rama ruled.) One young man pointed out to me, however, that my geography was incorrect: the capital where Rama ruled was in Thailand, rather than in India. "The real Ayudhya is in Thailand. This is something that you will have to understand." I did not want to start an argument. I said I would have to go home and study further.

Such exchanges inspired the question in me: what was it that made it so easy for an Indian to assimilate in Thailand? I first learned of India's cultural influences in Southeast Asia during primary school at Choon Guan. I mentioned earlier that our class teacher, Tan Keng Kang, had started a magazine for which he asked students to contribute articles (I had written on the American presidential elections). This time, I wrote a one-page paper grandly entitled 'The History of India'. When I presented the paper, Keng Kang commented flatly, "I thought India's history was longer than that."

In university, my knowledge of India's forays into Southeast Asia expanded to encompass the commercial and military excursions of the Cholas. The Chola Empire was a trade dynasty of Tamil monarchs in South India, whose maritime kingdom rose to prominence between 985 AD and 1025 AD. Up till this point, the Cholas traded with the Sri Vijaya Empire, located in present-day Indonesia, which had "controlled temporarily the transoceanic trade in its central Strait of Malacca."[1]

The Cholas and the Sri Vijayas jostled for influence over the spice trade with China's Song Dynasty across Southeast Asia's lucrative sea-lanes. The Sri Vijayas were said to have "possessed the ears of the Chinese monarchs"[2] and used their frequent interactions with the Chinese to expand their commercial empire while "exert[ing] exorbitant tolls on [Chola] merchant ships."[3]

This irritated the Cholas, especially when it was discovered that "for several years the Chola state was wrongly described in official Chinese annals as a tributary or 'vassal' state of the Sri Vijaya[s]."[4] (The Sri Vijayas, apparently, had introduced this notion deliberately to sabotage their rivals.) The Cholas unleashed a naval armada to teach the Sri Vijayas a lesson and puncture their monopoly. I recall reading that the Cholas had actually informed the Chinese emperor's office of their impending attack. Notably, the Song "did not do anything in support of their vassals [the Sri Vijayas]", and were just "as annoyed at [their] rent extraction."[5]

I spent a lot of time trying to understand the legacy of subtle historical and regional nuances such as these in relation to my own experience in Thailand. Inadvertently, my curiosity raised my value as an employee, because another special duty I had at the bank was to relay Thailand's history in English to prominent visitors. English speakers were in short supply, and so I would be earmarked to accompany and educate senior foreign bankers on Thai history.

Our guests were genuinely impressed with the depth of my understanding and asked how I knew so much about another country's history when I was a Singaporean of Indian origin. "This is common knowledge," I answered them simply. "There is enough history you can dig up." I also found that it added to my quality of life.

Locating an English Tutor

Bangkok Bank's managing director, Boonchu, became the deputy prime minister of Thailand. He was quite friendly with me. Whenever he came to Singapore he would call me and we would have a cup of coffee. Initially, Boonchu was quite diffident about speaking in English, and asked for my assistance in finding him a tutor.

I found a young British hitchhiker in a coffee shop open to taking on his lessons. It was the sort of cafe where if you spoke any English, everyone grabbed a seat beside you and would try to strike up a conversation. "How do you fund yourself?" I asked him. He told me he taught for a living. Boonchu was pleased with my choice.

At one point, I asked Boonchu whether I could rent the bank's guest house in Chiangmai. He asked who was accompanying me there. I said my wife. He answered slowly, in perfect English, "You are taking coal to Newcastle!" At that moment, I realised that he had vastly improved his knowledge of English!

Boonchu remained a friend for some time. I used to write to him from Singapore, but our correspondence diminished as he became progressively occupied with political affairs.

On the Dragon Staircase, which leads to the temple built 600 years ago. Phra Dart Doi Suthep, Chiangmai, December 1963.

9

A "Homecoming" to Malaysia

"I did quite a bit of travelling for MIDF, which put me in contact with many Malaysian businessmen. The work started looking very attractive to me, and was actually to be the start of my love affair with business. Indeed, in short order, I was promoted as an investment officer for the region of East Malaya."

How I Came to Malaysia

Another friend I made in Thailand was the trade commissioner to Malaysia from Canada, Mr. Philip Stuchen. He was involved with work at UNESCO and had asked my wife to introduce me to him. We had a few coffees, and I found him to be an immensely knowledgeable person whose experience spanned several countries in Southeast Asia. He brought up a vacancy at an organisation called Malaysian Industrial Development Finance Bhd. (MIDF), to handle their public relations. Philip had connections at the World Bank, which partly funded MIDF.

I had heard about this organisation through my work at Bangkok Bank. Their main line of business was to study the funding of industrial projects and offer modes of financing. I told Philip that I was not particularly excited about working in public relations — the project evaluation side was more appealing to me. He advised that MIDF would offer plenty of opportunities: if I pursued the opening, for instance, it would allow me to work anywhere in the world, and even open doors to the U.S., where both my wife and I planned to pursue postgraduate studies. He was very persuasive.

With the help of Professor Menon, my wife by then had succeeded in securing a scholarship to study at the State University of New York (SUNY) at New Paltz for a master's degree in comparative education. Professor Menon indicated that he would try to get me a scholarship as well so that in six to twelve months I could also go and join her. My wife could not wait for me any longer than this, as she would not be too happy living for so long in New York by herself.

Philip and I left the conversation at that. Shortly thereafter, I received a call from a higher-up at MIDF with a job offer from Malaysia. He planned to pass through Bangkok and asked if I would like to chat. When we met, I repeated what I had told Philip: I was not too enthusiastic about public relations.

"Why don't you take charge of public relations?" he asked. "Then after a short period we will make you a project officer?" I was puzzled as to why they were pursuing me so keenly. There was no shortage of English speakers in Malaysia, and I said as much.

"But they are not so well travelled." In an attempt to win me over, the gentleman then emphasised that one cannot control every situation in the future. "Situations just evolve and you have to see where they lead."

During my recruitment, it was hinted that I would likely be sent at some point to head their newly established Singapore office in the Malayan Bank Building in Battery Road. First, however, they wanted me to earn my stripes and see how I would fare in my early years. I had been in Bangkok for nearly two and a half years by this point, and felt I had gathered the maximum amount of knowledge I could from the experience. Since Shyamala and I had not yet started a family, we were still mobile and could take a chance with new pursuits.

Another reason for deciding to break new ground was that although I could imagine a secure future for us in Thailand, I could never envision myself becoming a Thai citizen. One thing my wife and I realised halfway through living there was that while we had many Thai and foreign friends, developing deep-rooted relationships was not easy. Furthermore, Thailand was quite far from our families. When I spoke to my wife and her parents about returning "home" to Malaysia, they were excited by the prospect. We decided that I would take the job while Shyamala pursued her master's degree in America. I would then join her in the States as soon as it was feasible.

When we finally left Thailand in May 1965, Bangkok Bank and our friends gave us an amazing send-off. We had more Thai friends than friends of Indian or Chinese origin. We travelled by train from Bangkok across the border to Kuala Lumpur. It was a two to three day journey. The MIDF executive who interviewed me, Mr. Chai Fook Loong, soon to be my immediate boss, checked us into a hotel.

"You rest for a day," he said. "Then come around to the office and we'll talk about the position."

Job Developments

Due to my initial lack of enthusiasm for pubic relations, they adjusted my formal title, as an act of goodwill, to 'Deputy Economist'. I would support the economist Bill Stewart, an Irishman. However, the writing portion of public relations deskwork fell under my portfolio (an instance in which my title changed but my actual responsibilities remained the same).

I had dreamed of quickly joining my wife in New York. But reality set in when Professor Menon informed me that going to America was not immediately on the cards, as he was experiencing some difficulty getting me a scholarship. Philip also advised that I should stay and work for some time in Malaysia. Perhaps, as he had suggested, some other opportunities would reveal themselves to me there.

My engagement with MIDF, however, evolved faster than I ever expected. Within a few months of joining, I was shocked when Singapore was asked to leave Malaysia on August 9th, 1965. Overnight, I became an expatriate. Chai Fook Loong (the company's operations manager) and Mr. Ladislav Svoboda (the general manager, seconded from the World Bank) made special efforts to reassure me that my job was secure; they said the fact that I was not Malaysian would not affect my position or prospects of future promotion. Moreover, my wife was also Malaysian, which perhaps offered a modicum of security.

I did quite a bit of travelling for MIDF, which put me in contact with many Malaysian businessmen. The work started looking very attractive to me, and was actually to be the start of my love affair with business. Indeed, in short order, I was promoted as an investment officer for the region of East Malaya.

~

The circumstances surrounding my promotion came as a stroke of good luck. The central bank had been pressuring MIDF to look at industrial projects in the not-so-developed areas of East and North Malaysia. The general manager, Svoboda, a Czechoslovakian, was preparing for a tour of East Malaysia for his first visit. He requested that I accompany him.

Fook Loong, my senior, was initially slated to go. But at the last minute an unexpected family issue arose, and he was unable to make the trip. As Hokkien was the primary dialect spoken in East Malaysia, the management actually preferred Fook Loong (a Malaysian Chinese) to accompany the General Manager. I was called in as a last resort.

"You don't speak the language or know the country," my colleagues said. "But try to understand things as quickly as possible. Go and support the General Manager and don't make a fool of yourself. We hope you come back in one piece."

The briefing left me nervous. However, I was determined to show my mettle. I had a chat with Svoboda to say that I would be grateful if he could sanction a two-day visit prior to his trip to do some groundwork before his arrival. "I will get a feel of the place and, if I am lucky, make a friend or two to help us. If you allow, I might be able to gather some information to better serve you."

He thought it over. "It can't get any worse than this," he said, and approved the request.

So I set out for Sarawak and Sabah. For my background research, I read up about the politics in Sarawak. The political situation was quite active there. I thought I would attempt to make use of my professional affiliation with MIDF to make contacts. My gamble paid off, and I succeeded in connecting with Mr. Ong Kee Hui, the leader of the Sarawak United People's Party.

"Your first time in Sarawak," I recall him saying. "You are a brave fellow." And he invited me to his house.

He was pleased by my visit and revealed he would be going into projects in seafood and fishing. Right off the bat, I had two projects to present to the General Manager. I could tell him that I had not been sitting idle.

I went to my local contact's office and, using my credentials, accessed a typewriter to prepare an overview of the situation and the potential projects which seemed attractive. I then prepared a draft of a press release. The next day, by lunchtime, my boss had arrived. I remember him giving me a piteous look that said, "He is in over his head." I requested a short meeting with him alone for about five to ten minutes after he landed.

By that time, many business people in town knew my name and that I came from Kuala Lumpur. "Luck seems to have been on my side," I told Svoboda. Maybe I can introduce you to the two clients I met and we can organise a press conference."

"A press conference!" he exclaimed. "For that I need a press release, and don't have one."

"But I do," I said, handing him a copy.

He was overjoyed. He said quite seriously, "You have done well."

The rest of the trip lasted three to four days. One contact led to another, and our network grew. They hosted a grand dinner for Svoboda — an extravagance he had never expected. When we returned to Kuala Lumpur, the first thing he did was request for me to be transferred from my current post as 'Deputy Economist' to 'Investment Officer' in charge of East Malaysia. He felt that training a new officer simply because he speaks Malay or Chinese would have been a waste. In his opinion, the aptitude of the employee was the most important.

He said I seemed to know what I was doing and that I should look after the funding for the region.

~

Fook Loong, who had taken leave, resigned from the company. Svoboda recruited his replacement — a former permanent secretary of finance in Singapore, Mr. H. F. G. Leembruggen, a Eurasian of Dutch extraction (a Burgher). Leembruggen was reputed not to have got along too well with the establishment in Singapore, and resigned from the government to start afresh in Malaysia.[1]

Leembruggen decided to restructure MIDF. Svoboda and I provided him with our recommendations. He appointed three coordinating investment officers under him — one for North Malaysia, one for Central and South Malaysia and one for East Malaysia. At Svoboda's request, I was appointed to cover East Malaysia. I enjoyed travelling all over Sarawak and Sabah, including to Kudat, Tawau and Sandakan, evaluating projects that ranged from plywood and seafood to real estate.

A Significant Change in Plans

By this time, it became clear that I would not be able to join my wife in New York as quickly as we had envisaged. Also, I felt that I could not now throw in the towel regarding my new responsibilities and say, "My wife is waiting." This would have looked irresponsible. People had entrusted me with important tasks to be done. So I told my wife to carry on with her studies; I would meanwhile work in Malaysia a little longer. "You may have to stay by yourself for a time. But during the holidays I will visit you," I said to her.

Shyamala was not too impressed. She did not like the idea of being all on her own in New York. (She had no problem settling down in Thailand, as I had been with her then.) One of the primary reasons she decided to pursue her postgraduate degree in the U.S. was that she thought I would eventually join her. By moving to America, she thought she was helping me to achieve my ambition of completing my master's degree while furthering her own studies. She must have suspected that my interest was now less in holding a degree than in advancing my business career. Putting my study plans on hold, to her mind, meant I would never resume them. (Indeed, I had learned that I could do well and get promoted without a postgraduate qualification. The same urgency was no longer there, and she probably feared she would be lonely in the States for a long time.)

From her letters, I also gathered that she was having difficulty making friends. She had a few close acquaintances, but they were all adult part-time students who came to the campus only in the evenings. Otherwise, she was miserable. I thought, "She is the most important person in my life. I must bring her back." My parents said, "Oh, what a waste of money." (My mother was disappointed Shyamala did not complete her studies.) But her parents were ecstatic that she would be coming home and would soon be reunited with her husband.

Shyamala at State University of New York (SUNY), at New Paltz, United States of America, December 1965.

Shyamala therefore gave up her studies at New Paltz and settled on returning to Malaysia. "If you are not coming to me, then I am coming to you," she said. "Let's not do something artificial, like living in different continents while maintaining a marriage. It is time we start a family."

That was that. Even today, when I look back on our decision, I think we made the correct one. We valued being together and, even if we could not both follow an academic career path, we settled on carving out a future suitable for us and our family.

Starting a Family and Race Riots

Malaysia was by no means a new country to us, which is why it felt like a homecoming. To our good fortune, MIDF gave generous loans for staff that enabled us to purchase a house at a reasonable price. We bought a nice house in Petaling Jaya. Shyamala, in short order, also got a job at Assunta Secondary School to teach English and English literature. Meanwhile, a tutor came by the house to teach Malay to my friends and me. Everything was wonderful. My eldest daughter, Preetha, was born in Petaling Jaya in August 1967. I felt extremely lucky to have had so many little pieces come together in my life, and to have arrived at a situation where my

Me as a first-time father with my eldest daughter, Preetha, at our house in Petaling Jaya, Malaysia, 1968.

wife and I were employed and enjoyed our work and life together.

Then tragedy struck on May 13th, 1969, after the general election in Malaysia. The country exploded into a racial conflict. The conflict was between the Malays and Chinese, but the riots soon engulfed the entire country. Sometimes, a race riot would happen and then things quickly returned to normal. But this time, something was different. There was a discernible change in attitudes. Even for those who were not Malay but born in Malaysia, like my wife, there were real or imagined problems.

The May 1969 riots were not a one-off event but unfolded over several days. When my wife was at an advanced stage of her pregnancy with our second child, Prakash, the two of us had been out on a shopping expedition one day at the department store May May on Batu Road to buy baby's clothes. Suddenly, there was a resounding bang and the rioting resumed. The police arrived at May May and ordered the doors shut. We were caught inside.

The owner, an elderly Chinese gentleman, approached us to tell us not to worry. "My wife knows how to deliver babies. In the worst case, if she suddenly goes into labour, tell me and we will look after her." It was a very humane thing for him to do.

Fortunately, we were allowed to drive back to Petaling Jaya once everything was in the clear. We had hired three or four construction workers for refurbishment work at our house. When we reached home, however, we noticed one worker was missing. "What happened to your colleague?" I asked them.

"We don't know," the workers replied. "He disappeared."

Then, before the riots ended, came the most harrowing event of all. Shyamala was soon to go into labour, and the authorities had put a night-time curfew into effect, which required us to acquire a special pass to visit the hospital if the baby happened to arrive after dark. I had a problem with the officer-in-charge of police district (OCPD) — an unfeeling man who would not budge an inch to issue us the pass that we required. "If you have any problem," he said dismissively, "you call me, and I will have a car take you to the hospital."

I pointed out that it was unlikely he could do this in the time proposed, identifying the right type of vehicle and so on while navigating the curfew and the rest of it. But I sensed he was looking at our dilemma purely through a racial lens. We determined to seek help from a more senior officer.

We went back to the house and rang all our friends. Eventually, when we rang the police station again, another police officer answered. He confirmed that this was an emergency and requested a pass on our behalf. Sure enough, my son, Prakash, was born during the curfew hours. After that scare, we soberly reconsidered our position living in Malaysia.

Aside from this episode, my wife had also in her regular work life started to notice a change in attitudes. "Why should we be learning English literature and poetry?" her students asked. English was the medium of instruction at Assunta Secondary School for subjects like literature and history. It was expected that English would soon be phased out and substituted with the Malay language (though English as a second language would have remained in the curriculum).

We felt that our inability to speak Malay would have hindered our children's education. We noticed that even signs in public were starting to appear in Malay, with a few translations into other languages. We feared the language barrier would dim our children's prospects and compel them to move elsewhere.

When I told Leembruggen that we were thinking about leaving the country, he was shocked. "I don't think you know how badly things are going," I said. He asked me to speak with the chairman of MIDF, Tun Ismail Mohamed Ali.

Tun Ismail also tried to bring me around. "You have already been here for six years or so. If you stay on for another two or three, I will get you citizenship." But I told him honestly, "People like you are from the older generation. The young generation has a different way of looking at things and a different political agenda. It might be difficult for us to become citizens."

The incident with the curfew pass had made Malaysia feel like a different world to me. There were also extraneous factors: my parents were getting older and had no one to look after them in Singapore, since my sister was working in New York. Weighing everything in the balance, we decided to go back to Singapore. This was one of the best decisions of my life.

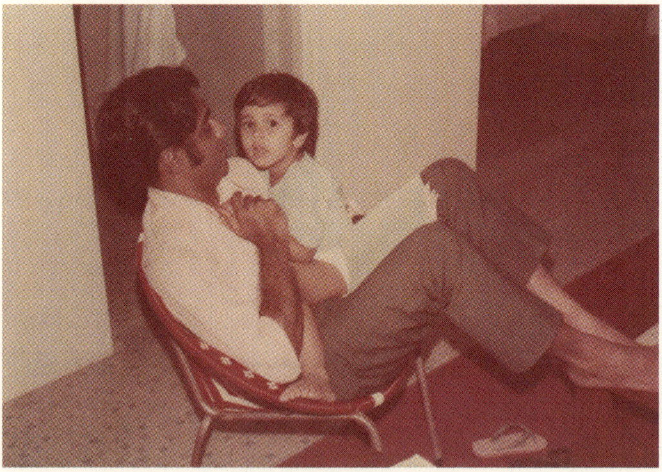

With my son, Prakash, 1970.

10

An Unexpected Return

"Before this, I had never been deeply involved in industry: I had only interpreted data — analysing economic statistics, writing reports and columns about trends and so on... A job in manufacturing would be more dependable and a novelty... On returning to Singapore, I was determined to take my new circumstances and make them a success."

New Commitments

We knew that it would be possible to stay with my parents temporarily while we found our feet in Singapore. Many school and university friends also helped with the transition, and I was fortunate to find a job in a relatively short period.

One friend who came to my aid was a senior member of MIDF, Mr. Cheam Tat Pang. He reached out to a senior officer in the Singapore government service, Mr. Ngiam Tong Dow, the permanent secretary at the Ministry of Communications, about job openings.[1] He was also a few years my senior at university. He called me after hearing from Tat Pang to say that he was looking for a general manager to run operations at a garment factory called Raya Mills Corporation Ltd. Raya Mills was owned by the government with private sector investment.

I told Tong Dow I had never run a factory, and would have to learn along the way. He assured me that the duties were not overly complex — the key would be keeping up with the operations. He took a tremendous risk offering me the job, as I had no experience whatsoever in running a company.

The factory was small and underperforming; Tong Dow wanted to use my background experience in industrial finance to turn the company around. He felt my background was relevant, as I had earlier evaluated the finances of companies to advise on how best to improve their work.

The factory was not yet profitable, but with good management he believed it could become lucrative. If I did not succeed — or if I was not up to the task after some time had passed — he told me he would have to reconsider. I would too. There was no long-term contract, but we were both prepared to give it a go.

~

A major asset my wife and I had acquired in Malaysia was our house in Section 5 of Petaling Jaya on 12,000 square feet of land. I needed to sell the house and settle the soft loan provided by MIDF so that we could use the residual amount to buy a new house in Singapore. After the May 1969 riots, the prices of property had plunged, however; and those who came to view our house only offered a pittance. Nobody wanted to buy a house in a riot-torn city. One major disturbance during the riots had, in fact, erupted on a highway not too far away from our house.

I shared my situation with a good friend and former classmate, Mr. R. Balakrishnan, who offered to lend a hand. "I am looking for a house

My daughter, Preetha, in front of our old house at Section 5 of Petaling Jaya, Malaysia, 1969 or 1970.

just like this one," he said. He explained he could buy the house at the price I had paid for it, provided I found him a 100 percent housing loan. "Then I will then take it off your hands."

This was a tall order. Luckily, a friend and former colleague from MIDF who had left the company to join a bank was prepared to grant Bala a loan for the full amount. Bala was already known to him: he was the Indian section head of Radio Malaysia and had a good reputation. Further, he was an excellent sportsman — he had acquired the distinction of being the goalkeeper for the University of Malaya football team which had scored an incredible long goal on the opposite side in the university's inter-varsity match with either Macao or Hong Kong.

Thus, it was through the kindness of two Malaysian friends that I encashed my asset and exited Malaysia intact. The company released the mortgage, and my friend took over the house. The house was then worth the equivalent of forty-eight thousand Singapore dollars. Years later, I paid a visit to Bala in Malaysia, who had by then remodelled the house. I told him I would never forget the favour he had done for me. "I didn't do you a favour," he stressed. "You did me the favour." The house was worth less than fifty thousand dollars when he bought it; it had since appreciated to one hundred thousand dollars. "I have more than doubled the value!"

In January 1970, we returned to Singapore. I purchased another house off Dunearn Road in Bukit Timah — a detached single storey house, more modest than our old home in Petaling Jaya. It had three bedrooms. By this time, I had two children who required the extra space. Luckily, I was able to shift everything without much hassle. My parents lived a short distance away. They helped to get us set up and ensured that the children were well looked after.

I had come to Singapore somewhat anxious about my job. Then there was the problem of funding the new house and meeting the family's expenses. This episode is only but one example of my friends' ready support during a time of trial. My entire life, I can honestly say that I have been truly blessed by the trust and love of wonderful parents and good friends.

From Writing to Business

The head of *The Far Eastern Economic Review* (for which I had continued writing while I was in Malaysia), Mr. Dick Wilson, was astonished that I should give up journalism to enter into manufacturing. "You have never run a factory!" He said incredulously. "And there are nearly three hundred workers there. How are you going to manage this?"

"It's just common sense," I replied. "It is difficult, but it will pay much more."

Frankly, I was ready to try something new. I had thought about becoming a journalist full time, but I found the opportunity of running a factory more appealing. Before this, I had never been deeply involved in industry: I had only interpreted data — analysing economic statistics, writing reports and columns about trends and so on. The problem with a journalist income, however, was that it was not very stable. A job in manufacturing would be more dependable and a novelty. I felt it would be more interesting to work at a manufacturing outfit when Singapore was emerging as a regional manufacturing hub. There was a great deal of effort to get the economy moving and to create export markets. The opportunity appeared to be significant.

Around this time, Dick Wilson retired. They would have recruited me as a *FEER* columnist, but I did not think they were in a position to offer me a job on a full time basis. I had written a number of articles for *FEER*. But aside from developments in Jurong, there were not too many events one could write on which would have made for compelling reading. Building a factory, on the other hand — looking at the labour laws and the various problems that arose — would ensure steadier engagement. I was relieved when Shyamala also resumed teaching, as our joint income would be sufficient for our needs.

I was put in a somewhat challenging situation. But as they say, beggars cannot be choosers. I had previously been sitting pretty in my house in Malaysia. On returning to Singapore, I was determined to take my new circumstances and make them a success.

Life Transitions and a New Frontier

Many of my socialist friends during this transition began to feel I had undergone a transformation — a political mind shift from socialism to capitalism. Even earlier, around the time I had moved to Thailand, I had decided that I would continue to hold onto all my friendships but, politically, would withdraw (although this did not affect my interest in politics). My reasoning was that a person has obligations after he marries. Looking after my family would be my primary duty now.

These were friends I knew well and, to their credit, they tried to empathise with what I was experiencing. Many also held down various jobs and did not see what I was doing as strange. But I think they were perhaps watching to see how far I would stray — how much of a capitalist I would become. Occasionally, snide remarks were made in jest, like "our friend who is waiting to become a millionaire!"

There was no significant or overt antagonism in comments like these; but adjusting to others' perceptions of my recent major life choices still caused me a degree of mental distress. It seemed that some were disappointed that I did not become a part-time politician. Their statements like "Now he has become a capitalist" were perhaps motivated by the gains they thought I sought to accrue.

But this view was not quite correct; I have never been fond of accumulating money for the sake of it. I wanted to be financially comfortable so that my children would be comfortable and equipped to pursue a university education. By the time I had returned to Singapore, Operation Coldstore had also shaken up the political scene significantly — there were no longer quite as many strident political activists out in the open.

Finally, I was probably willing to take on jobs that most people would find rather onerous. For instance, turning around the garment factory. I have never shied away from hard work while doing something I found interesting. Furthermore, by this point in my career, I had built up resiliency. In the future, I would have to make sure the workers would be paid, the shareholders would be given their dividend and that a product would be produced that the customers wanted. I saw this as a bit of an adventure. I liked doing things I was not familiar with, and to make something new from the opportunities that came my way.

Part II

Professional Life

Former Minister for Finance Hon Sui Sen (centre) visiting the Raya Mills stall at the Singapore Fair, 1973.

11

Raya Mills: The Internationalisation of My Outlook

"Singapore in the 1970s was embarking on major new industrial policy initiatives that would steer the trajectory of the country's future economic growth... Tong Dow warned me that Singapore's industrialisation policy was undergoing a review: the EDB was examining it to figure out how best to proceed with its economic mandate."

A Government Warning

I was very lucky to get the job at Raya Mills at the time that I did. Although I had cut my teeth in industrial finance at MIDF, I soon discovered that running a company presented an entirely different set of challenges from anything I had faced before. My experiences at Raya Mills, for instance, would guide my future career direction and assist in the early internationalisation of my outlook. As general manager, I would direct employees, decide on union matters and oversee the company's work streams. All my friends sort of teased me at the start: "Since you are always pontificating to others about how to run their companies, now you finally have the chance to run one for yourself!"

I was ready for the challenge and was not at all intimidated by the new job. I saw significant growth potential for Singapore and myself in manufacturing. Garment making was fairly straightforward: making yarn for fabric, and from that fabric cutting and sewing it into garments. Raya Mills owned one unit based in Singapore.

Nevertheless, this did not mean running a garment factory would be easy. Several workers were skeptical about whether I would succeed. The factory had hundreds of workers — mainly Chinese, with a sprinkling of Indians and Malays. In my heart, I thanked my father for his wisdom in making me study at Choon Guan until Senior Cambridge to familiarise me with the Chinese environment. Ngiam Tong Dow, after hearing from Cheam Tat Pang, set down his expectations for me. "The company is small and losing money. The most important thing will be keeping your eyes and ears open and dealing with situations as they arise. If you succeed in turning this company around, we will all applaud you."

Indeed, Singapore in the 1970s was embarking on major new industrial policy initiatives that would steer the trajectory of the country's future economic growth. The government had two nominees on the Raya Mills board: Ngiam Tong Dow (then Executive Director at Intraco, the state's trading company) and Jurong Town Corporation (JTC) Chairman Woon Wang Siang. The Economic Development Board (EDB) had a direct share in the company, and 50 percent was owned by an entity called Minister of Finance Inc. Tong Dow warned me that Singapore's industrialisation policy was undergoing a review: the EDB was examining it to figure out how best to proceed with its economic mandate.

"Priorities will change," he said. "You need to be careful about that — be able to handle it."

I did not know what that meant in real terms at the time, but was soon to find out. The Singapore government was examining economic diversification and the transition from low-value manufacturing towards the production of higher-end products. Manufacture upgrading required replacing labour intensive industries like garments production with enhanced mechanisation. Although it may not be apparent when we look at our vibrant, bustling metropolis today, we were a backwater economy then and aspired to climb into a new world class.

Assessing the Problem

My work schedule, up until I joined Raya Mills, had been more or less predictable. I knew that at six in the evening I would be off the clock and could spend time at home with my family. That lifestyle, however, changed. After entering the private sector, I learned that I was no longer the sole custodian of my time. For instance, the demands of energising the factory would compel me to miss my son's birthday and instead attend an important meeting with two Swedish businessmen. They would, in fact, prove instrumental later in reviving the factory's fortunes.

From day one, Tong Dow set high targets. As one way of monitoring my progress, he advised that I should reach a break-even position within the company in the first six months. The factory — in addition to the couple of hundred workers it employed — had four salesmen, three of whom were old hands. As I launched off the block, not sure whether I would sink or swim, they too were curious to see how I would fare. One worker who had been trained in textile engineering in Taiwan, Mr. Lim Swan Teck, supposedly joked, "If this man lasts three months, I will be surprised!" When I heard this, I thought wryly, "Well, now I have a minimum deadline to beat!"

When I made it through the first three months still breathing, and had achieved the target that had been laid out, Tong Dow was well pleased. "Next," he instructed, "I want you to show a 30 or 50 percent profit in the remainder of the year," and directed my attention closer to the bulls-eye.

Revamping the Factory

Throughout my first year on the job, most of my attention was focused on solving one main question: "Why is the garment factory failing?" After spending many hours mulling this over, I concluded that the factory's underlying structure was what made it difficult to earn a profit.

Raya Mills concentrated on the Singapore market, specialising in the production of low cost garments like T-shirts and underwear. We were dependent on domestic buyers and could only manufacture small quantities. Our stocks, for example, were sufficiently large to replenish the salesman when he came around, but never big enough to produce the volumes needed to break out in a substantive fashion. There were no economies of scale. One could manufacture ten or a hundred dozen shirts, but the market was not going to budge.

A visiting Swedish gentleman by the name of Mr. Forslund suggested to me a way out of Raya Mills' dilemma. Singapore had just begun to channel its energies towards starting up new cooperatives to attract foreign investments. The Swedish Cooperative, Kooperativa Forbundet (K.F.), in particular, had a strong global reputation. Mr. Forslund had been invited to participate in a conference in Singapore focusing on cooperatives. He was using his trip to explore the prospect of whether Singapore could become a viable alternative source of products for Sweden.

Once the conference concluded, he met me at Raya Mills to discuss developing an export market together. "I see that you are young and eager to build up your factory. But you will not succeed with the volumes you have now. Your inbuilt capacity is too small. First, you will need to secure orders for bigger volumes, then install the requisite equipment." He stayed and offered me some good advice on how to do this. I owed him a tremendous debt of gratitude.

Trade relations between Europe and Singapore in the early 1970s, I hazard, were not very significant. But Europe was hungry for new products and not many manufactured items at that time were coming out of Asia — maybe some from Hong Kong and Korea, and to some extent China (though its economy was still getting off the ground). Singapore was not yet developed, but one point in our favour was that we offered lower prices than our European competitors.

Forslund's advice seemed sound, and so I took the risk of approaching the Chairman and the board of Raya Mills to propose an overhaul of our operations. "Selling the products locally is not viable," I argued. "We should be going out into the world market."

Friction at Work

Metaphorically speaking, ripping out the floorboards of a company is not feasible without incurring workplace friction. In addition to shifting our focus to international markets, I also set about changing salary incentives. I explained to my salesmen that, in the long-term, small-time buyers were unsustainable for a business like ours. To succeed, we needed to go after the bigger fish.

"What I will do is put you on commission with a small monthly allowance. If you get good orders, you will make an income that is higher than your current salary. But if you don't," I stressed, "you will not get paid."

This announcement elicited a little hue and cry from our three senior salesmen, who went to the Raya Mills board to complain. On the Board sat an Indian gentleman — a textile merchant — to whom they pleaded their case. They attested that I had never sold anything before in my life and was driving the company into the ground. I was doing something highly dangerous by entering unknown international markets, and they felt whatever gains we had made in the past year would be lost.

"This young fellow knows nothing and wants to experiment with people's lives!"

The textile merchant also happened to be the managing director and a large shareholder of the company; he owned about 20 percent and held considerable sway. His primary income must have derived from the interest he charged on the imported woven fabric that he bought and supplied from India and China. Many of the Chinese retailers who dealt in the sale of fabrics and garments were beholden to him. (As a sign of his influence, he had his own office on High Street.)

He decided to throw in his support with the senior salesmen, and advised our Chairman to be careful and not to waste his money. He perhaps also hinted that, keen to show results, I was taking risky shortcuts by wading into international markets.

I must say that the Managing Director's stand puzzled me, because his line of work — that is, buying from one country and selling to another — was not so different from my proposal. He essentially felt I needed the wisdom of the three senior salespeople, who had implied that if I did not change course, they would resign. The Managing Director also did not think the youngest salesman was experienced enough to guide me.

The three veteran salesmen finally took matters into their own hands by marching into the Chairman's office. But Tong Dow remained level-headed and stood his ground in face of their complaints. "Look, we are stuck in a hole and don't seem to have any way out. This young man is offering a solution according to his experience. We are losing money and are trying something new. If we don't do anything, we will lose even more money and shut down. But if he succeeds, we all benefit. I am ready to support him and give him the full benefit of the doubt."

But even Tong Dow must have privately worried, because he went to consult the factory's yarn supplier at South Grand Textiles (Private) Ltd., based in Jurong. "Unless you expand, you won't survive," the yarn supplier counselled. "What this young man is proposing is sensible. Singapore cannot absorb all the products you make. Europe could be an option. You can try what he is proposing, and if it doesn't work out, you can always go back to the old way of doing things." He said to leave matters in my hands.

In what might be read as a compromise, the Chairman agreed that big markets might be too unwieldy to handle and steered us instead towards a focus on middle-sized countries and cooperatives.

The World Market

The Chairman's support was the break that really saved me — I felt this decision actually transformed the entire character of the company. The garment factory took off after we looked abroad. We went from being a small, parochial factory, catering to domestic buyers, to a larger enterprise focused on foreign exports.

Through my correspondence with the Swedish gentleman, I made various contacts with European clients who placed larger orders. This way of doing business was an eye opener for me and set a new standard for doing business with which I had been unfamiliar. I went on a three-week business trip — to countries like Sweden, Germany and the United Kingdom — to gather requests for my order book.

As one small anecdote from the trip, I recall visiting the East End of London to collect orders, when I stopped by the office of a particularly parsimonious buyer. He asked me for my price, and after I quoted him my figure, his eyes widened. "You're telling me you actually sold these undergarments for that much?" He tapped his finger on his desk. I replied that I had. He whistled and scribbled something down on a sheet of paper. He stretched his arm out in the direction of his secretary.

"Margie, please take this letter to the Queen! Tell her I have met the most marvelous young man who has come to England and achieved the unachievable" (he cited the price of my garments) "which I think is worth half as much. Inform her he should be given an award!"

I watched these theatrics until he stopped. Then I quietly packed my bag to leave. He rushed after me. "Don't be angry, I was only kidding. I will buy your product. I just wanted to see how you would react." He promised to place a generous order.

But I said, "No, I don't like the way you handled the negotiations. I would rather not proceed."

Thinking back on the exchange, I feel I was too hasty in my reply. In business, while interactions of this sort do not crop up all that often, they can knock your ego. You have to harden yourself and build resilience. For instance, if that had happened to me today, I would not have walked out; I would have made light of it and taken a more mature attitude.

Despite this minor setback, my trip to Europe was a success, and I returned to Singapore with a full order book. The Europeans had never seen a Singaporean selling garments and were intrigued! Perhaps this is why, even though I was a novice, they supported me by placing decent orders.

I was also grateful to the Chairman and yarn supplier for backing me. The Managing Director was similarly pleased when the company did well and agreed I had done the right thing. But I never had any doubts that going global was the right thing for us to do, because, honestly speaking, our alternatives were very few. My belief was that we could make it. I was convinced that if we worked hard for our share of the market, there was no good reason why we could not succeed.

Hard Decisions and Hard Knocks

After I returned from Europe, the three senior salesmen resigned. Their work habits, from what I could tell, consisted of a relaxed routine. They had a telephone from which they would contact the head office, and through which they could be contacted. Otherwise, they were supposed to be out in the field, gauging the market.

I had been told by reliable sources, however, that during the day two of the salesmen went to their clan association to play *mahjong*. When evening came, they would call one or two retailers to transmit their purchase orders to the head office; and then they might report, for instance, that they had secured an order of ten dozens. This maybe explained why they did not appreciate that I had put them on commission. From another angle, their lugubrious work style could have been explained by the same constraint the whole factory was facing: a limited market.

On a separate but somewhat related note, the government's disciplining of the labour movement — that is, inculcating the values of hard work and the desire for more modern business standards in the workforce — was, I believe, to Singapore's overall benefit. The government understood the problems accompanying the economy's transition and, to my mind, handled the shift quite shrewdly. They calculated that if one manufactured sophisticated products, the workers' salaries would increase, potentially offsetting any job disruptions that were being caused.

From far-off Thailand, I had felt the reverberations of some of the governments' foundational decisions in the 1960s. For instance, I mentioned the launch of Operation Coldstore in 1963; I had been unsure at that time whether such assertive political control would lead to the abuse of power. (Fortunately, legal procedures have since been frank and open, and such abuse has not occurred.) As the PAP entrenched itself in power (especially after Barisan Sosialis boycotted parliament in December 1965 to protest two bills on independence and the constitution) the party gained a free hand to guide the future direction of the country. Indeed, the PAP's policies were successful in the medium term in putting a lid on subversive revolutionary fervour and laying the groundwork for a politically stable, economically viable and socially cohesive society.

The stability being created in Singapore, I saw, would indeed be a boon to the nation's prospective economic growth. During the 1970s and 1980s, foreigners were becoming more confident about investing here and felt more assured that the number of strikes in the country was dwindling; everything was under control. After the 1969 Malaysia racial riots, my own politics evolved also; I realised that there was a need to factor in the racial element and not just socio-economics. Lastly, I saw people of impeccable integrity joining the PAP. This made me feel that the new system being created should be analysed and given the chance to show its strengths.

On the economic front, the government meanwhile determined not to make it easy for workers to keep doing the same work while the country's leaders built up a new model for doing business. This resulted in some unhappiness. But the government took measures to ensure that the workers were fairly treated by implementing fair rules and policies. In my personal capacity, I also made efforts to ensure that my workers were well treated. The youngest salesman who stayed on with Raya Mills, for instance, changed his attitude towards me and became the supervisor of my sales team.

In terms of my workplace philosophy, I may not be able to get along with everyone; but if a person does or articulates something useful, I am always open to their ideas. I tend to struggle most with bosses who become overbearing as opposed to those who guide you through the process but leave you to make your own decisions — while all the time expecting a high quality of work and output. Tong Dow had a strong personality, but he was balanced and an excellent chairman. If you gave him a work document that needed his attention, he would get back to you in half an hour. No matter how busy he was, he was responsive.

With bigger orders, I got better staff and credit for yarn and fabric as it was now trusted we could pay our bills. With relatively greater prosperity came the opportunity to upgrade the factory's capacity. Modernisation would also be required for our expensive dye treatment plants. After returning from my European business trip, I took the Swedish gentleman's advice to upgrade our production facilities. In the second year, our profit more than doubled. The Chairman gave me a bonus for what I achieved — a country club membership to host our foreign clients for golf and entertainment when they visited Singapore.

12

Transitioning to a High-Value Economy

"This is when we entered Malaysia. The Directors were in favour of the move: I was in a confident frame of mind, and by now they felt I had the ability to show positive results. So I built a second unit for sewing garments in Johor, in southern Malaysia, to expand our labour-intensive garment department... I later started a third unit in Malacca."

Opportunities in India and Malaysia

My Swedish contacts brought Raya Mills more clients, allowing us to expand our operations. I am forever grateful to them. Apart from the cooperatives, some reputable retailers also came to see me, the most well known being the German department store "Hertie". Mr. Ralph Swagger, their regional manager, offered me a position to start up another factory if I agreed to run the enterprise as manager. The factory would be based in India. They were prepared to pay my full salary.

Ralph must have had a demand that he needed met; but I also felt I should take time to carefully consider the proposal and my future. I did not fancy living in India while my young family remained in Singapore. I felt I should instead sink my roots in Singapore and show that what I had achieved was not just a flash in the pan.

"I've barely just started in Singapore, and through the grace of God some good things have happened," I told them. If Hertie were to withdraw, and the operations faltered, I would be in a bind. Finally, I felt it would be tricky to run an outlet successfully in India — it would be wiser to source material from other manufacturers than to start my own production unit.

The Germans understood. But they cautioned that my production costs were becoming high in Singapore and suggested I look at Malaysia to possibly manufacture my garments there.

Around the early 1970s when I had shifted Raya Mills' outlook towards the international market, some large import-export houses were making efforts to monopolise the import-export business in Singapore: they wanted sizeable manufacturers to sign exclusive rights with them. Hertie, the company with which we had worked for many years, chose to drop us because a bigger multinational player had entered the scene.

I went to speak to the bigwigs at the German office and argued that this was not ethical. They folded their hands: there was not much they could do. I was at a loss — forfeiting to the multinationals would have meant selling to Hertie at a cheaper price. I reminded Ralph of the special deal I had signed with Hertie to supply their materials. My tenacity fortunately won the day and, subsequently, he signed a new deal with us.

I am glad I pressed my case, because the new deal gave us the best of both worlds. I held onto my business while our new deal with Hertie was regional; also, Malaysia was familiar territory where I had contacts from my time at MIDF. The Germans' suggestion to expand was therefore timely, and I asked the Raya Mills board for its approval.

This is when we entered Malaysia. The Directors were in favour of the move: I was in a confident frame of mind, and by now they felt I had the ability to show positive results. So I built a second unit for sewing garments in Johor, in southern Malaysia, for our labour-intensive garment department. That was a success, allowing us to cut our costs. I later started a third unit in Malacca.

One of the factories I purchased, I was pleased to discover, was built by an MIDF subsidiary company called Malaysia Industrial Estates Bhd. The company was involved in building modest units for small companies to jumpstart production. The MIDF Chairman happened to be visiting the area and was delighted when he heard that an ex-employee was buying one of their semi-detached factories.

I remember him declaring to his team, "This young man went through the paces with us." He seized the opportunity to show off a bit and suggest to his employees that if they worked hard, they might also be in a position to buy a factory one day.

Intervening on Behalf of Employees

Within a couple of years at the garment factory, the Raya Mills board determined that the company would let me buy a company car. I appreciated the kindness, since my second unit in Malaysia had sprung up so quickly and required repeated trips across the border.

"But I have one request," I told the Directors. "Would you also consider providing my factory manager a car, even if just a small one? He oversees the technical side of operations and has to travel to as many as three factories. I am quite comfortable; but if he has to travel by bus, it will be a hardship. He needs the car most; if you help him, I am sure he would be grateful."

I had promoted my factory manager, Lim Swan Teck (the man who at the start of my tenure had speculated that I would not last for more than three months): I found him to be capable and talented. Not many companies in those days bought factory managers their own cars, and the Directors grumbled at my request. But I argued that within the next year or so, the company would have recouped the money; and so the purchase should not be viewed as a debit.

"Look, you will be giving him some stake in the company." I recommended that he get a Volkswagen — a small but sturdy car.

My factory manager was touched that I had intervened on his behalf. He pointed out that a car of that size would not allow him to carry very much of our products. Still, I advised him against petitioning for a bigger car since he would not get it, and tried to convince him instead that if he did have excess items in need of transport, we could hire a van. I gently reminded him that there was an element of status even in a car like a Volkswagen: it was a sign that the company valued him.*

---

* My tendency is to intervene on my employees' behalf. Another memorable episode occurred when, as the chairman of NTUC Fairprice almost a decade later, I tasked our chief operations officer with overseeing nearly forty or fifty outlets on the island. I felt a driver would ease his burden immensely. Again, several members on the Board opposed. "We are a trade union movement," they said. "We should not be hiring drivers for our staff." I presented the merits of my case. "Not only does he have to visit all these sites, but simply finding a parking spot costs him half an hour." I managed to convince them why a driver should be deemed an essential service and to help him.

The Raya Mills board finally conceded, and my factory manager received a Volkswagen while I got a Volvo. The Chairman gave me a bit of a dressing down for my car choice. "When a company lets you get a car, the person generally gets a Mercedes!" But I thought a Volvo was more than adequate for my needs.

After completing three years at Raya Mills, I held a little get-together in my office. I asked my factory manager vaguely, "How do you feel?" I did not want to remind him of his forecast when I had first joined the team, but he knew what I was talking about. We had become good friends and worked closely together. Treating employees well, I believe, brings out their full potential.

Selling Raya Mills

The factory was running smoothly, but it was not long before what Tong Dow had said on the government's industrial policy review came true. The Economic Development Board believed that with Singapore's small population base, we should be equipping our citizens with all the benefits and skills necessary to manufacture more expensive items for a world market. At the appointed hour, Tong Dow thus called me into his office and asked me to find a buyer for Raya Mills.

"You have done well," he said by way of congratulations. "Now your job is to look for a buyer for the company and sell it. Then we'll see where to place you." I could remain at the factory, leave or do whatever I liked afterwards.

Finding a buyer was a little embarrassing and tricky, because I had just rebuilt the place from scratch. The factory was humming along smoothly and had expanded its customer base. Understandably, our clients were a little upset when they got the news. "You are one of the new and better garment makers!" they exclaimed. "We are dependent on you because we have a market in our countries to fulfill!"

It was meanwhile conveyed to me that if a buyer were to be found, the Chairman would recommend me for a job in one of the government-linked companies. This was to provide some cushion in case I fell on hard ground. I had two choices: to stay on at Raya Mills after the sale or find a new job.

I felt myself strong enough to decide when the time came. But I was not fully convinced we would succeed in finding a buyer; I had the uneasy feeling this task would be hanging around my neck for some time. Regardless, I saw my first duty as fulfilling my clients' orders; second was keeping an eye on how the situation evolved, to determine how best to proceed. After all, it was my own career that was at stake.

We scouted around and fortunately convinced a well-known tycoon from Malaysia to buy the company — the founder and chairman of a public bank who had a very large knitting factory in Malaysia, which I believe was called Wingmai. He had the idea of establishing a fully integrated cross-border enterprise and made an offer to buy the government's share in Raya Mills, which was readily accepted. We worked out a phased withdrawal.

He requested that I stay on and offered me a much higher salary than what I was earning at the time, but I had by then already decided to cast my sights elsewhere (although I had no other jobs lined up). It was while selling Raya Mills, in September 1973, that my third child, Priya, was born.

Singapore's Manufacturing Evolution

Despite the minor inconvenience that this caused, I think that the government was wise in deciding to phase out low paying, labour-intensive industries like garment manufacturing: in the long-term, the transition towards high-value products transformed the economy. Truthfully, I had initially wondered whether it would be successful, since the investments required for the plans were not at all guaranteed. The economy, I think, was fortunate to emerge from the turbulent 1970s as well as it did. The government, too, should be credited for having made every possible effort to push for a sophisticated manufacturing model which would lead to a better quality of life for its citizens.

Some background might be required about what this manufacturing

My baby daughter, Priya, with Preetha and Prakash in Raya Mills tee-shirts, 1974 or 1975.

evolution entailed. Garments were at the bottom end of the spectrum. Adjacent industries included the manufacture of fabrics, finishing, dyeing, spinning, knitting and weaving. Up-scale garment manufacturing also existed — for instance, for clothing that had intricate patterns and designs on them. However, what moved Singaporean manufacturing was the tilt towards the production of aerated beverages and processed foods.

After garments, these items galvanised the second phase of Singapore's manufacturing evolution. Several large Singaporean manufacturers at this juncture included Fraser & Neave (beverages); Yeo Hiap Seng (beverage and food products); and Chuen Cheong (soya sauce, chilli sauce and other condiments). While Yeo Hiap Seng was a Chinese family-owned business (many Chinese family-owned small and medium-sized businesses around then were involved in the manufacture of various products), Fraser & Neave (or F&N as they were known here) operated with foreign counterparts. This company was European owned; this meant that they were able to attract higher investments and sell their products at a higher price. F&N was the dominant manufacturer on the island. The channelling of higher investment into contract manufacture for foreign producers set the stage for the third level of Singapore's manufacturing story, which eventually transitioned into heavy-duty equipment such as tyres and auto parts.

This tiered process is typical for how many countries move up the value chain. The manufacturing evolution unfolded over many decades — it was not all achieved in the 1970s. I learned quite a lot about it as a member of the Singapore Manufacturers' Association (SMA). I had started on the textile sub-committee and, after a few failed attempts, was elected to the main council. I later became one of SMA's two deputy presidents, working closely with Michael Yeo Chee Wee, general manager of Yeo Hiap Seng Limited and SMA chairman (1978–1979).[1] When I was told the industrial review was underway, many industrial plans had been conceptualised but were not yet implemented. But it did not take long for Singapore to get the projects off the ground.

SMA Mission to the Middle East, November–December 1974, with me (left) and Michael Yeo Chee Wee (centre).

13

United Industrial Corporation: My Engagement with Taiwan

"I explained that he should gauge his decision more holistically...'This is a Taiwanese company, partly owned by the Singapore government. The Taiwanese shareholders will feel upset that you are bringing a non-Taiwanese into the top echelon of management... I suggest you appoint your son-in-law, Mr. Feng, as the general manager, and I will be his deputy.'"

A Private Sector Man

After selling the garment factory, I was offered a job by Ernest Wong, who had been my senior at university. He was the general manager at United Industrial Corporation Ltd. (UIC). Ernest convinced me that I was not really suited for a government institution and was at heart a private sector man. UIC was a publicly listed company with offices on Shenton Way. He offered me a position as a corporate finance manager but at a lower salary than what I would have received at a government-linked company.

"Time to celebrate!" Ernest said. "You should have never gone into garments. There is no future there. You should instead join me!"

Managing Raya Mills had nevertheless done me some good. I had earned a strong reputation in the business community from having turned around a cash-starved factory. Indeed, this experience proved invaluable, as many other challenges lay ahead. UIC was keen to leverage my experience for two of their pre-existing operations in food and polyester (UIC had invested in a large polyester plant for the knitting and dyeing of garments).

UIC was a wealthy company, substantially owned by Taiwanese shareholders. It was the largest manufacturer of detergents in Singapore and manufactured under licence for Unilever and Colgate. In addition, it produced its own brands. For example, UIC signed a joint venture with the British company Albright & Wilson to manufacture the chemicals for their shampoos and detergents. I negotiated the joint venture with them, becoming the chemical plant's first executive director. Mr. Goh Chok Tong, who was then Senior Minister of State for Finance, opened the plant in Jurong.* The Board was disappointed that Mr. Hon Sui Sen, the Minister of Finance (whom they had wanted to attend) could not make it. Finally, along with its detergent business, UIC also owned a handsome property at No. 3 Shenton Way from which it rented out floors.

The chairman of UIC then was Permanent Secretary of Defence Pang Tee Pow. Temasek (an investment company owned by the Singapore government) held a large stake in UIC, and Mr. Dennis Lee Kim Yew, the younger brother of Lee Kuan Yew, was an independent director on the company's board. He ran the family legal practice, Lee & Lee. At that stage, Dennis Lee did not participate too actively in UIC's affairs and mostly dealt with matters that arose at the board level.

Official opening of UIC plant in Jurong on May 10th, 1978 with me (second from left), Dennis Lee Kim Yew (right), Goh Chok Tong (centre) and other staff members.

* I recall then SMS Goh Chok Tong walking outside the plant as it began to drizzle. I had a couple of assistants stationed outside on the pavement to hold out umbrellas for him, should he need them. "Did you check the weather forecast before I came?" the former Minister of State asked. I had. "You also knew you needed *three* umbrellas?" he pressed, teasing me. "Yes," I answered with a laugh. "Given your height, we had to factor in the width and breadth of the umbrellas!"

Negotiating Against Promotion

Ernest was the driving force for my joining UIC. But I did not get the chance to work with him for as long as I would have liked, as within several months of my start date, Ernest and the Chairman got into a big argument. Ernest was by nature a headstrong person. He and the Chairman struggled to see eye-to-eye, and Ernest decided to wash his hands of the company. "I'm leaving," he declared.

Mr. Chuang Wen Lian, the company's major Taiwanese stakeholder — who spoke little English but still managed to communicate effectively in a mix of English and Mandarin — was very fond of Ernest. After Ernest announced his departure plans, Mr. Chuang asked me what we should do. "We cannot go and tell the Chairman to apologise."

"I know Ernest quite well," I answered. "He is a stubborn person. If he has made up his mind, then there is little chance we can change it. I think it is best that you start to look around."

Mr. Chuang followed my advice and my friend resigned. When the question of a successor arose, the Chairman put forward my name to Mr. Chuang as their new general manager. He said that he was not at all worried about my doing the job. To my surprise, Mr. Chuang also agreed that I should take this plum post.

I was shocked for several reasons. Firstly, I had only just started and felt that it would have been a bit of a novelty to have a Singaporean Indian running a Taiwanese company. But when I raised this concern with Mr. Chuang, he dismissed it: I had been with them for six months and he was fine with the selection.

Secondly, Mr. Chuang had a son-in-law named Mr. Feng, a sincere engineer employed at the company whose name the Chairman had also suggested. I argued it would be more appropriate for him to take the position as general manager. My intention was to make sure that Mr. Chuang was respected and seen to be observing modern principles of management, as well as Taiwanese expectations of supporting one's kith and kin (provided they were strong performers). Again, Mr. Chuang's answer surprised me. "I like my son-in-law, but he is not suitable for the role. I believe that you will be most effective in running the company."

I surmised that Mr. Chuang was afraid that if he did not support my nomination promptly, the Chairman might spring another name. The Chairman likely had other candidates in mind; I am not sure whether he expected Mr. Chuang to take the proposal of my name seriously. However, the Chairman did not want to upset the process that he had set in motion. I asked Mr. Chuang if we could speak informally.

I explained that he should gauge the appointment more holistically, as it was a matter of some cultural sensitivity. "This is a Taiwanese company, partly owned by the Singapore government. The Taiwanese shareholders will feel upset that you are bringing a non-Taiwanese into the top echelon of management. This is not good. They will think the control of the company is slipping away. Then they will start selling their shares. I suggest you appoint your son-in-law, Mr. Feng, as the general manager, and I will be his deputy. I can help him look after this area."

Mr. Chuang turned my proposal over in his mind. "No, I don't like the idea of you being a deputy."

"Okay," I answered, "but give me some time to think the problem through. The answer I come up with will not be that I take over as general manager!"

"All right," he said, "but come back this afternoon." It was at that time early morning.

When I returned, I recommended asking the Chairman whether he would be fine with appointing both Feng and me as joint general managers. Mr. Chuang looked down at the floor, then at me, and said, "You are a wise man." I took this as an endorsement! I felt I had been presented with an insoluble puzzle and found the solution!

Feng and I ran the company together happily for several years; he became a friend with whom I occasionally played golf.

Working with Dennis Lee

Meanwhile, Chairman Pang Tee Pow became sick and died of cancer. His position was filled by Dennis Lee. I hadn't worked with Dennis Lee extensively before this; I only knew him from my time at UIC. He had inherited the staff infrastructure more or less intact; any orders he had were sent to me to be carried through. He requested that I work closely with him on all matters.

With Ernest's exit and the Chairman's passing, there were now quite a few gaps in the company that needed filling. One of these was to find someone to run UIC's restaurant, Southron. I had mentioned that UIC's property on Shenton Way had floors available for rent. A Singapore businessman with Taiwanese connections approached Mr. Chuang one day to persuade him to start a Chinese restaurant there. He spun all the usual stories — UIC would take 50 percent of the shares while he would take on the major responsibility of running the restaurant. The businessman argued having a restaurant at this prime site would benefit the Group.

However, time soon proved this to be quite the opposite. The operating partner who had pitched the Group the idea of this restaurant failed to make it profitable and quit. Ernest had been the chairman of the company which owned the restaurant, and had been overseeing the area of food operations before he resigned; a part of his responsibilities was assigned to me. Now that he was gone and the restaurant was losing money, nobody wanted to touch it. The polyester company, too, was struggling. It was a messy situation and the Directors started to get restless, although our detergent business was doing fine and funded the company's other ventures. Dennis Lee called me in to discuss what should be done.

I did not feel comfortable supervising the restaurant; we were landlords rather than restaurant managers and, in my view, each of our businesses should stand on their own merit. If it could not, we should write it off. Also, the problem with the polyester company was of a different order than the problem of supply and demand that I had dealt with at Raya Mills. UIC had overinvested; I concluded it would be very difficult to save the polyester company because of the large amount of resources required to salvage it — unless we could pump in money for the restructuring, it would be difficult to turn the company around.

I therefore had two tough decisions to make, and I shared my assessment with Dennis Lee. "We can sell ourselves as a manufacturing and property company, but I don't see how the restaurant business fits anywhere into this. The restaurant business is notoriously corrupt — everyone wants a cut. I will find it troublesome to run. I suggest we take the loss."

I also suggested that we take the loss on the polyester company, because I knew that Singapore had little interest in this kind of low-value manufacturing venture. I recommended we look for a partner in Malaysia or Thailand instead.

He agreed. Dennis Lee was an excellent chairman who came to rational conclusions. The final story was rather gory, in terms of the deals and sub-deals we made. But I feel that UIC came out of the situation extremely well.

Changing the Old Guard

While all this took place, the episode of the Chairman's passing had done a different damage: Mr. Chuang was becoming more and more introspective. He was spending more time in Taiwan and Nevada and away from the company. In the past, he had done this intermittently, perhaps only once a month. But at this point, he had started to spend time away from the company more frequently, suggesting to me that his mind was no longer on work. I started to get the feeling that he wanted to exit.

I saw that it was only a matter of time before potential buyers swooped in to make an offer. Mr. Chuang was a wise, honest man, and I was disappointed to see him cut himself off this way. Later, my hunch proved correct when an investor from Southeast Asia started visiting Feng for meetings.

One day, this investor struck a deal to jointly run the company with Mr. Chuang. He said he would bring his own team, which required a staff overhaul, and that he and my Taiwanese friend would run the company together. I felt now would be a good time to leave; I did not want to stick around now since Mr. Chuang had withdrawn and Ernest had left. Concurrently, I also received an offer to join the government-run company Intraco.

Dennis Lee wrote a very kind letter, asking me to stay; he reassured me that amidst the restructuring by the new investor, nothing would happen to my position: "Under whatever circumstances, I will ensure that you are not affected by this." But I felt it was time to move on.

I did not want to be a burden. Better for the new investor to bring in a fresh team to restructure the company in alignment with the interests of the new shareholders. They would not want me to interfere. Dennis Lee was very sorry to see me go; I had been with UIC for two and a half years, and a degree of warmth had grown between us.

Divergent Manufacturing Paths

I appreciated the experience working with the Taiwanese. Singapore and Taiwan had strong people-to-people relations, and Taiwan was undergoing a revolution in manufacturing similar to ours, although in policy it took a different path. One thing I have always admired about Taiwan is how they were able to nurture small, promising businesses into small and medium-sized enterprises (SMEs) and eventually larger companies, which helped Taiwan to catapult its manufacturing profile.

Singapore too had a nascent engineering industry on Lavender Street with several engineering workshops, which I believe had the potential to become thriving private sector businesses. However, the workshops were virtually wiped out because the rental costs became too high and the environmental requirements too burdensome: they could not survive. Today, only a few workshops can be found on Lavender Street, which perhaps adversely impacted our private sector's development.

Apart from the government- and Temasek-linked companies (GLCs and TLCs), I do not believe we have a private sector comparable to Taiwan's. Singapore was more interested in bringing in competitive goods that fit into the existing manufacturing landscape than in nurturing the producers of those materials. Due to limited land and labour resources, Singapore had to efficiently attract products — a gadget, for example, which the Taiwanese would have designed locally. Our business federation thus hunts high and low to see who and what we can admit while we lack homegrown companies into which some of these engineering workshops could have been developed. This is one underlying economic problem that we are dealing with today, people say: bringing in foreign workers for employment at multinationals who then take money out of the system.

In education, however, Singapore has been quite successful. After school, if a young person attends university, the sky is the limit in terms of the types of jobs he or she is able to access. For those without university education, Singapore innovatively opened polytechnics and equivalent institutions that impart skills "to support the technological and economic development of Singapore" through vocational training.[1]

For instance, if a young person wants to be a technician, he can join the Institute of Technical Education after completing his "O" or "N" Levels, graduate to a higher-level polytechnic and head straight into work. It is also possible to join a university and complement practical workplace experience with a higher education. From there, obtaining a better paying job is fairly easy. Employers actually prefer hiring workers with knowledge-based and accrued real world experience.

14

Intraco: Forum for the Unheard of and Unexpected

"My job at Intraco was to identify new markets and products overseas and to see how we could penetrate those markets. Those of us who worked at Intraco were united in our buccaneer-like spirits. We had a common approach towards the conduct of business abroad. We went into promising, diverse foreign economies to trade; and, if there was something that we wanted, we did the deals to make that possible."

Singapore's Trade Policy

As Singapore was building up its manufacturing base it was also venturing into unchartered waters with a forward-looking trade policy. Singapore, being a late industrialising nation cut off from Malaysia with limited resources, needed to establish connections with the global economy and open new markets as part of its strategy of export-oriented industrialisation. Dr. Goh Keng Swee established Intraco (or International Trading Company) in 1968 against the backdrop of other government-linked companies being created to foster critical sectors in the economy. Intraco was founded to "blaze a trail overseas" and expand Singapore's trade.[1] For doing unheard of things in far-off places, Intraco was the head of the spear.

Before joining Raya Mills, I had reached out to Tong Dow to see whether there were any openings at Intraco. Intraco was recruiting young talent to be posted outside of Singapore as special trade officers. They had advertised for individuals with international experience to build a specialised team and "create export markets for Singapore products and source for imports for the domestic market".[2] My return to Singapore came on the back of seven years in Thailand and Malaysia; I thought

Intraco would be an ideal fit, given my background. But my life took a different direction when Tong Dow directed my talents towards Raya Mills. After a diversion, however, I found my way back to Intraco.

Intraco was the state's "premier trading enterprise", substantially owned by the Singapore government and tasked with facilitating commercial ties in the international market during the Cold War. According to Faizal bin Yahya, a senior research fellow in the Governance and Economy Department at the Institute of Policy Studies, Intraco was created to navigate trade amidst a tense geopolitical climate and shore up Singapore's entrepreneurial and financial capital. Providing political context, he writes in his book on Intraco that "distrust of the communists prevented Singapore from establishing any political or diplomatic links with China and other socialist states",[3] but that as part of "its role to diversify procurement of raw material from new sources and demand from emerging markets", Intraco was consequently encouraged to "trade and explore business opportunities in… [closed] socialist economies or emerging markets such as the Middle East or Africa."[4]

Mr. S. Chandra Das, then the managing director of Intraco, offered me a job. Chandra, a close friend, is a remarkable person. He was a former government official who had served as a trade representative to Moscow. I first knew Chandra through the teaching profession, although both of us had taught in different schools. He left teaching to join the Export Promotion Centre in the Economic Development Board. In 1980, he entered politics as a member of parliament.

Chandra originally joined Intraco as an assistant to the head of operations. With senior management retiring, however, he quickly ascended the ranks to occupy the post of managing director by the time he brought me on in 1980. Intraco was not only looking at trading then but also at getting involved in manufacturing and investments. With expansion in mind, Chandra appointed me as one of three general managers in charge of manufacturing and trading of chemicals and garments. My title was 'General Manager (Manufacturing and Investment)'.

My position built on my work experience at Raya Mills and UIC. I also added new commodities to my portfolio such as rubber, paper and steel. Intraco had a strong international orientation, with factories based in Singapore as well as Bangladesh and trade missions in West and East Asia. It also looked at development and property. The other two general managers were Mr. Charlie Phua, a trusted lieutenant of Chandra, and Mr. Rex Shelly, in charge of administration. Both were friends of mine.

Trade Mandate

My job at Intraco was to identify new markets and products overseas and see how we could penetrate those markets. Those of us who worked at Intraco were united in our buccaneer-like spirits. We had a common approach towards the conduct of business abroad. We went into promising, diverse foreign economies to trade; and, if there was something that we wanted, we did the deals to make that possible. Intraco was unique in being allowed to trade in specialised items. Furthermore, if there was a security problem in any country that was seen to be a deal breaker, our group was expected to step in and have a handle on the political situation.

Many of the countries we traded with, as mentioned earlier, fell under the Socialist Bloc. This included China, whose trade with Singapore was restricted. Trade with other countries, such as South Africa, was restricted as well due to apartheid: Western countries treated it as a pariah. Big countries like America and Britain could release fantastic rules about which countries the international community should trade with, while they could do as they pleased whenever required.

Singapore also needed to survive, and they say that when necessity calls, invention follows. Intraco's distinguishing contribution was in finding workarounds; as Yahya explains, this was by taking on the role as a sort of middleman or intermediary for product exchange.[5] We were a cohesive bunch, and Chandra left a great deal for us to manage. Some said Chandra's leadership style could be tough to handle. But I found him to be quite reasonable. He set difficult targets for himself that he ultimately achieved. He expected his staff to do the same.

International Lessons

At Intraco, I learned how to deal with cultural environments far different from Singapore's, especially in the Middle East. We were more or less concentrated on Africa and the Middle East and were doing well. Chandra had one cardinal principle that he stuck to, which was that if a team was entering a foreign country — especially in a land rather difficult to live in and trade with — he insisted a senior staff member accompany and steer the mission. One of our trade delegations travelled to Tripoli in Libya. I was the senior staff member chosen to lead it.

Singapore Manufacturers' Association (SMA) Mission to the Middle East, 1976.

We surveyed the possibility of trading in oil and minerals in Libya, both areas in which Singapore did not have a sizeable record of business. Basically, for countries that were not very active in international trade, setting up a trade relationship entailed getting to know key actors in the sector, setting up trade ties and then inviting them to Singapore to look around — to convince them to invest in or identify industries that they might want to establish. Singapore in the late 1970s and 1980s was not well advanced, but these countries in the Middle East and Africa were even less so. They hardly had any industry, which made Singapore a viable investment destination.

I also visited another Middle Eastern, partially English-speaking country, Yemen, whose southern region in the early 20th century had been a colony of Britain. Intraco had a network of people moving around investigating opportunities there. I benefited from the exchange of information with them. If a colleague shared any promising news about Yemen, I mentally tucked this information away. I went into Yemen for several reasons: firstly, because I heard it had money and was open to business; and secondly, because, compared with its neighbours, it neither victimised nor mistreated foreigners, making it a more approachable market.

In other words, we followed a three-step model: we read the terrain, and if that was acceptable, we determined what products we wanted and studied if we could source them. Combining these factors, we devised our strategy for entering the market. If I followed these steps, I tended to come out okay. This is a type of sixth sense my colleagues and I developed through on-the-job training. Intraco was a hybrid company, appropriate for someone like me who had experience outside Singapore and a background in trade and manufacturing.

New Wonders

Many political systems in Africa and the Middle East were dictatorships. In Libya, for instance, I went on a sightseeing tour of a huge palace owned by a brazen man. I asked my guide, "Who lived here?" He answered, "Idi Amin," the notorious former president of Uganda. Idi Amin was the mastermind who orchestrated the extradition of 30,000 to 40,000 Asians from Uganda, mostly of Indian and Pakistani descent, when he expropriated their property in 1972 and distributed their businesses to his soldiers and cronies.[6*] Amin resided in Libya in exile in 1979.

I also visited Yemen's capital Sanaa, where the Queen of Sheba once ruled. I discovered during my trip that Yemen had a sizeable Parsee

---

* Financially, this backfired on Amin because the Indians and Pakistanis buttressed Uganda's economy, bankrolling his foreign mercenaries. Amin's soldiers were untrained and largely illiterate. The businesses were mismanaged when his cronies took over. Amin was ousted from power and fled to Libya after Tanzanian troops invaded in 1979.

population. In 1967, South Yemen turned communist after the departure of the British. Business declined as the port of Aden on the Arabian peninsula, which was once described as "a thriving trading port, a free port like Singapore… lost its position as an important trading post on both sides of the Suez".[7]

Foreigners chose to leave; in particular, the Parsees, who were afraid that their holy fire temple would fall into communist hands. As the book *The Flames of Faith: A Historical Saga* recounts, Cowasjee Dinshaw, whose family had built the agiary (fire temple) in Yemen, decided that "he would not let the Holy Atash (Fire)… die away as the one in Zanzibar had" and resolved to save it by relocating to Bombay.

The Parsees are now one of the most prosperous communities in India. If I ever had the option of choosing a business partner, it would be a Parsee, as I have found that a Parsee always keeps to his word. My good fortune was that, years later, in the 1990s (when my team and I began building up Gateway Distriparks Ltd. in India), one of our investors brought along a young Parsee gentleman named Mr. Saroosh Dinshaw. He later became a director. I found him to be quite capable and intelligent. Casually, Saroosh one day mentioned to me that his father was Cowasjee Dinshaw, the leader who made the plan to move the Holy Fire from Aden to India!

The curious part of his tale was that Zoroastrianism restricted "the crossing of the Holy Fire over wide expanses of water." Multiple rivers transected Yemen and India; crossing them would have presented "major difficulties."[8] According to the book, his father had therefore chartered an Air India Boeing 707 and arranged for a flickering flame to be flown over the desert with five priests, who needed to be aboard to attend to the needs of this "special passenger".[9] These were just a few of the marvelous insights I gained while employed at Intraco.

South Asia and China

As part of my trading portfolio at Intraco, I was responsible for the trade of palm oil. We sourced the palm oil from Indonesia. I recall the lukewarm welcome I received at the Trading Corporation of Pakistan when I first arrived at their offices. The Managing Director was outraged that Chandra had left them in the hands of a novice. The Pakistanis were conscious of Chandra's station and aware that I (being new) was of a lower rank, with little to suggest that I held comparable experience.

I explained that since Chandra was a member of parliament, he had a great deal of work to deal with. (He was the chairman of the Trade Development Board from 1983 to 1986, and would go on to set up the Parliamentary Committee for Defence and Foreign Affairs, which he chaired from 1985 to 1990 and into which I was inducted as a resource person in the 1980s. My involvement led Chandra to later gauge my interest in becoming a non-resident ambassador in the 1990s and, as a result, in 1994, I was appointed Singapore's non-resident high commissioner to Pakistan.) But back then, I was the new kid on the block.

Although the Pakistanis were stand-offish at first, I later found them to be quite easy to work with and accommodating. We built up the palm oil trade between us. I made good deals with Pakistan. Selling palm oil to India, on the other hand, was not so easy. The Indians contended that the palm oil Singapore exported was from a third country and that, because Singapore did not originally produce the material, they did not want to trade in it. I was confounded by this, as a country consumes products from third countries all the time. Meanwhile, I started experimenting with IT work in India, supervising several Intraco subsidiaries, the most prominent being a joint venture with Tata Consultancy Services (TCS). Before the Bangalore boom in the early 2000s, I saw the potential of knowledge trading but left Intraco before it became big.

I also proposed producing palm oil in countries with favourable growing conditions, such as Sri Lanka and China. We had gone to Sri Lanka to look at the prospect of growing oil palms — but the politics there at that time did not permit us to do that. Then, I remember, someone suggested that we look at Hainan Island in China. The atmosphere on the island is tropical and similar to a Southeast Asian country. We sent a team there with the idea of combining our resources with the Chinese Chamber of Commerce. Again, we met with some external constraints.

After the Chinese provided their inputs, we conferred and decided that Hainan Island would not have been a suitable site for such a large investment. Whenever we entered a country to invest, we tried to be circumspect. If the project was expensive, and we were unsure of its success, we risked losing all our money. Intraco never invested in plantations, but we did talk about it and spent some money researching the question.

The Rise of China

The world was changing apace and, within the near decade I had spent working in Singapore, China grew at a stretch. Intraco was one of the companies pushing hard for the opening of the Chinese market.

The government had acted cautiously towards communist China at first, due to the history of insurgency in Singapore and Malaya. Still, the government remained pragmatic and open to trade with major players in the region. Intraco's monopoly over foreign markets and materials, meanwhile, stirred resentment amongst the Singaporean Chinese traders, who felt it was unfair that they should be levied for their trade with China. The government observed this unhappiness and smartly revised the CESS tax system.[10] Although the tax remained intact, it was used to promote Chinese education, thereby curbing reasons for complaint.

Personally, my first professional engagement with the Chinese was in the 1970s through the Singapore Manufacturers' Association. I became chairman of the committee for the Singapore Fair, which SMA hosted annually. The fair exhibited Singapore-made products to the world; we invited countries from all over to participate. Singapore government ministers attended as our VIP guests, such as then Minister of Economic Affairs Dr. Goh Keng Swee (at that time the most powerful man in Singapore, after Lee Kuan Yew) as well as Hon Sui Sen. Later, the fair's inauguration ceremony was taken over by members of the next generation such as Goh Chok Tong.

The government agreed to allow us to invite a Chinese delegation to the fair. (If my memory serves, this was one of China's earliest

Opening of the Singapore Fair by then Deputy Prime Minister Dr. Goh Keng Swee.

trade delegations to Singapore.) We were delighted when the Chinese manufacturers chose to participate in our event for several years; this was viewed as a major achievement on our part, as Chinese attendance helped to put Singapore onto the world map. The Chinese had even on one occasion asked us to host a dinner, requesting the names of prominent Singaporeans who would like to attend. We consulted with the various governmental departments concerned and proposed our list.[†]

I have found that there are many benefits to working with the Chinese. They are very broadminded and quite friendly. Also, after having grown up alongside the Chinese community on East Coast Road, I never faced a scenario in which I was sidelined because of my race. China's way of doing business is different from Western or Southeast Asian countries where family connections and hailing from the same village or clan go a long way in forging common ties. Regionally, China became both a major supplier as well as a buyer after its free-market reforms in 1979, and absorbed a large number of traders who wanted to set up shop.

[†] I was tasked with reviewing the list with the Chinese delegation. I was impressed by how meticulous they were in questioning the credentials of each and every person we had suggested — not to mention why we had suggested them and what they were expected to contribute. Our job had been to draw up the list. The delegation really combed through it!

Indeed, by the time I had joined Intraco in 1980, China had shown its strengths, and many on the Board felt China offered a promising source of business and trade. China is exceptionally efficient at implementing projects sanctioned by the right people. Projects not easily implementable in other parts of the world are feasible there. One just has to start work and bring in the capital. From the time the first nod is given to when one begins manufacturing, I have observed that a lot of time can be wasted in other parts of the world.

Although Intraco wanted to focus on China, it nevertheless struggled to recruit talent with enough inbuilt experience to handle the market. And so, while we in management felt that, on the whole, we were doing well in our operations, a problem had started brewing amongst the Directors. They believed we were losing our focus on our chief area of concern, which was import and export trade, and were not focusing enough on China. My hunch was that some higher-ups were unhappy that we were not pulling our weight.

I was the person in charge of this area and began to feel that this criticism was more or less directed at me. To complicate matters, I had also taken on a voluntary basis the board-elected position of chairman of NTUC Fairprice in 1983 (although I was not a paid employee). Understandably, I came in for some criticism. I realised that I had better resign. "If you have a better way of doing it, then I will make way for someone else to take over," I said.

Exodus

Quite a number of others resigned after I left, including Chandra, who resigned a few weeks later. I believe the senior members of the staff were shocked by his resignation. A key reason for pressuring me, I suspected, was just to send him a broader signal about the kind of business they prioritised — cutting off the cock's head to frighten the monkey. Afterwards, the senior management approached Chandra to clarify that they did not hold him to blame. But he left the job anyway, in part to focus on his role as a member of parliament. Articles were written in *The Straits Times* documenting the names of those who resigned.[11] Chandra's resignation, for many, had been a deciding factor; several employees unhappy with the change of management left en masse. First, one or two assistant general managers left; then the other general managers, Charlie Phua and Rex Shelly. An entirely new management came in after that; reassembling a group of similar size took time and was harder than envisaged.

Intraco continues to operate; in 2003, the government divested its stake which was bought over by PSC Corporation Ltd.[12] It today describes itself as an "investment holding company", which deals mainly in the trading of materials like plastic resins, the provision of management services for mobile/radio infrastructure and crane rental services.[13] Several of us learnt valuable lessons from our time at Intraco. I learned not only how to trade but also to understand the mentalities of countries different than my own. Moreover, it gave me the opportunity to engage with India and Pakistan, which would prove useful years later as an entrepreneur and diplomat. I was at Intraco for three years. That encapsulates my short stint in the government sector.

15

Inno-Pacific: American Franchises and the High Court

"[I]t seemed that the prosecution had gone a little overboard with their accusations, assuming guilt before gathering enough evidence. This was the conclusion of Chief Justice Yong Pung How, who was known for being a strict judge. I recall him stating in court, 'I see the prosecutor has gone on a fishing expedition.'"

A Franchisee of Kentucky Fried Chicken

Anyone who has been in business long enough knows that there are moments when your friends become your major lifeline, helping you to navigate life's unexpected trials. This was not only the case when I was looking for a new job after moving to Singapore, but also after I left Intraco for a new job. Again, I gravitated towards friends whom I knew and trusted. As one particularly challenging episode in the 1990s reveals, such help was not confined to job hunts.

In 1986, I for a short time held the position of managing director of Ambassador Holdings Ltd. Ambassador Holdings was the owner of Ambassador Hotel in Katong, opposite Katong Park. Yet again, I was helped out by my old friend Bala, who had invested a large sum of money in the company with the belief that it had a bright future. But the company was not well run and had a few skeletons in its closet. Not long after I joined the company the hotel was sold.

Next, I received an offer from Inno-Pacific Holdings, a major shareholder of Kentucky Fried Chicken (KFC) in Singapore. Inno-Pacific was 51 percent owned by Innovest Bhd., the franchisee of KFC in Malaysia. Cash-wise, it was a wealthy company. The managing director, Cheam Tat Pang — my senior at MIDF, who had recommended me for the position at Raya Mills — recruited me to look after Inno-Pacific's trade as executive director. He was a brilliant man and my senior at university. Tat Pang completed his Honours Degree at the University of Malaya and his Masters at Williams College in the U.S. There were three of us at the top: Tat Pang, Mr. Thomas Chong and me.

I had two major responsibilities. My first was to oversee the trading company, Poon Guan. Poon Guan had a trading portfolio for South Asia with Bangladesh, Sri Lanka and India as well as Burma and some parts of Africa. By the time I joined the group, KFC had also proven to be quite lucrative, and its profitability inspired us to think about owning a fast food franchise of our own. My second responsibility was to purchase a franchise in the U.S. and to supervise its operations. One of the most memorable episodes of my time at Inno-Pacific was when the company bought one of America's oldest pizza franchises. Another less pleasant episode was when my co-directors were accused of mishandling company funds and taken to court.

Shakey's Pizza

The American franchise I identified for purchase was called Shakey's Pizza. Shakey's was one of the U.S.' original pizza parlours, based in Sacramento, California. The founder of this family restaurant had served as a soldier in the Vietnam War, where he contracted a malarial fever that gave him "shakes" all over. My role was to visit America each month to evaluate the franchise's size and pinpoint outlet locations.

We made the purchase in 1989, at the beginning of the unipolar period marked by U.S.-led globalisation and the fall of the Berlin Wall. Buying Shakey's was pioneering for a Singaporean company; its acquisition came on the back of many successful fast food restaurants spreading all over, such as McDonalds and Pizza Hut. Shakey's was a reflection of Inno-Pacific's ambitions to go global. We appointed our franchisees to run the outlets in the U.S. while we became the owner of the franchise.

By the time we entered the fast food industry, Shakey's had undergone several significant changes of ownership and had lost quite a

Inno-Pacific acquires Shakey's franchise

By MAGDALENE NG

"Inno-Pacific acquires Shakey's franchise", by Magdalene Ng, 1989

"Kentucky Fried Chicken (S) Ltd, now known as Inno-Pacific Holdings Ltd, has pulled off a coup in the international fast food franchising business… Executive director Gopinath Pillai said Inno-Pacific is the first Singapore company to acquire an internationally known franchise."

bit of lustre. We in management, however, saw Shakey's growth potential, and were not disappointed that its operations were predominantly confined to the U.S. We also felt that we would not have been able to handle a far-flung empire. KFC would help us to support Shakey's by generating supplementary cash flow.

We had high hopes to start. We targeted establishing several Shakey's outlets in the region: three in Singapore, five in Malaysia, three in Thailand, three in Hong Kong, three in Taiwan and four in China. We planned to build ten stores in Singapore from 1989 to 1992 and hoped to overtake Pizza Hut, our closest competitor.[1] While our benchmarks for Singapore and Malaysia were more or less met — Shakey's achieved a fairly good reach in the U.S. and the Philippines — our presence in the rest of Southeast Asia was at the end of the day not very significant.

Rubbing the shine back into the Shakey's brand did not, for various reasons, pan out as planned. Shakey's was not what you would call a *prosperous* franchise; although it was not generating a lot of money, it was, however, not losing a lot either. Our major challenge was that we were a small operator in a far-off part of the world, unused to handling a behemoth like the U.S. market. The franchise withered because of a lack of a united management and cohesive financial structure. Shakey's was also short on funds, which was why the Americans had decided to sell. We offered our best price for Shakey's International and Shakey's Incorporated — a combined price tag of S$11.5 million — but did not know at that time how much money would be required to rejuvenate the operations.[2]

A franchise, by its very nature, succeeds according to cash flow. If you do well, the cash funnels in to fund your growth. This did not happen in Shakey's case. We had a few outlets that were doing well; other money came in from our royalties and territorial licences. But that was not enough to thrive. Another impediment was our rivalry with Pizza Hut. They had better resources and deeper pockets. Thirdly, pizza was a new cuisine to Asia, whereas the chicken offered at KFC was more familiar to the Asian palette.

I will neither declare Shakey's a success nor failure. Dealing with the franchisees, however, and visiting the U.S. was an adventure. Every time I went to the U.S. during the 1990s I felt I learned something new. To help run our operations, we brought a few of our colleagues from Singapore and Malaysia to the U.S. They considered the Americans to be very hardworking and friendly. They found that the Americans were easy to get to know and that the country was convenient for settling down in. This made handling the projects amid our managerial issues a little easier.

Of course, there was a little "getting-to-know-you" on both sides. The Singaporean workers observed that the Americans seemed to have no other preoccupation besides work — to which I responded that this was only an artificial impression: Americans are also often on the lookout for relaxation and fun. The Americans were amazed at the English we spoke, and did not expect us to speak "American" quite so well.

"How come you speak such good English?" they asked.

"Well, many have no choice," I jested. "We were once a British colony too!"

The Court Case

While managing Shakey's posed a few challenges, problems started emerging in Singapore at the administrative level. Accusations were being made about how the company was run. Inno-Pacific was a public company, answerable to the shareholders. Several complaints were lodged against my fellow directors.

I will not go into the details of the case but, in short, they had gotten into trouble with the stock exchange, and were charged with a criminal breach of trust.[3] The Commercial Affairs Department had started an investigation claiming that they had overseen a questionable sale of property. The directors were charged with seeking to use the sale proceeds for their own advancement.

I was interviewed in connection with the proceedings. From our conversations, it was clear that the interrogators were suggesting that my co-directors had compromised the law. "I don't know about that," I told the investigator, "and in any case, I am not involved. But I do not think they would do anything criminal. They were classmates and studied together in Singapore."

The investigator found that funny. I said maybe he had not heard all the stories yet. For me, the fact that they had all studied together in Singapore was significant — I did not believe they would ever jeopardise their standing amongst their peers through questionable behaviour.

The lower court found my co-directors guilty and was prepared to hand down a sentence. Their lawyers advised them to plead guilty to a minor offence. But Tat Pang, who was strong-minded, declared, "There is nothing criminal in what we have done in this company. I have not done it; so if you are going to accuse me, I will go all the way to the High Court to fight it." They were keen on proving their innocence and clearing their names.

For one reason or another, the charges brought against them kept changing, and it seemed that the prosecution had gone a little overboard with their accusations, assuming guilt before gathering enough evidence. This was the conclusion of Chief Justice Yong Pung How, who was known for being a strict judge. I recall him stating in court, "I see the prosecutor has gone on a fishing expedition. If the prosecution had only been interested in looking at company law infringement, I would have had sympathy and granted them the case. But because they have gone for something bigger, I do not see the evidence."[4]

He was not at all convinced that Tat Pang and Thomas had been involved in criminal activity. His point was that irresponsible handling of fiduciary duties could not be equated to criminality — otherwise, this could have had consequences for the business community in Singapore.[5]

The prosecutor who put forward these charges was agitated by the Chief Justice's remarks and sprung to his feet, committing a fatal error. "Sir," he hastily intervened, "we will amend the charges."

Yong Pung How was infuriated by mention of the amendment. "You have been investigating this case for two years, and now you are jumping at this chance to charge them with a minor offence? No, I will let them go free, no strings attached."

Everything became quiet after that. The two gentlemen resigned and I was left to pick up the pieces. As far as I know, nobody pursued the case and no further charges were brought.

Resettling the Board and Paying Old Debts

The Inno-Pacific trial attracted a great deal of attention, and my friends were understandably concerned about me. They showed their support when the time came to appoint new board members.

It was assumed that no outsider would agree to direct a company that had been involved in a criminal court case. Nevertheless, I proposed several names — people with impeccable credentials: Mr. Lim Jit Poh as chairman (a well-known civil servant who was close to the political leadership); Mr. Haider Sithawalla (an ex-civil servant who later became my business partner); and Mr. Low Siew Joon (a prominent lawyer). They all helped to shore up faith in the company.

Later, I also approached our shareholders because we wanted to raise capital to pay off Inno-Pacific's debts. There are two friends who guided me through this crucible. The first hero worth mentioning is

Mr. Tow Heng Tan, who represented the investment bank that the company appointed to assist with the exercise. When the bankers did not want to do business with us during the trial, Tow offered his services for free. He was entirely selfless. The second hero deserving of praise is Mr. Sat Pal Khattar — the founder and then senior partner of the law firm Khattar Wong and Partners. He remained by my side during the trial and reviewed with me in minute detail the implications of the case.

Our capital-raising exercise to pay the company's debts was successful, and we repaid our creditors every penny we owed. I was determined for Inno-Pacific to be known as a company that paid its debts — only then would I be able to leave with my head held high. After significant wrangling, the company was back on track; once the creditors were paid, I left.

The key figures in the trial are today no more. It is said you know who your true friends are in times of trouble. Yet again in my life, I can vouch for this.

With Sat Pal Khattar and Sivakant Tiwari, a former senior legal officer of the Singapore Legal Service and former president of The Hindi Society.

16

Breaking into India: A New Era for Entrepreneurs

"My interest in investing in India began as its economy was opening in the 1990s... But access for outsiders was limited... Then came Prime Minister Goh Chok Tong's visit to India in 1994, not long after Narasimha Rao was elected as Indian prime minister in 1991... PM Rao was a far-sighted man and felt Singapore should be a target destination for Indian business. I found it timely that I was looking at India and started to think about how I could get my foot in."

Goh Chok Tong's Visit to India

If you give up when things have not been resolved, people may take the lowest level of gossip to justify their opinion of events. But if you leave a situation with a clear conclusion — and can confidently delineate a matter as either black or white — then there is a better chance your case will receive a favourable review. I am the kind of person who does not ever lose his fighting spirit; and so after paying back the company's debts and reconstituting the Inno-Pacific board of directors, I began to give serious thought to the idea of starting my own company — being part owner of a business rather than merely an employee. As I recount in the book *Gateway Distriparks: The Story of a Successful Singapore–India Joint Venture,*

> "One of the subsidiaries of Inno-Pacific that had been divested... was a trading company called Windmill International Pte Ltd founded by Mr. David Ho, who had retained 30 percent equity in the company... I suggested to David to buy out the 70 percent owned by Inno-Pac, which

he eventually did. Very much later, when I decided to leave Inno Pac, David invited me to become a minority 10 percent shareholder and be Windmill's Chairman. I accepted David's kind invitation."[1]

My interest in investing in India began as its economy was opening in the 1990s, and I started to look at the Indian market in earnest. But access for outsiders was limited and aside for a few families who had business contacts, personal connections or property, few were willing to take the plunge. Investors from Singapore and other countries were cautious about entering the market, not knowing how to judge business opportunities there and whether they were safe for investment.

Then came Prime Minister Goh Chok Tong's visit to India in 1994, not long after Narasimha Rao was elected Indian prime minister in 1991. PM Goh Chok Tong's high-level visit with a business delegation to New Delhi as chief guest for India's Republic Day celebrations in January of that year was a watershed moment in the bilateral relations of India and Singapore; it changed economic calculations between the two countries considerably. PM Rao was a far-sighted man and felt that Singapore should be a target destination for Indian business.[2] I found it timely that I was looking at India and started to think about how I could get my foot in.

Before that visit, India's relationship with Singapore evolved largely in the context of the countries' political development. Lee Kuan Yew respected Nehru — even if he did not fully embrace his views, he gave them a hearing. Many Leftist leaders early on also visited India, a fellow socialist country, for advice on models of governance. I am not sure if the same relationship which had cut across the entire political spectrum still exists between Singaporean and Indian politicians today in the same way that it did after India's independence, when Singapore turned to India like a brother for advice.

India had been exploring trade-related prospects with Singapore but made little progress, which was why PM Goh Chok Tong's trip was significant. India's opening provided opportunities that Singapore had not seen before. Its liberalisation was perhaps more significant than anything else that was happening in the region, and I believe Singapore responded to the shift quite well.

19/6/2009

review. THE STRAITS TIMES FRIDAY, JUNE 19 2009 PAGE A22

SINGAPORE'S INVESTMENTS

Time is ripe for India fever

By Gopinath Pillai

IT SEEMS obvious from the extensive coverage in the local media that Singaporeans have been watching the Indian elections with more than a passing interest. The spectacle of some four hundred million people voting over one month at about 800,000 polling stations for more than eight thousand candidates and at the end of the month, having the votes counted within 24 hours, was indeed an impressive sight.

The fact that the voting was orderly and peaceful despite a few attempts by Maoists to disrupt the elections was also noteworthy. Furthermore, despite the participation of a large number of candidates with criminal records, the electorate, a third of whom are poor and illiterate, handed power to a man who is universally considered to be a decent human being. All this would have been noticed by meritocratic Singapore.

In the early 1990s, then Prime Minister Goh Chok Tong started a "mild India fever" in Singapore which was well received by Indians. It did not, however, take off because Narasimha Rao's government, which had initiated reforms, went into a tailspin and what followed would not have given comfort to any investor. Then came the Atal Bihari Vajpayee government.

Singapore shared in the sense of "India shining" and began negotiations on the Comprehensive Economic Cooperation Agreement (Ceca). However, Mr Vajpayee's government too lost its shine and was replaced by a left-supported coalition led by Congress. There was some danger of the Ceca languishing because of strong opposition from some sections of the Indian bureaucracy.

However, a strong push from prime minister Manmohan Singh and commerce minister Kamal Nath led to the agreement being signed in June 2005, when Prime Minister Lee Hsien Loong visited New Delhi.

There was some flutter of activity after this but no real breakthrough for Singaporean investors in India. However, in Singapore itself, there was a noticeable increase in Indian activity. The number of Indian expatriates working in Singapore, especially in finance and IT, increased dramatically, so much so that more Hindi was being heard along Robinson Road than Mandarin. Some 3,000 Indian companies were registered in Singapore.

But the Singaporean presence in India lagged far behind the Indian presence in Singapore. Apart from Temasek Holdings and perhaps Ascendas, very few among the larger Singaporean companies were prepared to get their feet wet in India. Why was this so?

If I were to give a one-line answer, I would say it is because Singaporeans do not understand India. Despite a common British heritage, Singaporeans do not understand how India works. The result is that the problems they face in the country are magnified and look insoluble. And there are problems.

First there is the visual impact. The squalor that hits you as you drive from the airport to the hotel creates a powerful first negative impression.

The meeting with the Indian counterpart comes next. It starts with a high degree of mistrust. Can this guy deliver all that he promises? Does his obvious entrepreneurial flair vary inversely with his integrity? Only time can tell.

Congress supporters celebrating in New Delhi after last month's polls. Singapore's presence in India has lagged far behind the Indian presence in Singapore. It may be time for Singapore to step up its investments in the country when the economic mood is positive. PHOTO: ASSOCIATED PRESS

Then there is the labour situation. Work stoppages are common. Why don't they have an NTUC, wonders the Singaporean.

The final blow comes when you have to deal with the myriad rules governing investments. Is all this worthwhile, you ask yourself. The answer usually is that it is not.

Problems can be managed and solved but it is more difficult to change deeply ingrained perceptions. In my view, none of the problems one is likely to face in India are serious enough to decide not to invest there. The return of Congress to power with a stronger mandate is being touted by Indian commentators as a "game changer". It is possible that there will be some positive changes. But they will not be dramatic.

Do we wait for these changes to be in place before moving in? Rather than wait for changes that may or may not occur, it would be better to move in when the economic mood is positive.

Let me give three reasons why I think Singapore investors should look seriously at India. First there is the "profit" motive. Most businessmen who have invested in India will tell you that India gives you a better return than many other countries. It has a large, fairly wealthy middle class which provides a good market.

The second reason is strategic. Singaporeans should look beyond their comfort zones so as to diversify their investment locations. India is among the few countries that show positive growth despite the global economic melt-down. This in itself should be a good reason to consider India.

The third reason is the human resource that India offers. If you are looking at entering the Middle East, Africa or Central Asia, the best source of personnel to run these offices is India. An operation in India gives you entry into the Indian labour market.

I see two possible dangers facing India that can change the present positive mood. First, terrorists in the neighbourhood may be looking for an opportunity to create havoc in the country to counter the electoral success of the ruling coalition. The second danger, less serious, are attempts by parties defeated in the elections trying to disrupt the working of the government. The only comfort I can suggest is the fact that Indians are adept at handling crises and foreign investors should learn to take these in their stride.

Senior Minister Goh has said that he would like to see an iconic Singapore project in India. Some discussions were held to establish a free trade zone in India but the idea did not progress because land acquisition is a problem in the politically charged atmosphere of India.

I would like to float another idea: Dr Singh has expressed a wish for Mumbai to become another Shanghai. Perhaps the governments of India and Singapore, together with their private sectors, can work towards making this dream a reality. If it materialises, it will bring about a paradigm shift in investors' perceptions of India. We will not stop at a mild fever.

The writer is the chairman of Institute of South Asian Studies, National University of Singapore. He is also chairman of a port-related logistics company listed in India. The views expressed here are his own.

I reflect on this juncture in the 1990s in "Time is ripe for India Fever", *The Straits Times*, June 19th, 2009.

Once when I was in India, I happened to cross paths with Mr. Goh Chok Tong who was on one of his trips to Delhi. He was keen to tour several states in India, and had one extra day on his itinerary. He shared with me his plans to visit the Golden Temple in Amritsar, and asked if there was anywhere else that I thought he should visit. I suggested that he explore Ahmedabad in Gujarat. The chief minister of Gujarat at that time was India's current prime minister, Narendra Modi.*

To my delight, PM Goh Chok Tong took my advice and boarded a flight to Gujarat. He managed a full-day trip and returned to Delhi

* The first speaker we invited for the inaugural forum organised by ISAS around 2005, in fact, was Chief Minister Modi. Many were unhappy about the invitation, and I was challenged for my choice. These critics referenced the Gujarat riots, in which many Muslims had been tragically killed after a train carrying Hindus was burned. The critics' concerns were genuine, but I replied that Gujarat was one of India's most attractive business sites. Their sale of land for industrial purposes and utility management is so prompt and professional that I thought we should offer encouragement. I explained, "This man is transforming a major state in India and we wanted him to share his experiences and thought processes with us."

that same evening. He was impressed with what he saw there. This impromptu trip helped him cement a strong and lasting relationship with Mr. Modi. Modi refers to Goh Chok Tong as the "tall man of Singapore". It might not be wrong to say this helped lay the foundation for a healthy relationship between our countries as well as a friendship that continues to this day.

Obstacles to Doing Business in India

Thanks to PM Goh Chok Tong's visit in 1994, a new link was forged, and a number of trade missions started travelling both ways. Such missions, as I knew from my days of establishing IT subsidiaries through Intraco in the 1980s, were useful for understanding the Indian market and deepening our connections. The Indians knew relatively little about Singapore and, even earlier, they had started to make an effort to build relationships with Singapore companies and businessmen.

Indeed, before Goh Chok Tong's visit and India's implementation of market reforms, several factors played a part in making it difficult to do business in India. Certain Indian businessmen before liberalisation suffered from a "protectionist mindset"; they clung to the safeguards that the government afforded them, which they had vested interests to preserve. The trade delegations travelling from India to Singapore also gave relatively limited exposure to foreign products, which stymied trade. Business leaders feared that if international companies entered the Indian market, these companies would dominate the field and force smaller local traders out of business.

The second problem outsiders encountered pertained to funding. If the foreign party did not have sufficient funding or local connections, it was difficult to make headway. If one compared "ease of doing business" in India with China, China performed more favourably. The Chinese were keen to finance, so long as one purchased their products. In India, funding depended on factors like whether one's local partner could get a good deal from the banks.[3]

On the Singapore side, there were other issues. To an investor, India was like a black box and he was uncertain about the rules. For example, there had been no requirement in the past for an Indian company to consolidate financial statements; and, as a result, inconvenient loans and poor performances could be easily tucked away in subsidiary companies. The Singaporean investor also often entered with overly optimistic expectations. After finding his reception only lukewarm, he might then encounter problems in obtaining reliable information. For instance, there was no agency (at least to my knowledge) back then that provided information to foreign investors on which states were open for investment.

If special rules and facilities are not available to oil the runway, business can become daunting. Fortunately, the government has since rectified some of these practises. Persisting issues, such as scarcity of land for industrial projects, are also being addressed.[†]

The People Who Helped Me

During the early trade missions that I went on to India in the 1980s, I developed a reliable network of business contacts who helped me establish robust Indian and Singaporean collaborations, which in turn improved my fledgling understanding of the market. While I was at Intraco, one reliable colleague I had, for example, was Mr. Tarun Das, then the secretary general of the Association of Indian Engineering Industry. He shepherded my team in our early years. Another was Mr. Syamal Gupta, the head of Tata Precision Industry, with whom I became almost instant friends. Tata had deep connections and they came forward with valuable advice whenever we needed direction.

My approach to the cultivation of contacts in India was two-fold: I looked at what people were interested in and the kind of businesses they were doing as well as public figures eager to see Singapore and India build a rapport. I built my first network through Syamal. It is no exaggeration to say Syamal (an Indian based in Singapore and one of

---

[†] Gujarat's policies, as a positive example, were well calibrated: nobody cut into others' paths. If an investor wanted land and was serious about starting an industry, the State Government helped him. I understand other State Governments are also now taking the initiative to attract investments.

Tata's first employees to be deputed here) was a pioneer in Singapore–India business relations. He helped to lay the groundwork for my understanding of the Indian market and introduced many of his friends and business counterparts to me, which culminated in a joint venture between Tata Consultancy Services (TCS) and Intraco in Information Technology processing.

Not many expected India would grow so fast in the field of IT. But my experience was that India had an intelligent population that took to the latest innovations. I also got good support from my friend and the former managing director of Intraco, S. Chandra Das, who encouraged my plans. As I briefly touched on earlier, some at Intraco maintained that we were strictly a trading company and should confine ourselves to commodity-based trading. But Chandra's stance was that if you had a good idea, he would back it. The hard commodity-based trading that Intraco practiced was, I privately felt, in the long-term unsustainable and needed to evolve into other areas of business. I gravitated towards training in knowledge products and software development.[‡]

Companies like TCS took full advantage of India's demographic dividend, and knowledge trading in subsequent decades has thrived. Till today, Indians largely from the southern Indian states continue to migrate to Silicon Valley. The migration from such states as Andhra Pradesh and Tamil Nadu to the U.S. is even more remarkable, when one recalls that there probably were not even any special government schemes to recruit IT talent back then: it was almost entirely spontaneous. The Americans are very good at recognising an individual's worth — they saw that if an Indian was mathematically and technologically inclined, then he should be given a chance to pursue his talent. Both India and the U.S., I believe, benefited from the exchange of knowledge and peoples.

[‡] This proved to be partially true, in that the middleman role we had built up changed considerably after the Cold War. The hard commodities trading we did at Intraco depended heavily on a specialised knowledge of the global scenario which was disrupted by the Internet and, as Yahya argues in *INTRACO: Blazing a Trail Oversees for Singapore?*, the liberalisation of markets in former socialist countries. Now, you can check your phone for the latest price sold in New York or Beijing: the manufacturer can simply supply the buyer directly. The old role of the middleman from that period is lost, although middlemen have emerged in our new interconnected environment in novel forms.

Another reason I left Intraco was that I had been accused of being a bit too gung-ho, I think, in venturing into areas that were not Intraco's traditional domain. My understanding, however, was that I had not been hired for traditional business but rather to take charge of investments and manufacturing. Experimentation is at the heart of trading and entrepreneurship — one may get brick bats one day and kudos the next. Fortunately, in India we met with early success.

Well Wishers for Singapore

Syamal helpfully arranged for me to meet the chief executive officer of TCS, Mr. Faqir Chand Kohli. Mr. Kohli was a serious man; his habit was to stare directly at you, and he could become upset if you stumbled over your words. I also met the chairman, Mr. Nani Palkhivala, a renowned lawyer who took on then Prime Minister Indira Gandhi in court in defence of the constitution and civil liberties after she declared the Emergency (1975–1977).

The Indira Gandhi government, in 1973, had introduced amendments that "granted unlimited power to Parliament to alter the constitution" of India.[4] Thanks to Mr. Palkhivala's landmark Fundamental Rights case (otherwise known as Kesavananda Bharati v. State of Kerala), the Supreme Court upheld that "basic features and the basic structure of the constitution could not be changed".[5] In 1975, after announcing the Emergency, Ms. Gandhi's government attempted to reverse the decision and suspend fundamental rights, which Mr. Palkhivala and his fellow lawyers opposed. Their robust legal challenge reflected the growing and extensive resistance to Ms. Gandhi and her Emergency rule, which culminated in her defeat in the 1977 national parliamentary elections.

I felt honoured that Mr. Palkhivala was prepared to spend ten to fifteen minutes with me. After our meeting, Mr. Kohli agreed to come to Singapore to meet my colleagues. They were also flattered that TCS wanted to work with us in Singapore.

~

At the dinner that our team hosted for TCS, Mr. Palkhivala related a humorous episode about a trial during the Emergency. Indira Gandhi had appointed a few of her friends as Supreme Court judges, and the customary lawyers were not too pleased with the development. A defence lawyer made his displeasure known during one hearing by quoting a precedent from a book, which the newly nominated judge requested to see. The lawyer focused his irritation towards the judge by thumping the book down loudly on the table. When the judge opened the book to read the precedent, he caught sight of a small insect inside — a weevil, ferried from the library.

Having now the opportunity to display his own annoyance, the judge drawled for the courtroom to hear, "Well, you can give me the book, but don't give me the insect."

The lawyer was waiting for just such a gibe. He stood up abruptly and apologised. "Your honour, I'm very sorry. It just seems that of late, many an insect has jumped from the bar to the bench!" The whole courtroom held their stomachs, on the verge of rocking with laughter, but dared not to.

Mr. Palkhivala later became ill. By then, we had become good friends. When he learned I was coming to Bombay, he informed Syamal that he wanted to see me. Syamal passed on the message to visit him at the hospital once I arrived. I went straight to his ward, where he was sitting up in bed. Despite his illness, he was his usual lively self — full of jokes. We talked a little, and then he paid Singapore a sincere compliment I will never forget.

"Gopinath, you are a very lucky man. You were born in a country where people respect the law, follow the rules and where the rules are chosen carefully for the benefit of the citizens. I would like to see a big country like India learn from a small country like Singapore, because there is much that you can teach us."

Pausing to catch his breath, he continued, "This is something you should mention to your senior leaders: please don't abandon India, just because there are some things that may not be quite right. I see your team has got Singaporean Indians and Singaporean Chinese. Yours is a multi-racial society. This is what we also want."

I was very moved by this. Not very long afterwards, he passed away.

I would like to say one last thing about Mr. Palkhivala. Every year in his private capacity, when the government announced its annual budget, he held a public discussion on the budget. It was a very well attended event held in a sports stadium; hundreds of people would gather to listen to him. He assiduously parsed through the budget's details for the crowd, answering questions and rebutting arguments.

It was a remarkable feat, I felt — surely one of the strengths of Indian democracy! — that he could hold such an important conversation in full view, without ever having to worry about the government intervening.

So this was my introduction to India, how I penetrated the market and some of the friends who helped me.

17

Observations and Lessons from Entrepreneurship

"I used to joke, 'India is on this planet but not of this world!' due to its highly unique ways of doing things. But from the exposure to global society, outsiders entering to invest and Indians returning to India from abroad, India has shown the potential to become an important trading partner and 'gateway' to new opportunities."

IT Processing Company for Utilities

Now for more about my own business ventures in India. In the field of IT, I have two examples, one good and one bad.

The company I am perhaps identified with most closely today is Gateway Distriparks Ltd. (GDL). GDL handles the transportation, storage and distribution of import/export goods and provides a nationwide network of cold storage, which it services through a fleet of refrigerated trucks. Before my partners Sat Pal Khattar, Haider Sithawalla and I went into GDL, however, there was a small IT processing company called Infotech that was not making very much money. If I recall correctly, the bank was unhappy with the shareholders, so Infotech approached my partners and me to indicate its interest in partnering with us. It was owned by a British company that was based in London but carried out its software work in India.

We studied the prospect and decided it was a risk worth taking. The chairman of Infotech was Rohit Chand and its managing director was Saurabh Srivastava. Mohit Goyal was another partner. An executive committee was formed, of which I became the chairman. We met once a month to review the operations.

Our first entry into India, due to the reasons outlined in the previous chapter, was very cautious and calibrated. We found that the old formula the company had adopted — in which London acted as the centre while India became the source for IT development — was not all that efficient. We decided to reverse the order by designating India as the centre and London as the marketing office. The company also had marketing offices in other parts of Europe which we closed down.

Very soon, the company became profitable. We were more elated still when, two to three years later, another British firm made an offer to buy us out. "Why don't you sell it to us?" they proposed. "We will expand it and make it thrive." We were thrilled! Our initial investment was minimal; but within a short time, the business had shot up in value. We made good money and were able to exit.

Now for the bad example. Having cut our teeth on Infotech, some of my partners and I decided to go bigger with a company to teach and conduct IT training. We signed a memorandum of understanding (MoU) with a successful Singapore-based company that provided training in software development and had a good record in Malaysia and China. They were all over Southeast Asia. We went into India with the model of franchising because this private education company had already established a franchise in India. We bought out their Indian partner to become the majority shareholders.

We quickly established two hundred and fifty training centres in India and felt that we had done very well. Unfortunately, we ran into a few snags. The franchise model, we soon discovered, was not a suitable approach to education. In 'Chapter 15', I had related what it was like running the Shakey's pizza franchise. If a Shakey's branch closed down, it was not a grave concern, because tomorrow one could open another outlet somewhere else. Such manoeuvres are frowned upon in education since one has a moral obligation to students to uphold. If the franchisee closes down, we as the franchisor are held responsible when the students complain and beg us to complete their course to obtain their diploma.

We had many problems with IT training and lost a lot of money. Our main difficulty was that the stock of the parent company (which was based in Singapore and had set up the franchise) collapsed: they had a change in ownership and struggled to carry on. We had to wind up the Indian operation and write off our investment — everything we gained in the first venture we lost in the second. This forced us to apply our minds to something else.

Container Freight Stations

My next major experiment with my partners Sat Pal Khattar and Haider Sithawalla was in logistics. Mr. David Ho, the founder and managing director of Windmill, also joined our team: "David as a trader," I write in the book on GDL, "was very familiar with India, and the sort of issues that troubled the average Singaporeans were to him matters that could be managed."[1] We also expanded our Indian partners. The start of Gateway Distriparks was in some ways serendipitous. I was in Mumbai assessing the prospect of entering the paper storage business when I was convinced to set up a project in a field a little unknown to Singapore and unfamiliar to me at that time: container freight stations.

I had a friend in the paper business, Mr. Prem Kishan Gupta. Prem was the first to introduce me to the term "container freight station" or "CFS". Prem was the Indian agent of Intercontinental Forest Products (IFP), a Singapore trading company dealing with paper. I was its chairman.[2] He was also the owner of Newsprint Trading and Service Corporation (NTSC) in New Delhi. The newspaper industry had boomed in the 1980s, and its voluminous imports of newsprint for the printing and publishing industry alerted Prem around 1993 to the need for efficiency and protection against damaged goods in the logistics sector.[3]

A CFS, basically, is a warehousing and distribution centre for both import and export containers, which protects products while easing the costs of transport. When a ship brings a container to the port, it is evacuated to a freight station, from whence it is forwarded on to the final buyer. Being a large importer of paper into India, Prem explained that there was a dearth of good container freight stations in Mumbai.[4] He suggested that I assess the CFS situation in the port city and arranged for me to meet the then minister of industry in the

Maharashtra government, Jawahar Darda, who he said could suitably advise me.

Minister Darda invited me to breakfast at his house and, as Prem had said, suggested that we invest in the CFS business. The Minister elaborated that when shipping vessels come into the Mumbai port to dock they cannot drop their anchors for long as they do in Singapore. They have to drop off their cargo at a freight station. Mumbai port would soon be expanding, he explained, alongside many other ports that were coming up in the region. He wanted India to be ready with a system of freight stations to accept the surge in cargo likely to arise from surfeit trade. Although the Mumbai port was not as swift in clearing ships as Singapore, Shanghai and Hong Kong, he was determined to pick up the pace.

Meeting with an Indian government minister, Sharad Pawar, in Bombay.

Mumbai only had one modern warehouse owned by the multinational company Maersk, which had a freight transportation company. I recall it mostly catered to its own shipping line. With the Mumbai port expanding, Minister Darda recommended that we consider setting up an independent CFS to attend to the needs of other incoming vessels. "We are going to have many ports but do not have enough freight stations to handle the cargo. If you can invest in one or two, it will be useful and you will benefit."

He advised us to apply to the City and Industrial Development Corporation (CIDCO) to lease around thirty-six acres of land for the construction. The idea and pledge of his support ignited a spark in me, and Prem and I studied the proposition in detail. We requested the support of Container Warehousing and Transport (CWT), a subsidiary of the Port of Singapore Authority and an established player with a firm understanding of the handling of containers in Singapore. I had known

CWT from my days at Intraco. They conducted a viability study.[5]

Indeed, the study came out confirming that the CFS business was a good idea. My friend Chandra also participated in the project as a minority shareholder. During the breakthrough visit of then Prime Minister Goh Chok Tong to Mumbai in January 1994, CWT, with its Indian partner NTSC, signed an MoU with us at the Gateway Room of the Taj Mahal hotel. We chose to call the company "Gateway Distriparks", firstly, because we had gathered in the Gateway Room of the Taj Mahal hotel opposite the Gateway of India (we pictured the company as being a gateway for Singaporean investments). Secondly, CWT had suggested we widen the scope of the project to include distribution parks.[6]

Within nine months, the MoU picked up speed and progressed into a Joint Venture Agreement with CWT, which was signed during Indian Prime Minister Rao's visit to Singapore in September 1994. We made an application to CIDCO, as Minister Darda had suggested, anticipating that the lease agreement would be signed in two to three months. Prem knew the area, and while we were purchasing helped us to get a good deal from the ground up.

But nothing is ever done quickly in India — you make a decision and the implementation takes time. The application took two years to be approved. The proposed parcel of land, as I recall one of my colleagues describing, was marshy and barren; apparently, I had remarked to another colleague that "in [the] early part of Singapore's history, sea pirates used to come ashore through such creeks" and that "we did not want that part of history to be repeated."[7] We rejected the piece and acquired another from CIDCO on higher ground.

CWT gradually lost interest because of the delay; they pulled out from the project and decided to relocate to Chennai. I tried to convince CWT that this was a mistake: although Chennai was India's second largest port, Mumbai had a larger deep-water port and therefore a greater number of loaded ships.

I was not able to persuade CWT; still, I persisted with my other business partners, and we organised for our major shareholderse to proceed. I thought, "Well, if CWT goes, this does not mean I have to change

Windmill evolves from a one-man show to mega-trader

Company now aims for S$500m turnover in 5 years plus expansion into new regions and markets

spotlight on SINGAPORE'S BEST

"Windmill evolves from a one-man show to mega-trader", *The Straits Times*, August 12th, 1996.

our plans." The next issue that arose was how to fill the equity gap after CWT's exit and that of our other minority shareholder, which was nearly 40 percent. Together with a replacement partner in Singapore, David Ho's company, Windmill, we took up 50 percent of the share while the other half of CWT's share was taken by Thakral. (Thakral was already a shareholder through its holdings in Parameswara Ltd, an investment company promoted by the Singapore Indian Chamber of Commerce.* Thereafter, a board representative of the new shareholders was formed, constituting PRISM (Prem's company), Thakral, Parameswara and Windmill.[8]

But the withdrawal of CWT caused another problem, as we now found ourselves bereft of operational experience. We brought in Brig. Gen. Kirpa Ram Vij as part of the new management after the restructuring of the board; he had headed Neptune Orient Line Logistics (NOL) and had "14 years of service with NOL… work[ing] mainly in the container marketing and container logistics areas."[9] To play it safe, we further arranged for a parallel technical team in Singapore to provide input on the plans at the construction stage while our team visited the sites and spoke with relevant businessmen on the ground."[10]

Infrastructure Development Finance Company Ltd. (IDFC) funded our second and third phase of expansion, first by debt and later through equity injection to enhance the project's viability. In return, they got

---

* I had approached Parameswara after IFP's parent company, Inno-Pacific, encountered problems when the majority Malaysian shareholders transferred control of Inno-Pacific and its subsidiaries to new shareholders. Parameswara acquired Inno-Pacific's 20 percent in the company.

20 percent of GDL and a seat on the GDL Board. The speed at which they disbursed the funds was particularly invaluable; we signed the agreement at about 11am and the funds were credited to our account by the late afternoon.

I was lunching with an IDFC executive, Mr. A. K. T. Chari, to thank him for his timely support. He confided the reasons for disbursing the funds without delay. First was that "[w]e had a good project in a fast growing space and provided a service badly needed." Second was "a solid Board which was both conservative and aggressive." Third (though not as consequential as the other two factors) was "his trust in me personally."[11] I felt humbled and buoyed by his words, which I cherish to this day.

~

Our next major decision was to go for an IPO, which our advisors thought premature. They advised us to wait, as the profits from our two facilities needed time to grow. We feared, however, that waiting too long would be a mistake, and that by the time a few years had passed others might snatch this competitive position we had carved for ourselves in the market.

We decided to proceed with the IPO anyway, and, fortunately, delivered results. We brought in an institutional shareholder of international standing, Temasek Holdings of Singapore, which we convinced to take 10 percent in the company to enhance investor confidence. The IPO in 2004 was hugely successful and we were oversubscribed by almost thirty times.[12]

We then heard rumours that the Indian Railways were going to open up the movement of containers by rail to the private sector. We bid for a national licence. The rail business is costly and required us to raise additional funds of US$85 million. To raise capital, we issued Global Deposit Receipts and partnered with Blackstone GPV Capital Partners, a private equity company in the U.S., which invested 300 crore. A subsidiary was then established called Gateway Rail Freight Ltd. under Prem's chairmanship.[13]

Bombay park a success for Singapore

The consortium now wants to be national player in India and hopes to list the project to fund expansion plans

'We expect to have revenues of 50 million

"Bombay park a success for Singapore", *The Straits Times*, April 10th, 2000 (in photo, with the first CEO of Gateway Distriparks and [retd.] first Chief of Singapore Armed Forces, Kirpa Ram Vij).

We started our rail activity in Haryana but later expanded into North India and elsewhere. As of 2015, we operated rail-linked inland container depots in Haryana, Punjab and Mumbai and owned a fleet of twenty-one trains. We had six container freight stations — two in Navi Mumbai, two at Chennai, one at Visakhapatnam and one at Kochi.[14] The speed at which the company grew thrust GDL to a whole new level.

Snowman Logistics

The launch of another fast-growing GDL subsidiary, Snowman Logistics, was also the fruit of good timing. A cold store company, Snowman Frozen Foods, owned by Mitsubishi and Amalgam Foods, had been struggling;[15] the two owners were thinking about selling. The wastage of food in India is enormous, and we saw a gap in the market we could fill. Although cold stores and temperature controlled transportation differ from your regular brick-and-mortar warehouses and the movement of containers, the basic principle for storage and transportation management remained similar. I viewed venturing into cold stores as a natural extension of our logistics platform.

In 1983, some time before this, I had separately become the chairman of NTUC Fairprice. The Australian company Davids Holdings Ltd. approached me in the 1990s with the proposition to offer their temperature-controlled warehouses for our retail business; their expertise was in building supermarket cold stores. Davids became our partner for NTUC Fairprice in Singapore. A lesser-known story was that the advice of the company's then Managing Director John David also subtly influenced Gateway Distriparks' expansion into cold storage in India.

In 2006, I approached Mitsubishi, saying that we would be willing to acquire majority interest from them on favourable terms — they would remain the minority shareholders while we built up the business. As of 2011–2012, our investors in Snowman Logistics included Mitsubishi Corporation, Nichirei Corporation and International Finance Corporation. The market was keen to support the growth of cold stores which were in demand. We dared to take a risk with a public listing, to see how Snowman would fare. (To ensure a successful listing, the product had to be good, whose shelf life is measured not just in months but also years.)

Receiving the Padma Shree in 2012 from the 12th President of India, Pratibha Patil. (The Padma Shree, the Fourth Highest Civilian Award of the Republic of India, was awarded to Sat Pal Khattar in 2011, and The Padma Vibhushan, the Second Highest Civilian Award, was awarded to George Yeo in 2012.)

Like with the Mumbai land application, the usual processing time was taken; but then, all at once, they said you are passed. The public offer was tremendously oversubscribed by almost sixty times: we were shocked! When we launched the IPO in 2014, it just so happened that Modi had also become prime minister. The post-election market was upbeat and we became its indirect beneficiaries. As of 2014–2015, Snowman held twenty-eight temperature controlled warehouses spread out over fifteen locations in India, in addition to a nation-wide network that connected over four hundred cities, from Kochi in Kerala to Guwahati in Assam as well as Calcutta in West Bengal and the capital city of New Delhi.[16] (Amid the recent COVID-19 pandemic, cold stores are in increasing demand for vaccines.)

I am not a significant shareholder in Gateway Distriparks or Snowman Logistics any longer: I exited from both companies in April 2015. The chairmanship of Gateway Distriparks was taken on by Prem, my former partner and the company's then managing director, with whom my friends and I had started the company.

Lessons from Doing Business in India

I have always been very positively inclined towards India, its politics and culture. I have often wondered why Singapore has not done better in India than in China.

Singapore is spoilt for choice as to which country to do business with. Some linguistic and cultural similarities between Singapore and China make it easier to do business there. Our neighbours Indonesia, Malaysia and Thailand also offer opportunities. Singaporeans continue to have certain reservations about doing business in India. This is not only because of unfamiliarity with the terrain (the contours of which I addressed earlier) but also the trust factor. Trust is very important, and sometimes both sides are concerned about whether promises will be kept.

The second issue that often becomes a sticking point for Singaporeans is cleanliness — or the occasional lack of it. A third reason Singapore struggles in India, from my perspective as a practitioner (although in-depth studies might nuance these observations), is that the Singapore investor's appetite for risk has diminished. Generally, I feel Singapore investors have become risk-averse. I believe investors are worried that if they take a chance, all that they have accumulated will be lost. They must therefore be sure of the outcome before they proceed.

Exposure to international markets has made it necessary for governments to make rules more acceptable to foreign companies. Maybe because of successes internationally, some Singaporean investors equate success with the benefits of openness and transparency, and are looking for safe investments. Younger people, too, are now growing up in a more affluent environment — it is difficult to tell whether they prefer adventure or safety. Although conditions for Singapore–India economic cooperation have improved since the 1990s, some additional special effort, I think, should be devoted to advance conditions for trade on both sides — from India, to make it easier to do business, and from Singapore, to develop a greater willingness to take risks.[17]

One aspect benefiting anyone who wants to do business in India is that when you run into snags, there are multiple avenues for resolving issues. In China, crossing swords with the wrong person can spell the end of the project. In India, the pressure points are many: you can go to newspapers, politicians, civil servants — the sky's the limit! Undoubtedly, for talent and labour, India remains an attractive site. (I have already mentioned India's potential and acumen in the field of IT.) And if you look not just at India but throughout the South Asian region, labour remains relatively cheap.

From the vantage point of an observer, one approach India could take, to capitalise on Singapore's trade networks, would be to develop a relationship with Singapore's trade organisations and brainstorm ways to cooperate to break into third countries where both have limited access. Just as we have Singapore government-sponsored trade organisations, India too has several well-funded groups in the private sector. The two could look at developing a three-cornered partnership to reinforce one another. India is fairly strong in Africa whereas Singapore is not. Similarly, India could work with Singapore, Malaysia and others to maximise prospects in China. By using Singaporean business contacts, Indian businesses could unlock unexplored potentials.

The strong ties between Singapore and India, which hail back to British colonialism, have been strengthened through economic engagement. As geopolitical challenges intensify, Singapore will need to expand its trade relations not only with China but also with other South Asian countries. Given that close to 9 percent of Singapore's population is of Indian origin and that Little India is one of Singapore's popular local tourist and recreational destinations, I think more effort could be dedicated to understanding the Indian mindset.

I used to joke, "India is on this planet but not of this world!" due to its highly unique ways of doing things. But from the exposure to global society, outsiders entering to invest and Indians returning to India from abroad, India has shown the potential to become an important trading partner and "gateway" to new opportunities.

Official visit of HE Dr. Manmohan Singh, Prime Minister of the Republic of India and Mdm Gursharan Kaur, November 19–20, 2011. Official lunch at the Istana, November 20th, 2011.

Part III

Public Service and Extracurricular Activities

NTUC Meritorious Award 1990.
(From left) Ong Teng Cheong, Goh Chok Tong, me, Haider Sithawalla and Lim Jit Poh.

18

Non-Resident Ambassador to Iran (1989–2008)

"So I answered Minister Wong, 'You may be right that Iran might not be one of the easiest places to work in. But there are several reasons why I have chosen this country. Firstly, Iran has an ancient civilisation, of which I have some knowledge; secondly, their poetry is beautiful; and thirdly, Persian civilisation has a few cultural affinities with India. I know I don't speak the language, or have any qualifications to do this, but if you grant my request, I would be happy.'"

A Second Astrological Reading

While I pursued an active business career at companies like Raya Mills and UIC, I remained keenly interested in Singapore's politics and world affairs. During my time as an employee at Intraco, friends had even offhandedly suggested that I should enter politics. (Intraco, then, was a company close to the government, to which many senior civil servants had been seconded; due to a dearth in reliable entrepreneurial talent, civil servants had been recruited to staff Intraco.[1] Many mistakenly believed I too was a civil servant.) My parents were excited at the prospect that I might enter politics.

As a schoolboy, I vividly recall visiting the newly renovated assembly just before the Labour Front had come into power. I thought, as a childish sort of imagining, "One day, I will sit in this house!" I had done well as a debater at the Choon Guan Civics Club, and conjured up in my mind all the great British parliamentarians such as Edmund Burke, Benjamin Disraeli and Winston Churchill who commanded attention in the House of Commons. I envisioned how I too would one day hold the house spellbound with my oratory.

Over the course of my youth and professional development, however, my attraction and understanding of politics had undergone a gradual change. After returning to Singapore from Malaysia, I began to see how a strong, racially conscious but even-headed party was the only answer to politics in a multi-racial nation. (I believed the ruling party had to be strong, otherwise it might succumb to populism; and racially sensitive, in seeking to discern the country's community dynamics and how best to promote harmony amongst the various minority groups.) Finally, I believed that the party had to be balanced and fair in providing opportunities for advancement. The idea of meritocracy appealed to me greatly.

To divine the suitability of whether I should enter politics, two astrologers were again consulted at my home. For those unfamiliar with the astrological science, such readings can be mathematical affairs. To ensure absolute accuracy, the astrologers will request the time of one's birth and, according to a special almanac they have brought with them, check the stars' alignment and what that alignment indicates. (Due to the time difference between India and Singapore, they had to work two-and-a-half hours backwards.) The astrologers will then verify the details of several of your past experiences to confirm that these coincide with their readings. If your answers radically differ, they will redo their calculations.

The answer they pronounced after all this effort, however, was totally opposite to what my father had hoped for. Like my drama teacher Seow Cheng Fong had indicated when he cast me as the character Brutus in the play *Julius Caesar*, the first astrologer explained, "You will not do well in politics, because you are too honest. If you decide to pursue this path, you will get into deep trouble."

The second astrologer concurred. He, however, added, "Although politics is not for you, if you stay on the periphery and continue to be helpful, you will get many senior positions, and will be accepted by the government as a friend. You will go far. You will not be a politician but rather a respected person in society that people will listen to."

The astrologers who had "read" my future before my move to Bangkok Bank in Thailand also surprised me with their prescience regarding the launch of Operation Coldstore. Although I do not consider myself a superstitious person, I was not inclined to dismiss such insights either. For politics, I knew from the sacrifices of my uncle that I needed an objective I wanted to achieve — better not to launch out as a rudderless activist, parroting philosophies one was not keen to subscribe to. In my own way, however, as the astrologers foretold, I believe I have become useful to the community in Singapore.

A New Kind of Ambassador

In the 1980s, my friend S. Chandra Das had inquired if I was interested in becoming a resource person for the newly established Parliamentary Committee for Defence and Foreign Affairs. Chandra was recently appointed the committee's chairman, due to his international experience, having served in Russia and managed Intraco. After the proposal was made to me, I was drawn into foreign policy discussions on various countries in the parliamentary committee together with other recognised public figures serving as resource persons outside of parliament, such as Dr. Charles Toh, one of Singapore's early pioneers in the field of modern cardiology.

Later, Chandra shared that the government was thinking of gathering a small group of businessmen from the private sector to serve as 'Non-Resident Ambassadors' (NRAs). It was believed that their practical marketplace experience would serve them well in opening the economies of foreign countries and, as I remember one person putting it, "making an imprint in foreign lands".

Chandra framed the situation this way: "We are a small island, dependent on the rest of the world for our survival and growth. The question we have to ask ourselves is how to reach out to the world with the population that we have now." He listed Singapore's difficulties. "It is not feasible to have a foreign service that caters to the needs of every country with which we might have diplomatic relations. While it might be possible to appoint ambassadors for the bigger countries, developing relations with all the smaller ones likely to trade with us will be difficult."

For this reason, the government had developed plans to cover the shortfall by appointing NRAs who would administer their foreign posts while also continuing to reside in Singapore. That is to say, these non-resident diplomats would continue carrying on with their regular jobs, but when they traveled to their post country they would be called "ambassador" and paid their requisite expenses. Similar positions had been opened for civil servants, but this was the first time the expertise of others from outside the government would be tapped.

Chandra pitched it to me. "Would you be interested if they offered you the post?" I am always ready to embrace new roles and try new things. I said I did not mind. In actuality, I was pleased with the suggestion of becoming a diplomat. They decided to test out three "prototype" NRAs: Mr. Herman Hochstadt, Mr. Foo Kok Swee and me.

The Pitch for Iran

Singapore's foreign minister in 1989 was Wong Kan Seng, who later in the 2000s became the country's deputy prime minister. Amongst the areas for which he is most well known, he coordinated the nation-wide effort against the SARS epidemic,[2] presaging the nation-wide battle against COVID-19 that we have waged for more than two years now. He interviewed each of us in turn to assign us our respective foreign posts.

It was decided that Herman Hochstadt would look after South Africa. Herman, a top civil servant as well as a prominent figure in the Eurasian community, had been the chairman of Neptune Orient Lines.[3] Incidentally, he is another friend of mine from university. He was a philosophy major, given in his youth to being cynical about everything around him. He frequently gave his friends the impression that he was playful, but in reality he was a serious person with a deep understanding of the workings of the human mind. During the 1980s, we served together on the board of the Export-Credit and Insurance Corporation of Singapore (ECICS), where he was the chairman. He became permanent secretary of several ministries, and now, though retired, we are still in close contact.

Herman Hochstadt on my left.

Mr. Foo Kok Swee, a credit insurance executive and lieutenant colonel of the Armed Forces, was appointed the NRA for Ghana and Nigeria.[4] When I was called in, Minister Wong offered me a range of countries to choose from. "So far, we have only appointed two NRAs. Since the other countries have not yet been decided, you may choose whichever you wish." If I wanted any of the European or Eastern European countries, he said that it would not be a problem.

Without hesitation, I chose Iran. Minister Wong was surprised. "Why Iran?"

The Islamic Revolution had erupted a decade earlier in 1979, when Sayyid Ruhollah Musavi Khomeini had deposed the Shah and declared Iran an Islamic Republic. The Iran–Iraq war had been raging from 1980–1988, and furthermore, Iran had been receiving negative American news coverage. These incidents were fresh on people's minds.

"Iran is not the easiest country to operate in," the Minister continued. "Iran's culture is very different. I think it is going to be very tough on you, since you are not a Muslim." He referenced the prominent role that religion played in the country.

I stuck to my position, however, because I felt I had acquired some knowledge of Iran during my trade missions for Intraco to the Middle

East (Iran is situated between Central Asia, South Asia and the Arab States). Furthermore, as a child, I had developed a fascination for Iran's culture and history after hearing my mother recite the poem 'Sohrab and Rustum' during our sojourn in Kerala. The poem "recounts... the fatal outcome of Sohrab's search for his father Rustum, the leader of the Persian forces."[5] This eventually led to my reading other Iranian poems in English translation: surely the Persian language has some of the most beautiful poems in the world, to rival English literature.

Finally, my student interest in global politics through the USC drew my attention to Iranian political leaders whom I felt were worth their salt. Mohammad Mosaddegh, known to many as the "Weeping Prime Minister", cut an impressive figure. He was the Middle Eastern anti-imperialist who had started the real economic agitation against the colonial powers by nationalising the Anglo-Iranian oil company in 1951. This act, along with Egypt's nationalisation of the Suez Canal in 1956, delivered a crippling blow to Britain.

Indeed, Mosaddegh's gamble precipitated many recurring frictions with the West. Britain's exit from India in 1947 augured the former empire's decline; and both the U.S. and the Soviet Union had by the 1950s started to surpass Britain in absolute strength. In an attempt to cling onto its great power status — by maintaining its operations in the Gulf and Suez Canal Zone — Britain allied with the Americans to avenge themselves on Iran.[6] With the help of the U.S., the British painted Mosaddegh as a tyrant who had turned his back on the pro-Western Iranian elites.

The British acted as a guide and tutor to the U.S. (which after World War II had emerged as the global power best positioned to project its influence). According to the foreign affairs scholar William Wallace, for Britain, "[t]he process of postwar redefinition [of foreign policy] depended heavily on American partnership and support; that obtained, adjustment stopped short of matching Britain's global responsibilities and deployments to its sharply reduced economic circumstances."[7]

One might contend from these circumstances that Britain remained, during this historic transition period, more influential, even, than the Americans in manoeuvring within and exerting leverage over the international scene. In 1953, the American Central Intelligence Authority

(CIA) together with MI6 overthrew Mossadegh's popularly elected government and installed Mohammad Reza Pahlavi in his place, otherwise known as "the Shah".[8]

Mossadegh was imprisoned for years; he was held under house arrest until his death. Curiously, if you visit Iran, you will somewhat surprisingly find that a parliamentary seat is specially kept for him, so that visitors are able to straightaway see that this is where Mossadegh, the "champion of secular democracy" and defender against "foreign domination", once sat.[9] *The New York Times* reported that when the Iranian leader had first heard his prison sentence, he quipped, "The verdict of this court has increased my historic glories. I am extremely grateful you convicted me. Truly tonight the Iranian nation understood the meaning of constitutionalism."[10]

Personally, I had for a long time felt that Iran was exploited by the Western powers, whereas it should have been given the chance to grow. Starting from my first informal visit to Iran for ECICs in the 1980s, it seemed that it, like other civilisational states such as China and India, possessed an ancient heritage that gave it a long-term perspective to international affairs and governance. It was a mature nation, which I doubted would wantonly wage war. In fact, it is the only country I have ever visited where I did not see a single statue erected for a general or king! Most statues one sees are of writers and philosophers.

A statue commonly stationed in major cities is of the poet Abdul-Qasem Ferdowsi Tusi — "Ferdowsi", for short. His busts often come accompanied with lines from the *Shahnameh*, the national epic poem of Iran, from which the tragic episode of 'Sohrab and Rustum' is taken.[11] The Arabs invaded Iran between 633 and 654 AD and converted the country's Zoroastrian residents to Islam. The poet soulfully laments the soldiers and warriors enslaved by the Arabs after the invasion and the king's doctors who were openly sold in the marketplace.*

Ferdowsi was the poet who, of his contemporaries, most deeply internalised the humiliation of Persia's defeat. I thus sensed that the *Shahnameh's* acute expression of shame revealed something exceptional

---

* A verse widely known throughout Iran reads: "Damn this world, damn this time, damn this fate / That uncivilised Arabs have come to make me Muslim."

about Iran's complex national character. (Elsewhere in the Middle East, proselytisers of Islam had, to my knowledge, mostly been treated as saviours.) Iran was an interesting country in my view, different from its neighbours.

So I answered Minister Wong, "You may be right that Iran might not be one of the easiest places to work in. But there are several reasons why I have chosen this country. Firstly, Iran has an ancient civilisation, of which I have some knowledge; secondly, their poetry is beautiful; and thirdly, Persian civilisation has a few cultural affinities with India. I know I don't speak the language, or have any qualifications to do this, but if you grant my request, I would be happy." He seemed a little puzzled by my response but, mulling it over, said that he would approve my appointment as NRA to Iran.

Appointment as Non-Resident Ambassador to Iran, with President Wee Kim Wee and his wife, and me with my wife, May 12th, 1990.

I served as NRA to Iran for nineteen years, from when I received my appointment letter in 1989 to 2008, in one of the longest lasting tenures of any Singaporean NRA. I was carefully briefed for my first meeting with President Akbar Hashemi Rafsanjani (which I recall took place on March 17th, 1990) at which I was required to present my credentials.

My protocol officer was Mr. V. K. Rajan. He was the protocol officer not only for Iran but also many other foreign post countries. To prepare me for the presentation, he introduced me to the Norwegian ambassador to Singapore who had also served in Iran.† He also played videotapes for me of Iran's ceremonial procedures, which was helpful in shaping my expectations. Ministry officials then briefed me on what they viewed as Iran's major policy positions and granted me access to files through which I read up on important areas of our relationship.

Amidst this flurry of activity, my appointment papers were dispatched to Tehran for approval; but the Iranian officials took no action on them for months. It was in 1989, I think, that Mir-Houssein Mousavi Khameneh, Iran's last prime minister before the post was abolished, visited Singapore. During Mr. Mousavi's meeting with Goh Chok Tong, I suspect our then deputy prime minister referenced the delay in processing, because a couple of days later my papers were approved.

This delay had me rushing to Tehran faster than I ever expected. The 21st of March is Nowruz. Meaning "New Day", it is a pre-Islamic New Year of Zoroastrian origin, celebrated in Iran for over three thousand years. The Iranian public celebrates Nowruz with fanfare, shooting fireworks and playing music. After the 1979 revolution, the mullahs (educated Muslims trained in Islamic law and doctrine, some of whom became powerful in government) intervened, as they saw the festivities as too secular. But the people prohibited interference and their attempts failed. For Nowruz, everything is shut for two weeks. Officials on both sides pressed me to present my credentials as soon as possible.

A Tale of Espionage

When I landed in Tehran's airport, two Iranian officials were waiting for me. I suspect one of them was from intelligence because the younger of the two drew my MFA colleague away to collect our bags. The more

† When this gentleman was escorted to see the president, he had not been escorted to Rafsanjani but rather Ayatollah Ali Khamenei, Iran's current supreme leader, who served as third president of Iran (1981–1989).

senior officer hung back (from what I could gather, to evaluate me and gather information). It would be nearly an hour before the other officer and my colleague returned. The elder official asked if he could see my CV while we waited for our luggage to come.

The first line on my CV revealed my position as chairman of the Hindu Advisory Board. He was surprised that Singapore had sent a representative of Indian origin, and a Hindu. "How come you are chairman of the Hindu Advisory Board?" He laid stress on the word *Hindu*. "You are a priest or something?"

The credential would have impressed him. In Iran, religion is everywhere, and Iranians are strict in adhering to Islamic law. In their daily attire, they discourage short sleeves and restrict how much skin can be shown. Were a man to walk around in short sleeves baring his arms, he would be told to change his shirt.

"Do you need someone to take you to the temple?" he asked. He was very gracious. "If so, I will arrange for you to visit any time you want." He listed the names of a few temples in Tehran. I explained that I was not a priest and just advised the government on Hindu community matters.

His next question caught me off guard. Why did I wear a tie? He pointed out that this was not my national dress. I said in Singapore we wore ties for all our official functions. For us, it was not a badge of colonialism but a sign of professionalism. "We all adjust to these things. Even you are wearing a jacket, as far as your question is concerned, which is not the native Iranian dress. By this logic, you should be wearing a shalwar and long robes."

He continued cross-examining me on why Singapore was so close to the Americans. After our bags arrived, he then spent an additional thirty minutes plying us with routine questions before letting us enter the country. I found this questioning a little excessive, but also enlightening in terms of Iranian cultural worldviews.

Meeting the President

When the Norwegian Ambassador to Singapore shared his experience with me on meeting Iran's president, he had warned me to keep an eye out for the chief of protocol. The man wore a rain jacket or windbreaker, he said, with jeans and canvas shoes. He had allegedly risen to his official position by being the first to jump over the wall at the American Embassy when Iranian students seized the compound in November 1979, taking more than fifty diplomats and staff hostage. As the story goes, this early-mover inspired everyone else to too.[12] For his bravery, he was made "chief-of-protocol".

The ambassador's story should of course be taken with a pinch of salt, but his point was that I should brace myself for the unexpected. I was therefore primed to meet someone a little unconventional. However, the official who greeted me seemed quite the opposite. Iran's chief-of-protocol was well-groomed and spoke impeccable English; he professionally guided me through a series of events perfectly mirroring the scenes I had watched in V. K. Rajan's videos.

During the presentation of my credentials and meetings with the ministers, what struck me most was that their bureaucracy was extremely organised. If one was of high rank, assistants would stand by in the wings, ready to take notes. By the time I moved on to my next appointment with another minister, he would have already been well briefed about the positions I had taken in the meeting before.

Iran's governing structure is comparably systematic. The parliament, or Majlis, is perhaps one of the most democratic institutions in the Middle East. The Majlis legislates laws on issues within the limits of the constitution and parameters of Islam. Legislation passed by the Majlis moves up to the Guardian Council for review, which then checks for its compatibility with Islamic law and the constitution.

(The doctrine underlying Iran's political system is guardianship of the jurist; it maintains that "just government was possible if religious scholars sat atop it".[13] The supreme leader, presently Ayatollah Ali Khamenei, holds the most power and "has the final say over all government matters in the country".[14] For instance, he can ask senior state officials to be appointed or for laws to be reviewed. Iran's institutions, however, do possess countervailing checks and balances: Iran's parliament can call up the president or ministers for questioning, and if a minister is deemed unfit, impeach him. There is also an Assembly of Experts who have the power to appoint and unseat the supreme leader, although the latter has never occurred.)

President Rafsanjani, after accepting my credentials, requested that I sit and offered me a cup of tea. He spoke to me about Iran and Iran's expectations of Singapore. A translator interpreted his questions from Persian. He was knowledgeable about our affairs and said he would like to see Singapore become an important partner to Iran, due to our strategic location at the crossroads of East and West. The presentation was brief — probably no more than thirty to forty minutes.

A Curious Foreign Farmer

I had two main duties as Singapore's representative to Iran. The first was to maintain a cordial political relationship; and the second was to keep an eye out for what opportunities existed for introducing Iranian trade missions to Singapore. In 1995, for example, I became the mission advisor to the Singapore Trade Development Board (TDB), an agency developed to extend Singapore's relationships in international trade. We also ventured into the nearby country of Turkmenistan.

The TDB found new markets for Singapore and strove to establish Singapore as an international trade hub by welcoming foreign companies to set up base here. According to our mission brochure, the TDB's ambit "included third country trade, entrepot trade, counter-trade as well as regional warehousing and distribution."[15] We had brought in a group of businessmen to Iran involved in import-export from and into several industries and sectors: some of these included wheat and agri-products as well as yarn and fabrics, just to name a few. Other businessmen were involved in areas like transport and railways.

As one anecdote broadly reflective of the status of our trade relations, I had, in January 2002, visited the *Irani News* office to meet its managing director, Mohammad Soltanifar. We exchanged views on bilateral trade, around which a news article was written up. I cited economic data in the article which showed that our exchange of commercial goods was worth S$1.4 billion.[16] The direction of trade at that time was in Iran's favour, as

Singapore Trade Mission brochure to Iran and Turkmenistan, December 8–13th, 1995.

Singapore purchased more goods, including oil. Advocating for Singapore, I made it a point to promote our comprehensive telecommunication and banking facilities, which Iran could use to build links with our part of the world.

Not much came of the few working trade missions when I was an NRA; and on the whole, our economic activities in Iran were limited. With tension brewing between Iran and the U.S., sanctions were placed on Iran, which hindered activities by our government-linked companies. America was also an important partner on which we economically depended; we were, consequently, a little sensitive about pushing hard for anything that might alienate the Americans.[‡]

Beyond official relations, I personally did what I could to foster commercial ties and lower trade barriers. President Rafsanjani was from the province of Kerman, located in southeastern Iran; it is an area famous for its carpet-making and pistachio nuts. After Rafsanjani's imprisonment by the previous regime, I discovered a neutral trader from the nearby region had been given the keys to his household — he was assigned the critical responsibility of overseeing Rafsanjani's farm and ensuring his income was passed on to his family. I found it fascinating that Rafsanjani, who would become president, had handed over his personally accumulated wealth to a foreign trader rather than his own family members, whom the government might have targeted.

This trader — who became a foreign resident of Iran and a business

[‡] We did, however, let our trade grow naturally. During this period, there would likely have been an influx of Iranian tourists to Singapore, from what I recall. The Iranians had built up business in Dubai; and from Dubai, it is only one plane flight to Singapore. The tourism sector probably grew marginally, though I am not certain for how long this growth was sustained.

associate of Rafsanjani's nephew — must have proven he could be trusted. Kerman had an industrial reputation and was the origin of many of Iran's exports.[17] From Kerman, he bought, sold and ferried products to Middle Eastern countries and India. The trader had proactively read up on my arrival and, of his own accord, called on me to offer a favour: "I know the family. If you would like to meet with them, I can arrange it."

I did not expect to meet the President's family in so informal a manner; but not wanting to close the door on any opportunities, I replied that I would be quite happy to meet any senior people to whom he wanted to introduce me. The gentleman was a heaven-send and, thanks to his friendship, I received the royal treatment. After a few trips, I met with the President's nephew as well as the then deputy foreign minister, Alaeddin Borujeradi. He and I established a friendly relationship, and the President's nephew subsequently invited me to his home in Kerman.

In this way, my association with the trader proved beneficial, and my congenial relationship with the President's family grew. I also established friendly relations with the bureaucrats. As an act of goodwill, I introduced the foreign trader to NTUC Fairprice because of the pistachio farms that he owned. I explained that Singapore might be interested in buying for resale, and told him I could set up the meeting. But I caveated that he would be on his own as far as deals were concerned.

He brought a team to Singapore and spent three or four days here, visiting several places of interest — it seemed he wanted to establish more regular relations. But somehow, he seemed to never be able to clinch a deal or follow up on the opportunities presented to him. He visited Singapore several times and made an effort to say hello during each trip. I privately started to wonder if there was some other reason for his visits, such as side interests he was pursuing, perhaps. Borujeradi also visited Singapore to survey the market. After my term as NRA, he became an influential political figure in Iran; he was elected as a senior member of parliament and the head of the Majlis National Security and Foreign Policy Commission. When we met in Singapore, he was again quite friendly with me.

19

Friends from Far Places: Ministerial Visits to Iran

"Singapore had relatively good relations with Iran during the time of the Shah, and Lee Kuan Yew had also visited the country as his guest... But afterwards came a bit of a lull. The revolution disrupted relations, and we were completely shut out... Although I do not think I can credit myself for any major breakthroughs, rekindling the relationship is maybe one small area where I left a mark."

Travels through the Provinces

My diplomatic work mostly had me interacting with Iran's Foreign Ministry. But during my nearly two decades of service there, I made it a point to visit other ministries as well. With the appropriate permissions, I travelled all over the country. The Iranians ensured that I always had someone tagging along (probably to keep an eye on me). Eventually, they saw that I had a genuine interest in and respect for their culture, and their treatment of me, perhaps as one consequence, became warmer. Iran's Foreign Ministry provided me with a list of prominent people with whom I could meet whenever I visited a particular area. The Foreign Ministry was generous, and I saw as many people as possible.

"... they saw that I had a genuine interest in and respect for their culture... and their treatment of me... became warmer...".

I usually visited Iran two or three times a year. My travels through the provinces afforded me an opportunity to meet with a wide range of people who were involved with Iran's political, economic and social life.* For instance, on some occasions, I even met with the mullahs. Some mullahs (though not those I met) belonged to the clergy.

The clergy had gained a somewhat intimidating reputation in the West. I found those mullahs I interacted with, however, to be quite cordial in our encounters. To provide one example, I visited an institute named the Organisation for the Advancement of Islam. Its chief was a mullah — although from the civilian side rather than the establishment: "[m]ost of Iran's clerical hierarchy... remains outside the official structure".[1]

Expecting to talk about religion, you can imagine my surprise when the chief presented me with a trilingual collection of Omar Khayyam's poetry in English, French and Farsi instead, bound in an ornate cover. "I was told you like poetry," he said. "I would like to present this to you."

Omar Khayyam was a well-regarded 11th century poet and mathematician. In the *Ruba-iyyat*, his most well-known work, the poet reportedly challenges religious doctrines and alludes to hypocrisy amongst the clergy.[2]

Although Khayyam was an Islamic scholar, his work appeared at first glance to have little to do with religion. The chief, noticing my confusion, remarked, "You thought that I would preach to you about Islam. No, no, I want to talk about the world." He launched with me into an informed discussion on world affairs. Most of the mullahs spoke excellent English. However, even if they were fluent, many, like the French, preferred speaking in their native tongue as a matter of national pride. My conversations with officials were usually facilitated by an interpreter and recorded.

On another one of my visits, I met with a local mayor who was preparing a programme of city beautification. I came to learn that he had

* The temperature in Iran during the summers, as I learned, was unbearably hot, almost thirty-eight degrees Celsius. My trader friend from the region taught me how to battle the heat. Whenever I stepped outside, I first removed my jacket. Once, he spotted me doing this and asked me to put it back on. "Why do people need to wear coats?" he asked rhetorically. "To keep warm when it is cold! But here in Iran, we use coats for a different purpose. We also wear them when it is hot. When you sweat, it cools down the body. So you must keep your jacket on."

closely studied Singapore as a model. When I called on him, he asked, "How is it that the PAP, in spite of a very unpopular mission, manages to get elected term after term?" I found this to be a profound question; it confirmed my belief that the Iranians are serious thinkers who take a multi-dimensional governance approach.

A Struggling Economy

From my travels around the provinces, one problem that nevertheless became apparent was that everything in the country was predominantly sustained by one product, which was oil. Besides this singular income source, they seemed not to have devised a more comprehensive economic agenda. Indirectly, this observation has been corroborated elsewhere: a Brookings essay states, "the Islamic revolution ... did not bring a well-defined economic strategy to reorganise the economy", although it references other achievements, such as the Islamic Republic's relative successes "in the expansion of infrastructure for rural development and poverty reduction."[3]

The appointment of the oil minister, due to oil's sizeable influence over the Iranian economy (as of 2019/2020, nearly one-quarter of Iran's government revenue came from oil and gas),[4] was, therefore, a critical one, and became an issue around which there was a little jostling in parliament. The clergy also had a say in the proceedings as an extension of the supreme leader's power, whose authority encompassed "setting national policies and supervising their implementation."[5]

According to a study by Rand Corporation, Ali Khamenei "inherited the title and authority of the [first supreme leader's] position," established under rule by the jurist but not necessarily his "influence and power". Its authors Keith Crane, Rollie Lal and Jeffrey Martini state that his religious authority had been "purposefully upgraded [by the Assembly of Experts]".[6] While Ayatollah Ruhollah Khomeini was foremost among the Shi'ite clergymen, Ali Khamenei lacked equivalent credentials; I believe he is the second highest ranking. The Shi'ite leader with the widest following is Grand Ayatollah Sistani, from Shi'ism's theological center in Najaf, Iraq.[7†]

Beyond economic policymaking and planning, Iran's financial hardships were also due partially to the loss of many senior civil servants post-revolution. Many bureaucrats and businesspeople had migrated, leaving behind a vacuum. While the government replaced the civil service and built a new army, businessmen were not so easily substituted. Being an intelligent people, the Iranians prospered wherever they travelled — many migrated to the land of their so-called rival, the U.S. Finding success there, few had any incentive to return.

From the 1980s onwards, I had witnessed Iran's economic doldrums during visits to Iran for ECICS. At that time, the meal offered for breakfast in hotels was limited: typically two boiled eggs, some goat cheese and Iranian breads. By the time I presented my credentials in 1990 the situation had improved, but not drastically. Where in Tehran today restaurants with international cuisine abound, the menu in 1990 had expanded to only include a few extra items: an omelette or maybe an assortment of breads and cheeses. There were not many public restaurants, and one usually had to go to a hotel for meals.

Another problem was Iran's non-acceptance of American dollars. Exchange rates were unfavourable, and foreigners in the region opted to exchange their currencies under the table. I remember a humorous incident in which the MFA officer assigned to accompany me on a diplomatic visit chose to exchange our American dollars at the bank. The banker was shocked that my colleague had approached him and asked why he did not try the shop around the street corner, where the rates would have been much more attractive. My colleague replied, "No, I am a Singapore civil servant. Such under-the-table transactions are not allowed."

The banker was perplexed by the officer's response, wondering if he was alright in the head — especially since the exchange rate was as much as three or four times as high as what could have been obtained by taking just a short stroll! But reluctant to abandon his official instructions,

† My understanding is that the Shi'ite mullahs have rigorous methods of evaluating their religious leaders, according to their scholarly credentials, which are ascertained by a review of the ayatollahs' writings and papers. My impression was that this process was impartial and factual.

my colleague asked for the receipt. After that, every time we passed the shop around the street corner, a small crowd pointed at us and jeered, "Look, the stupid fellows who go to the bank!" I might have mildly suggested that we could relax our standards just slightly.

A Valued Hotel Manager

I stayed at the Royal Tehran Hilton, one of the country's pre-eminent hotels, which was opened in 1962. After the revolution, it was renamed the *Esteghlal* (meaning "Independence") when all foreign hotel management contracts were terminated. Its last international manager, I found out, was a Singaporean. When several of the staff learned I was a Singaporean also, they approached me and sung his managerial virtues to the sky. Since his departure, the hotel's standards had dropped; they complained to me, for instance, about room maintenance. The outlook had become grim.

Iran had a few huge organisations called *bonyads* or "foundations" — charitable trusts and semi-business organisations that played a prominent role in Iran's non-petroleum economy. As of 2008, they controlled an estimated 40 percent of the non-oil economy.[8] One *bonyad*, I seem to recall, was called the "Foundation for the Upliftment of the Downtrodden"; it had assets that had been taken over from the Shah. The Shah and his family had amassed a huge fortune that was divided up between the foundations in areas like housing, injury benefits and welfare. The Foundation for the Upliftment of the Downtrodden owned all the hotels in the country, which likely included the *Esteghlal*.

Where my accommodations as an NRA were at the hotel, the ambassadors of other countries had rented residences where they sometimes hosted dinners. Fellow diplomats like me would occasionally be invited to attend. But more often than not, we caught up at the hotel. During such meetings, the ambassadors apprised me of the turmoil roiling the country — such as from the People's Mujahedin Organization of Iran (PMOI), who called themselves freedom fighters and opponents of the Islamic regime and whom the clergy treated as traitors. Some reports suspected that the PMOI was behind the bomb blast that had paralysed Ali Khamenei's arm, clearing his path to power.[9] We also discussed Iran's economic prospects.

But when they were not discussing the country's current events, the ambassadors aired their personal complaints. The Foreign Ministry, for instance, had provided me with a car and a driver: this prompted the other ambassadors to ask, "What's so special about you?" I said that they perhaps did it to keep an eye on me, privately wondering why that was so.

The diplomat who left the strongest impression on me was the Ambassador from China. He was immensely knowledgeable and spoke Farsi like a local. During my first visit, I went out of my way to meet him by calling him up and inviting him to the hotel. When he arrived, I sensed the awe in which he was held by the staff, due in no small part to his excellent mastery of the language. So great was their respect that whenever he and I met for lunch, the staff made special arrangements for us.

China has a language college where over a hundred languages are taught — if I am not mistaken, it is Beijing Foreign Studies University. I congratulated China's Ambassador on his proficiency in Farsi and praised those whom I had met from China who spoke foreign languages like English so fluently. He modestly replied that Japan had an even larger school. For a Chinese official to cede such a victory, I thought, was highly unusual; his humility further raised my esteem for him.

Some years later when I travelled to China, I tried to meet with the retired diplomat in Beijing at the Singapore–China Dialogue. Professor Tommy Koh was leading the mission and I was deputy leader. The diplomat was out of town, but I was informed that he was still around and a senior figure at the university of foreign languages.

Anti-West Sentiment

In a roundabout way, my talks with the other ambassadors also nuanced my pre-existing understanding of Iran's hostility towards the West. My habit was to call on everyone: the Europeans, Chinese, Japanese — even the British. The Iranians did not approve of my meetings with the British, however. "What are you going to see the British for?" they would ask. "You are from Asia." They perhaps assumed all my friends would be the Asian ambassadors.

The Iranians have a saying that captures the then-prevailing anti-British sentiment in the country: "If you stumble on a rock in the road, it is most likely a Briton who put it there!" They viewed the British as an intelligent people. And this came with a modicum of respect — they acknowledged their shrewdness. They did not have the same respect for the Americans. In their minds, the British were the deep thinkers with the real potential to cause havoc.

Nevertheless, I strove to see the British ambassadors and, to the Iranians' credit, they never stopped me. I found that the British ambassadors, of all the ambassadors, were the best informed. I simply explained to the Iranians that they gave me another point of view, which helped me to keep my country up-to-date. The British ambassadors were very down to earth: when discussing the politics and economy of the country, they would tell me frankly, "this was good" or "that was bad". While the information was useful, their realism could sometimes come across as pessimistic.

Iran's anti-American feeling in the 1990s and early 2000s, to compare, was mostly at the official level rather than an indication of feelings on the ground. I remember in one of my outings I had been touring the National Iranian Oil Company. Upon entering a hall, I noticed a huge American flag painted on the floor. In a show of deference, I sidestepped the flag. But my manoeuvre caught the attention of a security guard; he pointed at the flag and gestured for me to step on it.

I then realised that the flag had been placed on the floor on purpose to insult the Americans: I found this rather petty. Elsewhere in the cities, big signs branded America as the "Great Satan" and depicted the "Stars and Stripes" with falling bombs. This jarred with conversations that I had with the man on the street who, if asked for his opinion of the Americans, would be likely to show a real, positive interest and inquire how he could get his green card. If I had asked the same question in

Kerala around the same time, I would have received a lecture on American imperialism with a full account of its faults.

Building Interest in Singapore

I attempted to persuade as many Singaporean civil servants and politicians as I could to undertake a trip to Iran whenever I returned home after one of my diplomatic trips to Iran. But in my early years, enthusiasm on the Singapore side was lukewarm. There were also external geopolitical constraints. Singapore knew little about Iran and, as I had mentioned earlier, many people's surface-level impressions were coloured by the Islamic Revolution. The first ayatollah passed away around the time I entered the service in 1989/1990; but his presence in Iran was all-pervasive. His image was everywhere, giving him a "god"-like status.

Singapore had relatively good relations with Iran during the time of the Shah, and Lee Kuan Yew had also visited the country as his guest. Lee Kuan Yew was impressed with the Westernised parts of Iran. One photograph was even taken of a suited Shah standing beside Lee Kuan Yew and his wife. But afterwards came a bit of a lull. The revolution disrupted relations, and we were completely shut out. We started to re-establish connections after the Shah's reign during my tenure. Although

Ayatollah Khomeini's presence was "all-pervasive". His portrait can be seen on the back wall during this ECICS meeting.

I do not think I can credit myself for any major breakthroughs, rekindling the relationship is maybe one small area where I left a mark.

A long time passed before I could arrange any high-level visits to Iran. Then, finally, in 2004, after a period of limited exchange, three official visits unfolded in quick succession. One was by Mr. Kishore Mahbubani, Permanent Secretary for the Ministry of Foreign Affairs — the first official senior-level visit from Singapore in a long time. Kishore received a grand reception. Looking down from our plane as we descended onto the tarmac, I could see a large entourage had gathered to meet him.

"He has brought the Deputy Minister to see you, which is seldom done for a civil servant," I said as our plane touched down. What most attracted the Iranians to Kishore was perhaps that, although he was of Indian origin, he looked fair and Persian. They happily pointed out that his name "Mahbubani" was of Persian extraction.

Then, one day, I had had a long chat with Mr. George Yeo, who was then Minister for Trade and Industry. In addition to being a scholar, he knew as much if not more than I did about Iran. George agreed to a visit, seeing the merit in such a trip, and thus became the first person of ministerial rank whom I accompanied to Iran.

Sometime before that, the Minister and I had gone on a trip together to India. This later furnished him with a colourful story to tell at my expense. George had lost his seat in Aljunied GRC in the general election in 2011. One day after the election, I met him for lunch where he remarked to an associate who had come with him, "This is the man who made me lose my seat."

He shared the legend of the Brihadeshwara Temple in Thanjavur, Tamil Nadu, which we had visited on our trip to India all those years ago. According to the legend, anyone who enters through its front entrance will incur bad luck.[10] There were, apparently, numerous cases attesting to the curse's credibility. These included the assassination of Indira Gandhi and the loss of former American Vice President Al Gore during the 2000 Florida election recount — both of whom had stepped through the main gateway of the temple. Tamil Nadu's Chief Minister Karunanidhi, who served between 1969 and 2011, was reported to have deliberately taken the side entrance to attend a dance programme: *The Hindustan Times* suggested that this was to avoid the curse![11] I had not been aware of this legend, which is why it took me by surprise when George informed me that he had been told, "Gopi lost you this election since he didn't warn you!"

On another occasion, I accompanied the Minister on a visit to Kerala. Our hosts had returned from honouring an austere Hindu deity, Ayyappan in Sabarimala, after an arduous pilgrimage to the Sabarimala temple, one of India's most famous pilgrim centres located in the mountains of the Western Ghats. George proved the virtues of culture-based diplomacy by asking so many penetrating questions about the deity and the import of the pilgrimage that our "hosts realised that he already had a great deal of knowledge about the Hindu deity, even though he is Catholic. One of the officials was [so] impressed… [that] he commented that he now understood why Singapore was successful!"[12] (I later shared this anecdote in a letter I wrote to young Singaporean public service officers to demonstrate the significant impact one can have through broad knowledge and interest.)

The Minister's trip to Iran proceeded along similar lines: the Iranians admired his deep knowledge and cultural insights. On the other hand, when I had first come to the country as an NRA, the Iranian officials were perhaps disappointed that I was a businessman rather than a career diplomat. However, my knowledge of Ferdowsi and Omar Khayyam helped to break the ice — another reason I am quick to extol the virtues of poetry!

~

Before George Yeo's visit to Iran, I knew that another high-level ministerial visit was also on the way. I thought that two high-level visits to Iran's capital city of Tehran in such a short time might be too much to swallow; another ministry official agreed that it would be wise to save Tehran for the next trip.

Given both George's portfolio and keenness for history, I felt it would be appropriate for him to enter Iran through a part of the country that was both economically and culturally significant: I inquired if he would like to enter through the gateway city of Shiraz. Shiraz, located in south-central Iran near the ancient capital of Persepolis, was also home to the classical poet Ben-Shams-ud-Din Muhammed Hafez-e Shirazi, or "Hafez". He wrote the *Divan*, which is seen as the pinnacle of Persian literature. His body is entombed at the site.

While we were touring the tomb, I shared with George a memorable episode from one of my previous excursions there. A student had approached me to test the depth of my knowledge on Hafez, and quizzed me on whether I remembered the lines of any of his poems. "Only in English translation," I answered. The student then asked whether I would like for him to recite and translate a few verses from Persian — he could sing it, if I preferred. I found this fascinating, as the singing of poetry is also a custom practiced in India.

As the student began singing, people crowded into the open hall. A guard then arrived, who informed me that the head of the organisation that oversaw the tomb was eager to meet with me. We shared the customary orange juice, as Iranians do not drink alcohol. What sticks with me to this day was the sight of that enthusiastic crowd and how appreciative they were that I knew of their heritage.

~

The surprise I never expected was when Prime Minister Goh Chok Tong himself elected to visit Iran. The Prime Minister's visit, in particular, was warm and informal. The Iranians were overwhelmed by his friendliness and informal approach. A key reason why the Iranians treated us so well, I believe, was that they felt that Singapore's attention showed — if not exactly their acceptance into the Western world — than at least acceptance into the modern global community. They had been ostracised, and I think that these three visits from Singapore provided them with a feeling of solidarity.

The Prime Minister came to Iran within two months of Minister George's Yeo's visit. As a group, we toured Isfahan together, Iran's second largest city and commercial centre. We had specifically chosen this location due to its specialisation in trading and industry. The governor of Isfahan received us. When greeting me, he asked, "Have you been here before?" I answered yes, "Several times," and recited a one liner in Farsi — "*Isfahan nesfe jahan*" — which means "Isfahan is half the world". This is tantamount to saying that if you have not visited Isfahan, you have not seen anything yet!

PM Goh Chok Tong, glancing at me, then quipped, "You must have learnt this just for the trip!" Everyone laughed and clapped. The governor was so thrilled by my recitation (and that I knew what it meant!) that he got up to hug me. They greatly appreciated the informality.

Elsewhere in Ifsahan, we met with the city's mayor, where I recall a competition staged in a large hall: if you whispered into the wall, someone at the wall's opposite end could hear you. An official from the Iranian party recited a couplet from Edgar Allan Poe's 'The Raven', and the challenge was cast of whether someone from the Singapore entourage could declaim any verses of Persian poetry.

The Prime Minister looked at me and asked if I could recite — if not in Farsi — a Persian poem translated into English. I delivered a couple lines by Omar Khayyam. The mayor was delighted. Along with my familiarity with poetry, he and the others were curious about my Indian heritage, which they were better acquainted with than other cultures. Indeed, during Mughal rule in India, Persian was the language spoken in the courts. It was also said that former Indian Prime Minister Narasimha Rao was friendly with Rasfanjani and could speak with him in Farsi. Rao was a scholar who supposedly knew several languages, including French.

Final Impressions of Iran

Of my life's major achievements, organising these ministerial meetings felt like some of the most meaningful. PM Goh Chok Tong not only fulfilled his duty by visiting but also enjoyed the experience. The Iranians appeared to have had no specific agenda when they met us; they did not even push trade, which they probably should have done. When we left, it felt as if the exchange was between friendly, neighbouring countries. The Iranians were surprised by our affability.

My experience in Iran is worth recounting, perhaps, because of the stark dissonance between my experience in the country and how it is sometimes portrayed in the press. Some Western journalists have spun the narrative that Tehran, a once idyllic metropolis, became a fear-ridden city after the revolution. But I do not think this characterisation is entirely accurate and gives the full picture. In day-to-day life, families would be out and about enjoying themselves in public parks, and children would be frolicking around. There are no policemen forebodingly hovering over your shoulders.

In an article that I wrote for *The Straits Times* in 2009 after I stepped down as NRA to Iran, I asserted that Iran had three major preoccupations. The first was their need for recognition and acceptance. Iran is one of the most important countries in the Middle East, and I believed that it should have been allowed a seat at the table for any pertinent discussion regarding the region. The second was what they saw as their right to develop nuclear energy, for peaceful purposes. (The West, of course, continues to view their motives, especially their nuclear programme, with suspicion). Third was their desire to lead the Muslim world, which is not easy to do, given that they are Shi'ites and the remaining 85 percent are Sunnis.[13]

DEALING WITH TEHERAN

Without Iran, M-E peace can't take flight

"Dealing with Teheran: Without Iran, M-E peace can't take flight", by Gopinath Pillai, *The Straits Times*, March 12th, 2009.

"[I]t would be timely for the West to understand the main preoccupations of the Iranians and to find ways to deal with them."

Over those eighteen years, I came away looking positively on Iran and its culture. The Iranians' long-term thinking, I would say, ranks with the Chinese; and in terms of global cultural knowledge, they are possibly even more erudite. Like Singaporeans, they are detail-oriented; during our commercial on-site visits, for instance, the Iranians were always ready with statistics on hand to notify us as about the latest trends and volumes.

I think that the West had done Iran a disservice when the liberal-leaning President Seyed Mohamad Khatami, a proponent of Iranian democracy, reached out in 2001 at the UN for collaboration with Western countries — a "Dialogue of the Civilisations". Iran, however, was rebuffed by the Americans in President George W. Bush's State of the Union Speech in 2002, where he linked Iran with North Korea and Iraq as part of the "Axis of Evil" and framed the war against terror through a "with-us-or-against-us" binary.[14] I think this negatively impacted U.S.–Iran relations. The lesson that the radical clergy perhaps drew from the exchange was that if the Americans ignored friendly overtures, it was better to take a hardline approach.[15]

The Iranians during our meetings sometimes referenced our close ties with the Americans; for instance, they were aware that the American Navy ships came to Singapore to be serviced. But they understood that such collaboration was in our self-interest. They respected it and made no attempt to interfere. They would occasionally try to influence one's views on the Middle East; if you were to discuss Israel, they would be well briefed. But knowing that Singapore had close relations with Israel too, our interactions nevertheless remained pleasant.

20

Non-Resident High Commissioner to Pakistan (1994–2001)

"The most striking aspect of my credential presentation was the way in which I was ceremoniously paraded. I recall being taken in a horse-drawn carriage, with a cavalry detachment of the Presidential Honour Guards, trotting on both sides... It was one of the most spectacular presentations I had ever experienced!"

Maintaining Good Relations

I was appointed in 1994 as Singapore's non-resident high commissioner to Pakistan. This was due to my South Asian origin and the trade activities I had started there while at Intraco. MFA briefed me on Pakistan as they did on Iran. But, already, my familiarity with Pakistan was greater. The country in the 1980s had been economically important to Singapore because of its large palm oil demands — Singapore was a big trader. I also knew more about Pakistan's history and culture — I was fond of *Qawwali* music and relished Pakistani cuisine.

Singapore sided with the U.S. during the Cold War, and Singapore and Pakistan had found common ground during the Afghan conflict during this period. Singapore was not so aligned as many other countries, so when the Cold War ended, one of the first things Singapore did in the 1990s was befriend other non-aligned countries like India. Pakistan felt abandoned by Singapore after we reached out to their rival. My job became assuring the Pakistanis that substantially nothing had changed between us, and that we did not see why opportunities could not emerge from both relationships. Singapore depends on the global economy for its survival; as such, we were keen to trade with whoever would receive us.

Pakistan might have had high hopes for Singapore in the early stages of our relationship. President Muhammad Zia-ul-Haq had visited

Singapore in 1982; and Lee Kuan Yew visited Pakistan in 1988. During his first visit, Lee Kuan Yew was impressed "to see Islamabad noticeably cleaner and better maintained than Delhi."[1] Pakistan underwent fast rates of growth in the 1960s and 1980s compared to recent years, in which Pakistan's growth rates have slowed[2] (one journalist reported that under Zia, the economy grew an average of 6.7 percent per year).[3] Lee Kuan Yew was also keen to look at areas for collaboration, because he saw Pakistan as a gateway into the Middle East. I believe he had once gone to Pakistan to carry out an economic study with a team of senior civil servants. Much of the Middle East, with the exception of Egypt, supported Pakistan.

At the governmental level, our understanding of the Pakistanis was also better than our understanding of the Iranians. This was largely thanks to our honorary consul-general in Karachi, Mr. Amin Lakhani, an American-trained Pakistani and extremely diligent worker familiar with all the ins-and-outs of the country. During an early diplomatic visit, I remember how he had come to pick up my wife and me from a hotel, arriving with two cars, out of whose windows four bodyguards could be seen in their black uniforms with rifles slung across their shoulders. I asked him if we could maybe proceed without the bodyguard contingent. He said the government insisted they accompany us wherever we travelled.

Besides this heavy firepower (which took some getting used to) Pakistan was easier to navigate for an outsider than Iran was, especially given my entrepreneurial experience in India and having studied Hindi as a boy (spoken Hindi is almost the same as Urdu). In Iran, however — not knowing Persian and, before my initial diplomatic trips, having had limited cultural exposure — I had to exert more effort to build my understanding from the ground up.

Presenting Credentials

I presented my credentials to President Farooq Leghari. He came from a wealthy family and had in 1983 participated in a national campaign of civil disobedience against Zia-ul-Haq's military government, which had temporarily resulted in his arrest in Lahore.[4] Benazir Bhutto was his prime minister in 1994, and both belonged to the Pakistan People's Party (PPP). Before being nominated president, he had earlier also served as defence minister in the cabinet of Benazir's father, Zulfikar Ali Bhutto.

The most striking aspect of my credential presentation was the way in which I was ceremoniously paraded. I recall being taken in a horse-drawn carriage, with a cavalry detachment of the Presidential Honour Guards, trotting on both sides. Afterward, the two platoons of the Honour Guards were reviewed on the parade grounds, followed by the official credential presentation and a meeting with the president.[5] It was one of the most spectacular presentations I had ever experienced!

President Leghari received me at the Aiwan-e-Sadar Presidential Palace in Islamabad. I then went to see the Foreign Minister, a post to which Leghari himself had been appointed before PM Benazir Bhutto nominated him for the presidency (requiring him to change posts). We exchanged pleasantries and views.

Unlike in the case of Iran, where I had the chance to visit many provinces, in Pakistan I did not travel much outside of Islamabad and Karachi, aside from a visit to Takshashila. Takshashila, located northwest of Rawalpindi, is a city said to be the location of one of the first universities in the world (although there is some debate as to whether, by modern standards, it would meet the definition of a university). The city sits near the Indus River on the Grand Trunk Road, an ancient trade route connecting South, West and Central Asia.

I also found Benazir Bhutto's husband, Mr. Asif Ali Zardari, the 11th president of Pakistan (2008–2018), to be remarkably friendly towards me. On one occasion, I was touched when he asked his mother to prepare some of her special family dishes for me. On another, when I went to pay his family my respects, he went as far as rousing everyone from their naps, entreating, "Come, come see Uncle from Singapore!"

Impressions

Pakistan, from my first impression of its Foreign Ministry, had an impressive civil service — amongst the most articulate, well-groomed and finely polished in their etiquette that I have seen within the region.

They were educated at the world's top universities in the U.K. and U.S., and had a strong command of the English language.

When I became high commissioner to Pakistan, the Pakistanis, as I had mentioned earlier, were not too happy that Singapore had started focusing so much attention to India. They were especially unhappy when India was admitted to ASEAN in 1996 as a dialogue partner.[6] In conversations, they signalled their displeasure at the increase in our engagement after then Prime Minister Narasimha Rao's economic reforms began to attract foreign investment, perhaps feeling they had been unfairly treated. "Pakistan was your friend during the Cold War. Now you are promoting India!"

Pakistan's hostility towards India is stark in the context of the countries' shared history. This animosity became especially pronounced during Kashmir Day, a Pakistan national holiday which is celebrated annually on February 5th; it is marked by rallies and speeches in protest of what they term the "Indian occupation of Kashmir". I recall that in Karachi the *Dawn* newspaper, one of Pakistan's reputed, liberal-leaning English newspapers, carried an article ridiculing the programme one Sunday, pillorying how the anti-India tirades (which blazed forth in the morning) would peter out by afternoon. By 12 o'clock, most speakers and their audience would have set off back home for their *biryani*, the article claimed, or settled down to watch a lengthy Bollywood film.

The Pakistanis were fond of Bollywood movies, and in fact remained dependent on India for a time for their melodrama, vibrant costume design and item songs. One day, a friend invited me for lunch and prepared a lavish feast. After clearing our plates, he good-naturedly invited me to spend the rest of the afternoon watching a Hindi film. Conscious of my ambassadorial duties and all the work that waited for me at the hotel — and not least the number of hours Bollywood films run! — I apologetically declined.

From what I hear, the media diet in Pakistan today is slowly changing, and is perhaps gravitating in cultural predilection towards a greater identification with West Asia. The Turkish drama series *Dirilis Ertuglul*, for example, has become increasingly popular; even former Pakistani Prime Minister Imran Khan promoted the show's Islamic values in a televised interview in 2019, where he recommend the show to the Pakistani public.[7]

Prospects for Economic Cooperation

Economic cooperation between Singapore and Pakistan began on a promising note. And, as I stated above, I was posted to Pakistan to assure the Pakistanis that we would continue to collaborate wherever opportunities emerged. But in all honesty, the opportunities were few: we did not trade in any major commodities like petroleum, and trade in edible oils tapered off.

I am aware that, in recent years, Singapore and Pakistan have tried to step up their cooperation. I was informed, for instance, that in 2019, a large Singapore business delegation visited Pakistan to identify areas for investment;[8] and that Mr. Imran Khan met with Prime Minister Lee Hsien Loong on the sidelines of the World Economic Forum in Davos in 2020.[9] According to an interview given by Pakistan's High Commissioner to Singapore Rukhsana Afzaal to *The Business Times* in 2020, Pakistan is also seeking to engage Singapore in several emerging sectors such as "infrastructure development, food processing, and logistics, smart city solutions, hydropower projects, and technology/knowledge parks."[10] Some of these commercial areas intersect with the Special Economic Zones arising under the China–Pakistan Economic Corridor (CPEC).

Lee Kuan Yew had seemed keen to develop relations with Zia-ul-Haq in the 1980s, a complex period of regional and world history after the Soviet Union had occupied Afghanistan in 1979. Similar to Iran following the Islamic Revolution, Zia felt religion could be a guiding light to state institutions.[11] Apropos this vision, he announced during his speech upon taking power on July 5th, 1977, "Pakistan, which was created in the name of Islam, will continue to survive only if it stays with Islam. That is why I consider the introduction of an Islamic system as an essential pre-requisite for the country."[12]

Despite promising signs under Zia, progress on economic talks with Lee Kuan Yew stalled. Zia-ul-Haq's plane crashed in Bahawalpur (some allege sabotage) in 1988. Prime Minister Nawaz Sharif, after taking office, had hoped to revitalise the relationship and Pakistan's economic standing. He later came to Singapore in 1991 to meet with Lee Kuan Yew to "study the reasons for our economic progress". In 1992, he even invited Lee Kuan Yew to visit Pakistan and advise on the opening of its economy.[13] Subsequently, when Benazir Bhutto became prime minister, she also tried to persuade Mr. Lee in 1995 to carry on with his economic study of Pakistan.

However, Lee Kuan Yew recounts in his memoirs how many of the economic recommendations he had shared with Sharif had not been implemented.[14] Many social problems were also erupting in Pakistan at that juncture, causing some reservations.

As a personal example, in 1996, one of my scheduled trips to Pakistan with Kishore Mahbubani was cancelled when Mr. Mir Murtaza Bhutto, the elder brother of Benazir Bhutto, was assassinated in Karachi; a hit job. The police officer tasked with investigating Mir's case also disappeared.[15] The Pakistani government warned that this was not the appropriate time to visit. Kishore and I were supposed to fly to Pakistan after visiting Iran but, after receiving the warning, had to reroute to Singapore through Europe.

Dialogue with the Pakistanis diminished after Mir's assassination. Then, later that year, as Lee Kuan Yew also recounts in his memoirs, PM Benazir Bhutto was dismissed by Leghari — the same president to whom I had started my tenure by presenting my credentials.

Relinquishing Posts

There were no major visits from Singapore to Pakistan since Goh Chok Tong visited the country in 2004, although Pakistani Prime Minister Shaukat Aziz visited Singapore in 2005 and Foreign Minister Makhdoom Shah Mahmud Qureshi came to Singapore in 2010. However, these did not lead to any major diplomatic initiatives. One hopes that Pakistan's economy will benefit from the enhanced connectivity spurred by China's Belt and Road Initiative and CPEC and attendant foreign investment coming into the region.

I relinquished my diplomatic post to Pakistan in 2001 and Iran in 2008. In the case of Iran, I had been serving for nineteen years and felt that the time had come for a new diplomat to take charge. I got along well with the Iranians and liked the country — but the same NRA cannot stick around forever. The Iranians used to joke, "We want you as our a permanent representative." But if we kept sending the same person, they would not take Singapore as seriously.

In 2008, I was made ambassador-at-large. But I should state in all honesty that my duties, compared with my service in Iran and Pakistan, have not been as intensive. While you are an ambassador-at-large, you do not have a particular country assigned to you but are still part of the senior staff at MFA. This year in 2021, while writing this book, my tenure with MFA has been completed.

I am grateful for my experiences as an NRA to both countries, as MFA exposed me to the chance to feel the textures of Iranian and Pakistani cultures and the heat of political sentiments unfolding at that time. If I had gone from a businessman to an ambassador without exposure to the MFA's way of thinking, for instance, I might not have fully appreciated the full significance of political events. Where a scholar looks at historical facts, a diplomat learns to weigh emotional depths.

21

Paying It Forward: A Guild House and Supermarket

"I have therefore always tried to make sure that the activities I took part in were significant to me as well as the people concerned — some goal that was slightly more meaningful than just making money. On the side, I have, for this reason, always involved myself in what I like to call 'extracurricular' activities — small projects that I found interesting and which, I often joke, helped to keep me out of trouble."

A Double Life

When Prime Minister Goh Chok Tong and I were on the plane departing from Iran, he paid me a compliment that I will never forget. "Gopi," he said, "you succeed in whatever you take on because you have the passion and you drive it with passion."

I have always reflected on this comment and whether it is true. I am the sort of person who — if I am not overly interested in what I am doing, or if I happen to be dealing with someone who does not want my advice — withdraws. I like to be involved with my work, but not in name only: I like to show that I have done something concrete.

I have spent the better part of my career as a businessman, and maximising profits is normally the key motivator in business. But for me it was not. Like when reflecting on my life's direction before joining Raya Mills, I wanted to provide a comfortable life for my family; but making money was never my chief concern. Just as I enjoyed drama in my youth, writing in my early career and world affairs throughout, I wanted to take pleasure from whatever it was that I was doing. I have therefore always tried to make sure that the activities I took part in were significant to me as well as the people concerned — some goal that was slightly more meaningful than just making money.

On the side, I have, for this reason, always involved myself in what I like to call "extracurricular" activities — small projects that I found interesting and which, I often joke, helped to keep me out of trouble. These "ECA's" gave me a sort of "double life" as I strove to fulfill the duties of my regular nine-to-five job as ably as I could. Perhaps PM Goh Chok Tong was on to something when he observed that when a person is passionate about something, he will find the time to set out and do it.

A New Guild House

One such "ECA" I pursued while employed at UIC was working with a team to build a new Alumni Guild House at Kent Ridge. During the 1970s, I had started to become active in the graduate body of my alma mater after the University of Malaya formally separated in 1962. The Singapore campus of the University of Malaya converted into the University of Singapore, which later merged with Nanyang University into the National University of Singapore (NUS) in 1980.[1] I had served as a committee member of the National University of Singapore Society (NUSS, formerly University of Singapore Society, or USS) for seven terms. I was vice president during the Guild House's construction in 1973 and 1984 and president from 1977 to 1979.[2]

I have always had a sense of closeness to my past, you see — whether it is with family and friends or the institutions where I grew up and studied. For example, I maintained my links with Choon Guan Presbyterian School and St. Andrew's Secondary School for a long time. With my primary and secondary schooling, however, I discovered that, although a sense of closeness lingers a while, it does eventually dissipate. My relationship with the university, on the other hand, goes on and on. It is a special relationship. Indeed, the community that the university creates — and the rapport established by it — exhilarates me; and I am sure that, up until the end of my life, I will continue to follow the university's progress.

~

At an NUSS Guild House dinner, November 5th, 2011.

After graduation, my interest in NUS was not for the pursuit of knowledge. I do not, by and large, consider myself a scholarly person. I mostly appreciated how the university provided me with an opportunity to keep alive connections with various people who hung around the campus long after they had graduated, curious to see what kinds of discussions were taking shape. Shyamala also keeps in touch with our old classmates, and meets them for lunch regularly.

I was part of a group of graduates in the USS under the presidency of Ernest Wong from 1971 to 1973. He had left UIC and started his own business with a partner. We kept in touch through the university and collaborated on advocating for a new Guild House at Kent Ridge. The university had secured a site for its new campus in 1969, and the society began to daydream about starting a new clubhouse there.

This was especially the case after 1971. The USS had relocated to a second Guild House on 15 Evans Road, but the furnishings of this bungalow, as some of my fellow alumni recount, were not entirely satisfactory. We had been put on short notice by the university to vacate our Dalvey Estate clubhouse and move to these new "run-down" premises.[3] Given how frequently we returned to the university to catch up and chat, we realised that a permanent guild house of higher quality was in order. Indeed, in 1980, the Evans Road Guild House burned down.[4]

The vice-chancellor, from 1968 to 1975, was Dr. Toh Chin Chye. If I might say so, Dr. Toh was not overly fond of the alumni, probably because we questioned a lot of things, which made us come across as difficult people. He did not like how the former students kept flocking back to campus to comment on official university affairs. The manner in which the USS, into which graduates were elected, flagged its concerns nettled him.

The graduate committee, to make our relations with the Vice-Chancellor more congenial, decided that it would be prudent to invite a person of stature — someone formerly a student but who also held the respectability of a professor — to become president of our alumni group. His primary duty would be to warm our relationship with the Vice-Chancellor. People like Herman Hochstadt (not a committee member but, nevertheless, a frequent visitor to the university) were also roped in to nominate this "skilled diplomat" who would persuade the Vice-Chancellor of our new Guild House proposal.[5]

The eminent professor we nominated was Maurice Baker, the head of the university's English Department. Professor Baker had, in fact, been a diplomat — along with being Singapore's first high commissioner to India (1967–1969) and ambassador to Nepal (1969–1970), he was the high commissioner to Kuala Lumpur after the 1969 riots. Speaking on the subject of his USS presidential nomination in the book *The Heart Is Where It Is: The NUSS Story*, Professor Baker jokingly describes the society's enigmatic attempt to court him:

> "They [Ernest Wong and Herman Hochstadt] approached me and sounded very mysterious. They said there was a meeting of the Society in Evans Road that evening and would I please come after dinner, they wanted to chat with me. And I went. I found that in my absence I had been elected President of the Society without my consent or knowledge."[6]

Professor Baker agreed to our request to become president but stipulated two conditions — firstly, that he should not be loaded with too much work; and secondly, that he should be flanked by a good number two who would do all the heavy lifting. Only then would he agree to take on the role.

The number two slated to carry that load, the USS decided, would be me. I was honoured to serve with Professor Baker. Under the leadership of our new president, the committee to build the clubhouse was formed, comprising Ernest Wong and myself. We had additional committee members who also joined us during various stages of the construction process: V. V. Giri, our honourable secretary, who secured donations and building materials; my friend Sat Pal Khattar, our honourable treasurer; as well as Anwarul Haque, S. Rajendran, Tay Soo Tee, M. Kishore, Chan Heng Wing and Dr. Philip Chen. More bolstered our ranks that year. As Peter H. L. Lim and Dana Lam smartly put it, we became collectively known as *The Baker's Dozen*.[7]

Hiking the Membership Fee

1981 was the year NUSS "embarked on its ambitious building plans for Kent Ridge".[8] Before that, however, our vision for the new Guild House — as faculties, departments and residence halls began to move[9] — was nevertheless close to failing; Vice-Chancellor Toh Chin Chye remained unconvinced. I sought an appointment with him to win him over to our side. He instructed me to meet with his number two, Reginald Quahe, who told me that there was no space for the clubhouse.

Then, as luck would have it, the government decided to recall Dr. Toh Chin Chye into cabinet. Lee Kuan Yew appointed Dr. Kwan Sai Keong as the new vice-chancellor (1975–1980), who resuscitated our dreams. In response to our request for a piece of property at the new campus, Dr. Kwan asked about our financial situation. I shared with him our plans to raise funds for the project. "We can give you the land, but we can't transfer it," he replied. "We will lease it to you at a nominal rate; then you can raise the money and build the clubhouse yourself."

We found the arrangement suitable. Raising the funds, however, presented the next obstacle. The membership fee for joining NUSS then was a paltry sum — S$15. We knew that with the fee at such a low amount we would never be able to finance a respectable clubhouse. We therefore took two steps to cross this hurdle: we commissioned a model for the clubhouse to bring around our club members; and, in 1981, we proposed a hefty increase in the membership fee from S$15 to S$1,000.

The graduate body practically booed us out of court when they got the news of the proposal. Actually, it had gotten to the point that the members wanted to call a meeting to pass a vote of no confidence against us. Professor Kiang Ai Kim (the head of the Chemistry Department whose research I had written about as a student in 'Campus Notes') recollects that the original budget was S$800,000. But as our ambitions grew, so too did the budget — to nearly S$4,000,000.[10] This is where the model saved us: we used it to explain to the others why the clubhouse would be so costly and how we envisioned the construction proceeding. Fortunately, the model brought the other club members around.

"If you think you can build this by raising the membership fee, we won't stop you," they said. Some skepticism remained, however, that anyone would pay such a princely amount.

Nobody bit at first — the project was too extravagant. We all became a little downhearted, wondering if our project would ever take off. Somebody then bravely suggested, "Why don't we request approval from the alumni body to include a provision that will allow us to further raise the entrance fee in the future, to cover any potential shortfall?"

This was a good move. In 1982, we boldly raised the entrance fee to S$2,000, anticipating that at such rarified pricing, interested parties would view belonging to the club as similar to an elite membership on a limited time offer. As Ernest Wong had noted, given the surge of other highly sought-after club memberships in Singapore at that time, the idea was that interested graduates would seize the opportunity![11]

So we put up some bravado and it worked. We announced that the membership fee would be raised from S$1,000 to S$2,000 and demand skyrocketed. 1,700 people signed up and we raised S$1,700,000 in only three weeks.[12]

In this manner, we successfully collected the amount required and then approached one of DBS's senior officers, Lim Yong Wah, about acquiring interim financing. He was initially hesitant: "The land doesn't belong to you, there is no tenure, and your office bearers get re-elected every year, so there is no permanence. What sort of guarantee can you give me that I will be paid back?" We waxed eloquent, and somehow managed to persuade him.

~

In 1984, the Kent Ridge Guild House opened. The project took nearly eight years to complete from the time the site was offered.[13] In 1994, NUS expanded and upgraded the old Kent Ridge Guild House, and in 2003, a "Project Committee… was formed to spearhead physical development of the Alumni Complex."[14] The book *True Passion: NUSS Fifty Years and On* details the new facilities that would be added: an "enlarged Guild Hall, rooftop tennis courts, new restaurants, outdoor terrace areas and [a] swimming pool."[15] The existing Kent Ridge Guild House, meanwhile, "expanded" to "form part of the complex" during the construction,[16] whose replacement was presented in December 2008.

Today, NUSS has become a fairly wealthy body. The alumni grant scholarships and financial assistance to students. Various academic panels and special events are held at the clubhouse, where I have sometimes been asked to deliver the opening remarks. Until such activities were curtailed by the COVID-19 pandemic, I regularly used to drop in at Café on the Ridge to grab lunch and a drink for old times' sake with friends. Whenever we take guests there, they marvel at how a graduate body could have such a magnificent building!

Chairmanship of NTUC Fairprice

Now for a different kind of "ECA".

One day in the early 1980s when I was at Intraco, Chandra Das approached me on a non-work related matter. He said NTUC would be merging a few of their supermarkets, NTUC Welcome and the Singapore Employees Cooperative (SEC) into one giant supermarket, to be known as NTUC Fairprice.[17*] Although I had never been involved with the trade union movement, Chandra said that they needed a new chairman and asked whether I would be interested in taking the post, adding that the position would be largely voluntary.

"I would be happy to do that," I said, and in May 1983 became the first board chairman of NTUC Fairprice. This was the same day, it so happens, that Mr. Ong Teng Cheong was appointed the secretary general of NTUC.

Merging the two entities presented some challenges; they were different entities with different work cultures. But bringing the two organisations together made NTUC Fairprice, in the long term, more efficient and prosperous. Our goal from the start was to make sure that NTUC Fairprice offered the best prices around. The problem in the 1980s (in which the world had just recently witnessed a recession and "spiralling inflation" caused by the 1973 oil crisis)[18] was that opportunistic merchants with a direct link to importers sometimes manipulated the prices of essential goods.

For many countries in the region, it was not uncommon for merchants to hoard products — such as popular and much needed items, like edible oil — while claiming that they were out of stock. After driving up the prices, they then dumped their goods onto the market. These practices drove up the price of essentials and, for this reason, the government decided it had to intervene and exert control. You can take any economic sector — if the government felt it adversely impacted the lives of the people, it got involved.

~

To deter such profiteers' questionable speculative practices, the government allowed NTUC Fairprice to buy all essential items from the source of those products directly. For instance, for rice, we dispatched

---

* SEC was set up by two other unions, the Singapore Industrial Labour Organisation (SILO) and Pioneer Industries Employees Union (PIEU).

buyers to paddy-producing countries such as Thailand to ensure that the prices we offered were the most attractive on the market. NTUC Fairprice, consequently, became known for putting out products that had both quality and economical pricing — whether for rice, sugar, oil or any other important everyday items.

The government's support of NTUC Fairprice had a beneficial effect on the market and largely helped to end price manipulation. For the first few years, Dr. Tony Tan (who became the seventh president of Singapore) was the chairman of the NTUC Fairprice investment committee. He monitored all the cooperatives and how they performed. I had to present my accounts to him. Once at a meeting, I remember him asking me, "What are your problems?"

"The problem is this," I replied. "How do I show and earn a profit, while maintaining optimum prices?" His answer was significant: no matter what our profit margins, we must not lose sight of our purpose. "Never compromise on your social objective," he said. "This is something we must always keep in mind. You have a daily collection of cash. Count the cash you have collected and you will find that you are profitable."

Maintaining the Social Mission

Just as Dr. Tony Tan advised, we never forgot our social mission, which was to provide access to essential goods at affordable prices to Singaporeans at all ends of the socio-economic ladder. As part of the government's support, NTUC Fairprice would be allotted a unit at the prime site of any Housing and Development Board (HDB) development on the condition that our pricing did not become too prohibitive. We were given HDB shop units at subsidised rates. They were not huge spaces, but enough to give us a leg up over our competitors. An outsider would have had to tender for it.

This had an unfortunate side-effect since there were smaller shopkeepers, in fact, who felt that the lower prices offered by NTUC Fairprice were hurting their business. However, nowadays, depending on one's location, it is possible to find even lower prices being offered

Official opening of NTUC Fairprice Jurong East by Prof. S. Jayakumar and NTUC Fairprice CEO Lim Ho Seng, January 6th, 1989.

by our competitors (some, for instance, argue Sheng Siong offers lower prices). If you reside in an area where property prices and rents are low, your average shopkeeper can also pitch their products attractively. However, this does not affect NTUC Fairprice's business too much, and NTUC Fairprice continues to offer reliable prices and bargains. One might argue that if other supermarkets lower their prices to compete, that would also fulfill our mission, as it equalises the prices of essential goods throughout Singapore: importers become conscious of the competition they face.

I was the chairman of NTUC Fairprice for ten years. As a decennial booklet presented to me by the NTUC Fairprice staff has it, 1984 was our "Year of Store Openings". We opened four branches that year, namely Tampines A, Potong Pasir, Jurong East and Bukit Permei. In 1987, we acquired a freehold property on Upper Thomson Road and, in 1988, officially opened our first Fairprice centre and launched our new corporate logo. By 1993, the 10th anniversary of Fairprice, more than ten branches had opened. Our fixed assets multiplied by ten times as much, and net profits went up by as much as sixteen times.[19] In recognition of our contributions to the community, we were honoured with the PRISM (Public Relations in the Service of Mankind) Award. We were also conferred with accolades for our contributions to national productivity and training.

~

1991 was a memorable year because of the rush on supermarkets sparked by the Gulf War crisis. Buyers were panicking due to rumours that the war had disrupted the supply of essential items. Several merchants (occupants of prime locations) unscrupulously held onto their products, declaring shortages. Conscious of our public duty, we responded by taking a few trucks, filling them with rice and parking them at various car parks. We kept our prices reasonable, to indicate that rice was available and to dispel the shortage illusion artificially created by the traders upselling their products.

NTUC Fairprice Co-operative (1983–1993) was successful because of our great team. Although not all are present in this picture, our team as of 1993 included our Board of Trustees, S. Jayakumar, Hsu Tse Kwang, Oscar Oliveiro, Zulkifli Bin Mohammed, Wong Nang Jang, Ivan C. Baptist, K. Durai, Goh Chee Wee, H. M. Sithawalla, Charlie Phua, Tan Soon Yam, and their Secretary, Lim Ho Seng; our Board of Directors, Chong Kim Chang, Ngiam Tong Tau, Leong Horn Kee, Ronald Ho, Tan Soon Yam, Belinda Teng, John De Payva, Yip Moh Wah, A. Rashid Hussein, Tan Kian Chew, Benedict Kwek, Lew Syn Pau, Annie Loke, and their Secretary Poh Leong Sim; the Executive Director, Lew Syn Pau; and the General Manager, Lim Ho Seng. With the future chairman of NTUC Fairprice, S. Chandra Das.

From a private sector point of view, this kind of market interference is not economically desirable. But to our minds then, we had a social mission to uphold: to ensure that the people did not suffer. If anything ever goes wrong in Singapore, the government is always the first to blame. Some might have complained that those who could have navigated the crisis dithered. We were determined not to stand idle.

The Evolution of NTUC Fairprice

Although some proposed NTUC Fairprice should become a public company, NTUC Fairprice is a co-operative, meaning that shares are traditionally held by the union members and are not openly traded in the market. If a member wants to sell, his option is to sell his shares to the cooperative. The price was not speculative.

Some outsiders argued that by offering NTUC Fairprice shares to the public in an IPO, we could have turned the enterprise into a commercial success. However, I felt NTUC Fairprice should never become a big company that benefited only a select few; NTUC Fairprice's policy was to benefit all its union members. In any event, a number of private-sector publicly listed companies today are successfully competing with NTUC Fairprice.

After I retired as chairman on June 11th, 1993, the group moved ahead to roll out a new brand called "Fairprice Finest", which ventured into more expensive products. With economic prosperity, I suppose that it is perhaps inevitable that some degree of social stratification occurs, leading higher income groups to scout for higher quality items. Consequently, one cannot stop NTUC Fairprice from responding to consumer demands. Indeed, in recent decades — as one byproduct of Singapore's economic success — people have developed an appetite for wines, cheeses, organic foods and the like. By adding luxury goods, the whole bundle of products offered by NTUC Fairprice appears more attractive. Without catering to market tastes, customers would otherwise run to our competitors or across the border to Malaysia to pick up the desired items for themselves.

I was appointed to the Board of Trustees of NTUC Fairprice after I stepped down as chairman. My new duties required me to attended board meetings and provide my inputs. I was also appointed as a director of NTUC Choice Homes, which built ECs (that is, Executive Condominiums), and also a trustee of NTUC Healthcare. These roles, however, were not as time-intensive as when I was the chairman of NTUC Fairprice: the scale of operations was quite different. As chairman of NTUC Fairprice, I was active in formulating decisions with my fellow team members.

Receiving the Meritorious Award from NTUC from then President Ong Teng Cheong in May 1990.

With Mr. Bobby Chin, Chairman of NTUC Fairprice (2014–present), and Mr. S. Chandra Das, Chairman of NTUC Fairprice (1993–2005).

22

Tradition and the Hindu Endowments Board

"Despite my roots and having special ways of relating to my ancestral tradition, however, I have always thought of myself as a Singaporean first, and a member of the Indian, or diasporic community, second."

Identifying as a Singaporean

Along with public service, I have occupied leadership positions of what one might call Indian or South Asian diaspora-related organisations. For instance, I have occupied the post of chairman of the Hindu Advisory Board (HAB); chairman of the Little India Arcade; senior advisor of the Singapore Malayalee Association; chairman of the Advisory Board of the Indian Heritage Centre (IHC) as well as chairman of the Institute of South Asian Studies (ISAS), a semi-autonomous research institute at the National University of Singapore. Despite my roots and having special ways of relating to my ancestral tradition, however, I have always thought of myself as a Singaporean first, and a member of the Indian, or diasporic community, second.

To mark Mr. Lee Kuan Yew stepping down as prime minister in 1992, the Indian community hosted a dinner in his honour on January 16th of that year, and we presented him with a book called *A Place in the Sun* with articles written in Tamil, Hindi and English. In my opening speech, I praised Mr. Lee for establishing meritocracy and multiracialism as the cornerstones of our Singaporean way of life. Much time had passed since we shared the stage when I was president of the USC. Over the intervening decades, I observed how every community, as the title of the book suggests, started to find their unique place in Singapore.

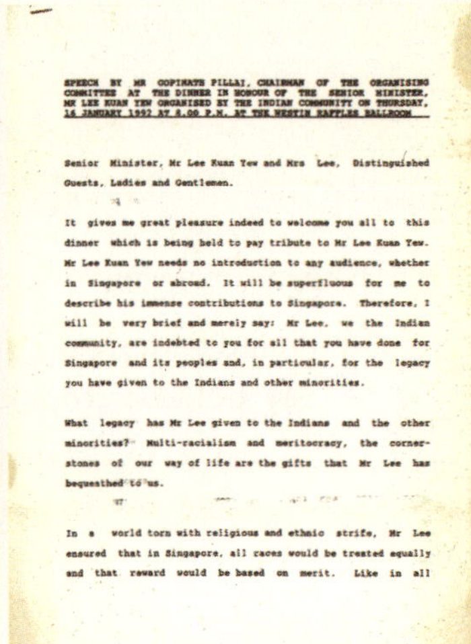

SPEECH BY MR GOPINATH PILLAI, CHAIRMAN OF THE ORGANISING COMMITTEE AT THE DINNER IN HONOUR OF THE SENIOR MINISTER, MR LEE KUAN YEW ORGANISED BY THE INDIAN COMMUNITY ON THURSDAY, 16 JANUARY 1992 AT 8.00 P.M. AT THE WESTIN RAFFLES BALLROOM

Senior Minister, Mr Lee Kuan Yew and Mrs Lee, Distinguished Guests, Ladies and Gentlemen.

It gives me great pleasure indeed to welcome you all to this dinner which is being held to pay tribute to Mr Lee Kuan Yew. Mr Lee Kuan Yew needs no introduction to any audience, whether in Singapore or abroad. It will be superfluous for me to describe his immense contributions to Singapore. Therefore, I will be very brief and merely say: Mr Lee, we the Indian community, are indebted to you for all that you have done for Singapore and its peoples and, in particular, for the legacy you have given to the Indians and other minorities.

What legacy has Mr Lee given to the Indians and the other minorities? Multi-racialism and meritocracy, the corner-stones of our way of life are the gifts that Mr Lee has bequeathed to us.

In a world torn with religious and ethnic strife, Mr Lee ensured that in Singapore, all races would be treated equally and that reward would be based on merit. Like in all

Delivering speech in farewell to Lee Kuan Yew when he stepped down as prime minister, January 1992. The book *A Place in the Sun* was launched on the same day.

I believe that multi-racialism and meritocracy are the twin ideals towards which Singapore should strive. The impartial attitude taken by the government has been a deciding factor for many in realising this Singaporean dream — where everyone would be treated equally and reward would be based on merit. In my view, the government implemented policies that rightly prioritised capability over other markers, such as skin colour, or, for that matter, birthplace or religious background.

In recent years, "identity" has featured strongly in global political trends. Although I may be criticised for saying so, I do not believe identity weighs so heavily on people's minds from day to day. That being said, facts of life must be faced and, inevitably, some individuals will prioritise certain forms of identification over others. Some individuals, for example, could give undue precedence to race, which, in its more intense manifestations, can create — if not necessarily anything as drastic as discrimination — at least a sense of asymmetry, in which differences supersede commonalities. Such asymmetry, I believe, should be prevented at all costs, and everyone should be treated fairly. People who are rational and have absorbed the lessons of history recognise that we must create an inclusive society that takes differences as part of our common social fabric — differences that distinguish without being divisive.

I was born into a family that honoured its long-standing traditions. But I would say, so far as it concerns my life, that I do not advocate for any one worldview or spirituality so much as try to follow a life path that acknowledges difference as intrinsic to the world and accepts the fundamentality of change. To provide one personal example, everyday, at the crack of dawn, I chant a prayer before I do anything else, beseeching for a mind better equipped to understand the complexities of the world.

My beliefs, from the teachings of my father and my own life experiences, are such that we should never sideline others or make them feel any less important because they might belong to a community separate or different in size from our own. Demographically, the Chinese are Singapore's largest group. Ever since making Chinese friends at Choon Guan Presbyterian School, I have also felt a mutual understanding between the majority and minority communities is essential.

As regards my own relationship with the Hindu organisations, I cannot honestly say that I was ever too active during my schools days or adolescence — with maybe the one exception during my USC membership when I had asked my friend whether my belief in God disqualified me from Marxism. But I will narrate just a few episodes demonstrating some significant lessons my father taught me.

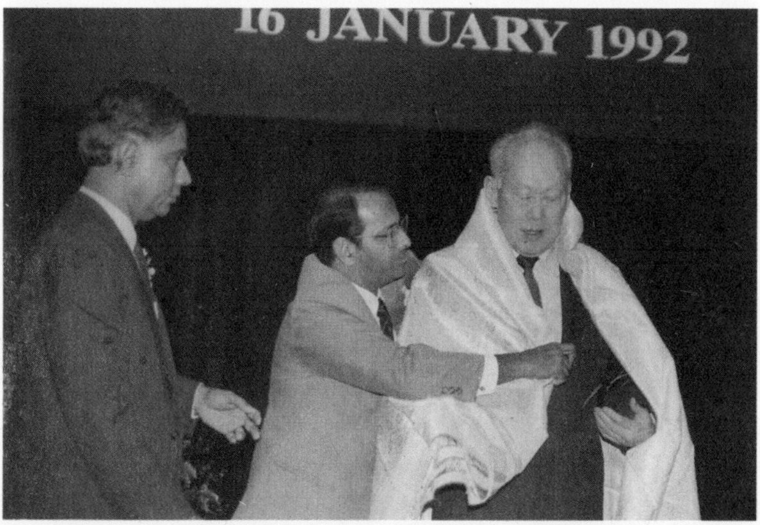

With Haider Sithawalla presenting a shawl of honour to Lee Kuan Yew.

~

At Choon Guan, one group that I had always desperately wanted to join was the Boy's Brigade — I thought that they looked very smart in their dark uniforms. The brigade was open to primary and secondary school boys. One day, I decided to approach the teacher in charge to ask if I could become a member. They would be delighted to have me, she said, but I had to be Christian. I thought, no big deal. "I will speak to my father."

But my father's answer shocked me. "No, you can change your religion when you are old enough to understand what that means. For now, you are just a schoolboy. God may have some purpose in having you be born Hindu — by our belief, he does — and I do not want to decide now just because you want to wear a uniform."

I was disappointed by this answer, but accepted my father's judgment.

Years later, a similar incident took place while I was at St. Andrew's Secondary School. We had a weekly assembly for prayers, hymns and bible stories. Canon Chelliah ("canon" means priest in the Anglican faith) conducted the assembly and explained to us the morals underlying certain Biblical parables. One week, I heard that the Malay students had been exempted from attending the assembly; noticing the Malay boys ducking out, I thought I should try my luck and see if I too could get an afternoon off.

I picked up my books and went looking for Canon Chelliah. When I found him, I put him on notice that instead of attending the weekly assembly he could find me reading in the library. Canon Chelliah, who was no fool, regarded me thoughtfully. "You've thought hard about this?"

"Yes. A lot of the Malay students are in study hall at this time. I think I can join them too."

"All right," he said. "Why don't you go home and ask your father to write me a permission letter?" The assembly was about an hour long, and I recalled how my father was always encouraging me to read. I thought convincing him would be a piece of cake.

"They're wasting time talking about St. Thomas," I explained to him when I came home, "which is not relevant to us. Probably better that I read a few books."

"Will this one hour a week upset your routine?" he prodded.

"Not upset, exactly. But it would be good to have extra time to do certain things."

"Well, it is also good to spend time thinking about God."

"But this is a Christian ceremony. It doesn't apply to us, because we're Hindu — so what does it matter?" I was surprised by the turn of events. I had been certain that he would say no problem, just carry on and play football.

"Can you give me the letter?" I repeated.

"No, certainly not," he maintained. "If you love reading so much, you can read about religion with the other students." He highlighted that there was no difference between "our" prayers and "theirs". Since in his opinion the traffic of prayers travelled in one direction, I could also recite Christian prayers. Being Hindu or Christian did not get in the way of God being able to hear them.

"You pray as you prefer to." He, however, cautioned that I should not sing or chant so loudly that I disturbed others.

I was puzzled by this seeming transformation in my father's stance. My first thought was that sometime when I was not looking he had turned into a different person! When I asked about this about-face, he said I was missing the point. "Taking a principled stand on the basis of religion at the age of eleven is a different matter from choosing not to attend an assembly. That is why I will not write the letter."

After absorbing his response, I steered away from Canon Chelliah for the next few days at school. I felt embarrassed since the prospect of a free afternoon had got me very excited. Then one day he caught me in the corridor. "Gopinath," he called softly, "Have you got the reply from your father?" I mumbled I had. "Would you like to come and discuss it?"

"Nothing much to discuss," I said. "My father said I should attend the assembly."

He smiled. "Your father is a wise man. You should appreciate that."

I had nothing to say — just then I was not appreciating too much of anything.

It had been difficult obeying my father. But as I matured, I began to understand that one's tradition is not something to be traded in exchange for an object of desire, and that it can also be flexible and did not preclude one from taking part in the ceremonies of others. Parental guidance, I learned from these episodes, is very important.

Nomination to the Hindu Endowments Board

In my adult life, I have observed that I have inherited some of my grandfather's fatalism. My life-long stance has been never to question the universe. If a task is set before me, I generally proceed to do it. One of Shakey's employees in America, in fact, had written a gracious letter conveying a similar opinion. He mentioned that if anything came my way, I did not complain but took it in my stride.

Once, however, I almost turned down an opportunity to participate more actively in the Indian community. In 1982, I received a call from the acting permanent secretary of the Ministry of Finance, Mr. Francis D'Costa. Francis informed me that a position on the Hindu Endowments Board (HEB) had opened, and that I was being nominated to fill the position. "Gopi," Francis said. "We are appointing you."

The Singapore Hindu organisations (the HEB and the HAB) oversee various temples — the Sri Mariamman Temple, Sri Srinivasa Perumal Temple, Sri Sivan Temple and Sri Vairavimada Kaliamman Temple. According to the HEB's official website, the HEB was established under the Hindu Endowments Act in 1968 and looks after any "endowment" placed under it — whether land, construction or temple patronage.[1] The HEB today also manages a half-way house and organises Hindu festivals. It is also involved in community service, such as inter-faith activities, health counselling and educational support for underprivileged children.

When I first heard about the nomination, however, the HEB was a different place; the Indian community in the 1980s was known for being a little quarrel shop, generating petty arguments that delayed decision-making and forward-moving action. My instinctive reaction was to say no — the HEB would be too time consuming, and I was anyway feeling slightly cautious. I said that I worshipped as a private matter but otherwise was not too greatly interested to take part.

Francis warned that if all corporate leaders kept shunning the organisation, it could backslide. I should therefore think over the matter carefully. He then shared a confidential piece of news: the government was examining the body and was likely to appoint a senior ex-civil servant to head the HEB. He said that this senior ex-civil servant had even suggested my name for membership. This revelation intrigued me: who was this person? I thought it over, and said I could join for maybe a year.

They revamped the board. The new chairman was S. R. Nathan, who would in 1999 become the sixth president of Singapore.

Family and Friends

I often tell my friends, "If you have a good, strong leader who is not biased but fair, and can deliver on work, then people will rally around him." Mr. Nathan was one such leader.

I had an earlier acquaintance with Mr. Nathan. S. R. Nathan was my father's boss at the Asian Seamen's Club. My father, thanks to his experience at the Adelphi Hotel, knew how such outfits were run, and was hired to lend his expertise. This eased our financial difficulties in the mid-1950s considerably. In 1956, S. R. Nathan was appointed the first Asian seaman's welfare officer. He was later seconded to the Labour Research Unit as assistant director before becoming director.[2] My father reported to Mr. Nathan and the Asian Seamen's Club board.

Mr. Nathan supported the government in the 1960s when the leadership of the Labour Union split up and left the Liberal socialists and Leftist socialists at loggerheads. As a result of Operation Coldstore, some in the Leftist faction had gone to jail. He used to joke that he could gauge the weather quite accurately. He still visited some of these Leftist faction members in prison, though he was careful about whom he met; he wanted to ensure that they were well-treated and were not uncomfortable. As a leader, he was quite conscientious and came to his own conclusions after listening to arguments worth hearing.

In 1983, he set about energetically reorganising the HEB; he was pleased I was so active. Many times, he rang me to pick my brain about some matter or the other. Even when he became president, I would once in a while receive an informal call from him to drop in at his office to say hello.

S. R. Nathan passed away following a stroke in 2016. I was one of the eulogists, the final speaker, at his memorial service. I represented the family and friends. What epitomised S. R. Nathan for me was the firm positions he took on matters which he felt to be morally right or wrong. He was not, in fact, very happy about certain religious practices at the Hindu temples, and felt more enlightened alternatives were needed to keep the congregation informed about what was happening in the world.

Although Mr. Nathan had his quibbles (he refers in his memoirs to "complaints from community elders, whose only claim to expert knowledge … was based on hearsay" and "advice [which] varied from individual to individual, depending on their whims and fancies"),[3] he was nevertheless quite sure our job was not to rewrite the religion.

All practices should be left as they are, he argued, unless they

Indian Community Dinner for President S. R. Nathan, April 2000
(S. Chandra Das on the left).

brought some harm to the people. He was adamant on the last. The most serious matter he emphasised on was that nothing should be done to foster animosity between the communities. I found this to be a rational approach.

In joining the HEB, I myself had no set agenda. But there were a couple of factors informing my involvement. I am spiritual in a sense, even if my understanding of God is slightly secular. I was also becoming concerned that perhaps not many highly educated people were being drawn to Hinduism. More often (as can be the case with other traditions) I saw hardcore people with very rigid views — the kind who believe in perpetuating and adhering to rituals above all else and dismissing others' beliefs.

Yet Hinduism is a complex tradition, whose teachings can at times be difficult to understand (I had mentioned my grandfather's elaborations on the *Mahabharata* when I was a boy). I felt it needed to attract followers who appreciated the nuances of its myths and rituals. My HEB membership, therefore, presented a chance to live by example of what I viewed to be a "Hindu way of life". Or, more accurately, a path to tolerance and a greater acceptance of differing worldviews.

For administration, S. R. Nathan brought in a sharp finance person, Mr. V. R. Nathan. (He had been a banking executive before overseeing the temples.)[4] Thanks to his diligence and competence, the Hindu organisations — according to Madam Yu Foo Yee Shoon, then Minister of State of the Ministry of Community Development, Youth and Sports, and a person with whom I consulted often — were said to have the most efficient accounting division of all the cultural bodies in Singapore. There were no scandals, which we strove to prevent from tarnishing the good name of the community.

S. R. Nathan served as the chairman of the HEB from 1983 to 1988 and also made key decisions pertaining to the establishment of the Singapore Indian Development Association (SINDA). Later, when he stepped down, V. R. Nathan (conferred in 1986 with the Public Service Medal) took over. I was nominated as chairman of the Hindu Advisory Board in 1990.

Accountability and Discipline

The HAB's job was to advise the government on relevant matters pertaining to Singapore's Hindu community. I worked side by side with V. R. Nathan for many years. He was a religious man and kind soul who attended most of the ceremonies. Aside from advising the government on Hinduism-related issues, we also oversaw the important function of distributing work permits for temple functionaries. (This was the only area that carried some teeth, as it empowered the Board to exercise a relative degree of discipline over the temples and those outside of the HAB's jurisdiction.)

The temples had to submit an application to the HAB to recruit priests or any other temple employees. I made it a point to ask for their balance sheets whenever they applied. We scrutinised the temples' accounts, deciding on how many permits to grant depending on their congregation size, sometimes providing advice on their accounts.

The balance sheets also had a secondary function, which was to assess the movement of cash. Some temples receive large donations and can be quite rich. This practice enabled us to keep the temple finances under control and prevented damaging scandals from emerging. Occasionally, the temples attracted unconventional characters.

One way that we tried to lead by example was by setting up a disciplinary sub-committee. Previously, we had a disciplinary sub-committee that penalised only the priests upon discovery of wrongdoing. On one occasion, we received allegations of abuse by a priest from one of the older temples that was not under the HAB's jurisdiction. Several devotees had approached the Board to ask if we could get involved. I was cautious about acting on it at first and said that we would monitor the situation. Then the accused was caught red-handed in an unsavoury act, and we packed him off.

We tried not to humiliate him or make a big song and dance out of it. We simply distanced him from offices of responsibility, such as the handling of funds in the temple and administrative tasks. However, he was allowed to come and pray as he liked. He resigned; I think he emigrated from Singapore.

I had also observed that the devotees of the temples could also be unexpectedly brusque at times towards the priests. Many pundits had just come from India and could be a bit doe-eyed regarding the ways of Singapore's city life. There were a few episodes in which the devotees spoke to them rudely, which called for our intervention and my cautioning them to behave. Finally, I went to speak with V. R. Nathan on the subject to persuade him that we should take action. "It's not just the priests — the devotees should come under the purview of the disciplinary sub-committee too," I told him.

Changing Traditions

In an interview I gave in 2011, I was asked about problems facing Singapore's Hindu community.[5] I mentioned how our lifestyles in the 21st century have changed, making it more difficult for children and parents to keep up traditional Hindu practices.

The established practices involved rising early in the morning, having a bath, saying one's prayers and in the evening visiting the temple for *puja*. I remember in Thrissur, where our family "tharavad" (ancestral home) was based, we would visit temples often. In Engadiyoor, my grandfather's village, temple going was less frequent. But every house had a little temple outside of it.[6] In the busy world in which we live today, modern life has made observing these practices more difficult. One instead rushes to get ready to leave for work, wolfs down one's breakfast, boards the bus or train to school or the office and rapidly becomes absorbed in the pressing duties of the day. The emphasis on prayer in the house is probably no longer as prevalent as it once was.

Amidst these constraints, some households remain steadfast in attending temples in the evening while others like my family only attend special functions. What, I wonder, do young people see during their temple visits? A lot of rituals, maybe. While they may impress some, to others the reasons for these rituals are obscure, since they have not been adequately explained. During special celebrations of a particular deity, for instance, it might not be entirely unexpected if a young person asked himself, "What is this fairy tale? What substance is there to it?" and became disillusioned. Not enough effort, I think, has been made to explain Hinduism.

When I was the chairman of HAB, I recognised that we did not have a good way of communicating to our congregation. Although we spent a lot of money renovating temples every twelve years or so, I began to think our expenditures could be more wisely considered, and brought up to the Board whether we could try to organise a programme around a few good speakers. "Why don't we get somebody to talk at the Mariamman Temple on Fridays?"

Friday is a special day for the female deity, Amman; it draws a big crowd and elicits high levels of participation, especially amongst women. The speakers would have to converse in Tamil because most of the congregation were Tamil speaking housewives. Next was the question of how to time the address. We decided that we would host the speakers after the prayers ended when everyone usually headed home after collecting their *prasadam* (sacred food). They would first have to wait and listen to the speakers.

I cannot declare the experiment a complete success. The devotees listened halfheartedly to the speakers and waited for them to finish so that they could pick up their *prasadam* and go home (I suppose this is only natural). My ongoing concern nevertheless remains that there is no concerted effort to energise the tradition. Increasingly, people are gravitating towards more accessible forms of worship. Perhaps we could also try to recruit inspiring speakers to engage the congregation on relevant, contemporary themes that the devotees understand, to keep them abreast of our changing times. Parents' free time is diminishing; but perhaps more attention could be dedicated to the interests of the young people and on sharing wisdom that can be applied to modern life.

23

Community Contributions and the Indian Heritage Centre

"The IHC has become a national monument operating under the aegis of the National Heritage Board (NHB), which oversees all the country's museums and art galleries... This is excellent because the NHB holds a high standard for all the organisations under it. For a small community like ours to be recognised in such a magnanimous manner by the political leadership, and to be allowed to examine the past and project it collectively and cohesively for times to come, is really quite significant."

Rebuilding the Little India Arcade

In addition to overseeing several temples, the HEB oversees a large shopping area called the Little India Arcade, which stands at the intersection of Selegie Road and Serangoon Road. Many of Indian descent run stores and restaurants there, preparing traditional, ethnic cuisine from all across India. The Little Indian Arcade is bustling: even when the rest of Singapore slows down economically, this place moves.

Little India was a congregation point for many Indians arriving in Singapore in the 19th and 20th centuries. As documented by Ms. Malvika Agarwal, they used the land for cattle trade and dairy farming.[1] Later, vendors and traditional tradesmen settled in the area after the swamps were drained. The increase in the size of the population had convinced colonial administrators to provide public infrastructure, whereupon shophouses sprung up for vendors, tradesmen and their families.[2] The name "Little India", however, was actually not given to the area until the 1980s when the Singapore Tourist Promotion Board made an "effort ... to promote the preservation and celebration of Singapore's ethnic quarters".[3]

After I joined the HEB in 1983, we noticed that shops in the Little India Arcade were yielding low rental income. Rent control on the premises blocked us from raising the rent for the tenants who had been living there for decades. To change the rent, the government required significant renovations. Meanwhile, some tenants sub-let their rooms to as many as three or four sub-tenants at higher rates than what we charged them. While they paid us peanuts and profited, we as the owners saw little benefit.[4]

I requested permission from the government to rebuild the Arcade, explaining that we would do over the insides and attract a new batch of tenants who would pay fair rental rates. The government did not ask for expensive renovations but required the refurbishments to be efficiently done, with one main condition: avoid touching or damaging the façade to protect this symbol of our community's heritage.

We agreed to all the government's conditions. But the HEB had no money. Where were we to obtain funding? "Why don't we ask DBS to partner with us?" I proposed. "We have the land. They will bring in the cash for the construction." DBS, after a few lengthy discussions, was persuaded to partner with us as an investor. They would take around 40 percent of the enterprise while we took 60 percent.

I cleared all of this with the Indian community political leaders and other prominent figures who needed to be consulted. But one group was upset with the plan. They felt that partnering with DBS was unwise — from a place of community loyalty, they believed that once we partnered with such a large and powerful company, we risked losing ownership of the land to outside interests. They argued that DBS would ask us to pay our share when further renovations were required. If we could not put down the money, we might find our control diluted.

The intentions of this group were well meaning. But the Little India Arcade had become a shabby building, and I feared it might remain an eyesore for prospective tenants and visitors. Furthermore, it was generating little income for the HEB. Although we could not touch the façade, we could still do wonderful things inside! And so, despite some chastisements I received for partnering with DBS, I was given the green light. I also cautiously inserted special clauses to safeguard our interests; for example, I stipulated that we had the right to buy back the property and raise money from others should the need arise.

May 1937 photo of Jawaharlal Nehru and Indira Gandhi's first visit to Singapore. The photo was taken with members of The Ladies Union, where Pandit Nehru and Ms. Gandhi motivated them to develop "self-reliance, character and beauty". To the far left, Malathi Pillai, pregnant with me. Next to her is Mrs. Ramamani Subrahmanyam, honoured with garlanding special visitors. *(Collection of Indra Iswaran d/o ES Muthu and Lavan Iswaran.)*

Incidentally, the Little India area intersects with my personal family history. During former Indian Prime Minister Jawaharlal Nehru's visit to Singapore in 1937, he was received by the Indian women's group and visited this Indian populated area not far from the Arcade. My mother was heavily pregnant with me at the time. Nehru was driven from the airport to the site of his speaking engagement. On the way to the speaking site, however, there was an accident en route. When Nehru reached and was sitting at the podium, he inquired considerately, "What happened to the lady who was pregnant? Did the accident have an adverse effect on her?" He asked for his *aide de camp* to go and check on how she was doing. "Are you all right, Madam?" the man asked my mother. "Mr. Nehru wants to know." She was touched such an esteemed, high-ranking figure would be so concerned by her mishap.

A Helpful American Architect

DBS employed an American architect who helped us to refurbish the Arcade. He was an ingenious person, fascinated by the possibilities for the building. Keen to eliminate wasted space, he advised us to seek permission from the government to use the two blocks behind it. These lanes were lying unused aside from drains and toilets — a vestige of earlier days when trucks collected the night soil.

The Singapore government does not give anything away for free; but they judiciously considered our proposal and explained that if the design was approved, they would let us blend it in. It was a sizeable chunk that we got. The Public Works Department was impressed with the American's design and developed a respect for us, observing that our requests were well thought through.

With the design approved and funds in hand, we rebuilt the Little India Arcade. My detractors boycotted the grand opening. Around six months after the Arcade re-opened, DBS approached me after the investment side of their operations underwent a restructuring (I seem to recall there was a merger of different companies and that DBS Land had been reconstituted). The new person-in-charge requested an appointment with me to chat about the remodelled building.

"Mr Pillai, we have a proposition," the bank officer said. "The Little India Arcade is small. We usually go for bigger pieces of land. But it is a good building, and easily saleable. Can you buy it back from us? We will give you a reasonable price, so that you can own it 100 percent." He added that if we did not want it, they would sell it for more than their original investment. Meanwhile, we would have first preference.

Thank goodness I had insisted on inserting those special clauses in our agreement with DBS: they actually required the bank to do this! The question of funding arose again but was soon settled when it was proposed that DBS could finance the purchase. I then announced to my shareholders the prospect of borrowing from DBS and becoming the Little India Arcade's sole owners.

With DBS's help and HEB's earnings from the temples and similar activities, we successfully transferred the debt to the HEB. Not long after,

A gift presented to me for the service rendered to Hindu Endowments Board and Hindu Advisory Board, May 29th, 1999 by then Minister of Community Development, Abdullah Tarmugi.

Sat Pal Khattar, the chairman of the Little India Arcade, retired from his position and I took over as chairman. I held the office for many years and stepped down on June 30th, 2018.

The Hindu organisations, as I saw it, had achieved their mission: the Hindu community owned a prime property in Little India; and thanks to V. R. Nathan's better management, we successfully secured two other small properties — one near the Chinatown Area and another not too far from the Sri Mariamman Temple. I am happy with the HAB and HEB's evolution; they became serious organisations, and today are guided by board members of sterling quality. I was honoured to be a part of the team under V. R. Nathan's leadership and to serve alongside many hard working people within the community committed to doing what was necessary.

Social Work with "The Community"

The achievements of Singapore's Indian community — which is only around 9.2 percent of the total population — are really quite significant. I have always approached the Indian community, or rather, the broader

South Asian diaspora, from this perspective. For me, Singapore's story parallels the story of meritocracy: if you are prepared to do the work and see how things can be done, you should do well. Both the community and I have directly benefitted from this.

Since Indians first started arriving to Singapore in the 19th century, they have made multifaceted contributions to Singapore's civic, cultural and professional life. As Ms. Shobha Tsering Bhalla writes in the introduction to a published interview I did for the Diaspora Dialogues in 2013, many lawyers and the heads of central banks are of Indian origin; these include "at least two past presidents of the prestigious Law Society of Singapore". Their diplomatic and bureaucratic service is also commendable; Bhalla writes that the Malayalee community, in particular, which numbers around 40,000, has "punched far beyond its weight in the development of the country".[5] To this, one could add the contributions of the Tamils, the Bengalis, the Maharashtrians, the Punjabis, the Telegus and the Hindi-speakers from Bihar, U.P., Madhya Pradesh, Rajasthan and other Indian states.

But the Indian community in Singapore, in some respects, can also be polarised — not necessarily in terms of linguistic or state origin but in terms of income. Although I have no official statistics to this effect, Rajesh Rai, a professor of Diaspora Studies at the National University of Singapore, states in the context of demographic change that "[t]here exists a general perception that the disproportionate increase in the education profile and income are largely the products of relatively recent immigration, and that comparatively long-term residents and their children have not fared as well."[6] Speaking in 2016 for an article in *Scroll.in* on the frictions between old and new arrivals, this same scholar reportedly notes that of Singapore's ethnic communities, income inequality amongst the Indians can be the highest.[7]

Indeed, the economic growth of Singapore's Indian community has not followed a straightforward line; and mobility between the lower and higher income earning groups, for social reasons and other factors, is not always fluid. Migrants of the generation of my parents and older, to provide one example, had largely shared a common background and the goal of improving their lot. The relative affluence of the Indian community was later buoyed by the country's economic growth in the 1970s and 1980s.[8] As I have stated elsewhere, I believe enhanced education and training in modern technologies will propel the prospects of the next generation.[9] Beginning in the 1990s, we also witnessed the arrival of a new cohort of Indians filling professional, technical and managerial posts in the fields of IT, banking and finance.

The Malayalam-speaking group have, along with the Singapore Indian Development Association (SINDA) (created, in part, to shore up a declining interest amongst Indian students in science and mathematics in the 1990s),[10] made important strides to level inequalities. Ms. Anitha Pillai reports that the Singapore Malayalee Association (SMA), started in 1917 as the Kerala Mahajana Sangham, is one of the country's oldest registered associations, and is hailed as the first Malayalee Association outside of India.[11] Further, since its founding, the group has gone out of its way to support the underprivileged and low-income families by providing children with a good education.[12] To provide an example, in 2016, Singapore's Malayalee community raised S$500,000 for bursaries for needy students at NUS.

The Indian organisations and groups have hosted additional social-based programmes and events that celebrate the community's diversity and engage other segments of the Singapore population.[13] Onam, the Malayalees' most important festival, has offered occasion for such social-based programmes. Referring again to Anitha Pillai's article 'SMA is 100' in *Tabla*, the Malayalee Association commemorated Onam in 1918 by offering meals to the poor and homeless at the end of WWI.[14] Onam is conventionally celebrated in Kerala in August or September each year — traditionally, all communities are welcomed to participate. Although it is a Hindu festival, the Muslims, Syrian Christians and Roman Catholics often attend. We have sought to bring a similar spirit to Singapore by inviting our Chinese and Malay friends to our meals as well as by honouring Singapore's senior leaders who have empowered the less fortunate.

A Friend of Computers

Our chief guest at the Onam Celebration Dinner on September 20th, 1998 was Deputy Prime Minister Lee Hsien Loong. We had wanted to do something special to honour the occasion of his attendance. I felt that, as Keralites had a keen interest in education, we should do something related to modern education or training.

Singapore in the 1990s saw people using computers for work, but many from the lower income group in the Singapore Indian community did not have their own computers at home (the home being where children develop an early affinity to technology). I proposed, "Why don't we roll out a programme to put a computer in every household?" IT knowledge was becoming indispensable for getting ahead at school and in the workplace. Technological awareness in needy households was not widespread at that point, and we feared that those without at least basic computer skills would run the risk of being marginalised.

I had seen that many companies tended to replace their computers after three or four years. We thought, "Why don't we try to refurbish these discarded computers and give them to those in need at a nominal price?" Unless one places at least a minimal value on things, human psychology is such that people do not value it. Next, we wrote to then DPM Lee to ask whether he would be supportive of the venture. If so, we would launch the initiative at the dinner that we were planning.

Happily, DPM Lee accepted — the government, he said, had also started developing programmes to encourage children to use computers at a young age. He said that people who could not afford them should certainly receive access.

We thus organised ourselves and registered an IT Co-operative. We set about trying to convince people to donate their used computers, which we would refurbish and make available with a little added pomp and ceremony. "Putting a PC in Every Indian Home" — to improve IT literacy rates and motivate some to aspire for better jobs — became our slogan.[15]

The project started off well. The proceeds from the 1998 Onam Celebration Dinner were used for refurbishing these used computers.

With DPM Lee at the Onam Celebration, September 20th, 1998.

The initiative became big news. But big success carries unknown pitfalls, because within a short period — only a few months after announcing the scheme — the Malay community decided to launch a similar programme. Then the Chinese community launched one too. People were now lining up outside of established companies to ask whether they had any old, used computers lying around that they could take away. This became embarrassing for us, as the supply of used computers was rapidly disappearing.

A computer programme was then finally announced at the highest levels: the government declared that it would also be making available low priced, new computers of decent quality to school children. Suddenly, our mission was gone! Although we were pleased with the result — with new, better computers coming straight from the government — there was not much left for us to do.

In an attempt to keep the mission alive, we rolled out tuition classes on IT training; but these did not generate much interest, because many such classes already saturated the market. I went to see the patron of our committee, Minister S. Dhanabalan, explaining, "We have accomplished our ambition, but have run out of computers to carry on." Minister Dhanabalan is one of the Indian political leaders who has dedicated significant time and energy to developing the Indian community. He said well done, you have achieved your goal: you can close shop and go home.

Generally, it is advisable not to start on another project unless you have an equally good idea to replace it. So we held a number of consultations with our members. Some were disappointed because the programme had had such a short life span. Meanwhile, we had a couple hundred dollars in reserve from our collections. I asked the board of the IT Co-operative what we should do with it. The Board told us that we should return it to the members. They added that because it was such a small amount, however, it might not be worth returning.

The IT Co-operative board instructed us to hold onto the funds for one or two years to ensure there were no claimants. If nobody claimed their money within that period, we had permission to give it to charity. We donated the remainder to the Sri Narayana Mission, one of the successful old folks' homes in Singapore set up by the Malayalee community. In the end, over 1,000 refurbished computers were distributed and, through the training classes that we offered jointly through the IT Co-operative and SINDA, we trained more than 2,000 people.[16]

That was that, except for one last thing. Because of this initiative that we had started, the Computer Association of Singapore bestowed me with an unexpected honour: "The Friend of Information Technology Award." My family regularly tease me about it, knowing that I am not particularly IT-savvy.

Indian Heritage Centre

In the preface to *50 Years of the Indian Community in Singapore*, I wrote that "[p]erhaps the most important single event from [2015] was the building of the Indian Heritage Centre (IHC) in the heart of Little India."[17] The IHC was founded to trace the history, progress and achievements of the Indian community and South Asian diaspora in Southeast Asia. It also serves as a node for the local Indian community as well as an attractive destination point for visitors keen to learn more about the history of the Singapore Indian community, from the pre-colonial era to Singapore's unfolding saga of nation-building.[18]

The kernel idea for the centre sprouted within the Indian community. It was a ground-up initiative, and in the early 2000s we decided to act on our wish to commemorate community heritage. The concept for the centre, we decided early on, would be derived by mutual consensus. We tacitly hoped that the government would help us by allocating a piece of land on which we could build, or through other financial assistance. But originally, the plan was to fundraise within the community itself.

We started by looking for a piece of land for the construction. Several community leaders, meanwhile, had approached political leaders from the Indian community to indicate that raising funds for a project on such a grand scale would be onerous. They asked whether the government would perhaps be willing to assist with financial support for the construction. The politicians pondered on this request. Lee Kuan Yew took the final decision, and argued that the IHC would become a legacy not only for the Indian community in Singapore but also for the whole country. By providing financial support to each of the major ethnic communities, he believed that such heritage centres could become national assets; the government would pave the way with funding and research.

This was a groundbreaking decision. With the meagre funds that we had at our disposal, constructing a respectable centre would have been very difficult — it might also have come across as a paltry affair. But now, we could flesh out our vision into a monument of substance, which would draw international attention and become a symbol of community pride. It is said that the IHC is the first institution dedicated to the heritage of Indians migrants in Southeast Asia.

How I Got Involved

Responsibility for the construction of the centre was placed in the capable hands of Dr. Balaji Sadasivan, a cultured and capable neurosurgeon who also served as Senior Minister of State, Ministry of Foreign Affairs. In addition to serving as the chairman of the IHC Steering Committee, he served as the executive president of SINDA and occupied important roles as president of the India Education Trust, member of the National

Steering Committee on Racial and Religious Harmony and advisor to the Indian Activity Executive Committee Council, amongst others.[19]

As a senior community member, I was recruited to lead one of the IHC's sub-committees. Three sub-committees fell under the IHC Steering Committee, whose job was to oversee the project's implementation. These comprised the Building and Construction Committee, which was tasked with looking after the building's structure, design and timeline (led by Mr. R. Jayachandran, the Hindu Endowment Board's current chairman); the Fundraising Committee, which was led by S. Chandra Das; and the Concept and Content Committee that was headed by me, with Mr. K. Kesavapany as its deputy chairman.[20]

Dr. Balaji felt content curation was the role best suited for me, as this area was closest to my interests. My committee had a heavy responsibility, in that we had to come up with the centre's unifying theme and designate what would be placed in the stalls. The sub-committees proceeded according to our grants and we submitted our reports to the Steering Committee, sometimes even to the PM.

Dr. Balaji, who commanded the driver's seat, specifically requested that I meet with all the Indian organisations (there are over fifty), as he was keen that we should engage the entire community. He said if the members of these organisations had any relics or oral history that they wanted to share, I should explore how such memorabilia could be accommodated. My deputy chairman, committee members and I tried to meet all interested parties and to honour their contributions.

Accordingly, we spent quite a few Saturday afternoons meeting with the organisations and their members. What is most remarkable about this process is that we must have met with almost every veteran community member, speaking for a couple hours with each person. Our interviewees recalled what they had seen and experienced in Singapore. I think the interviews went on like this for several months.

We succeeded in collecting many fascinating documents, artefacts and heirlooms for the centre. We found a letter, for instance, someone had written to Swami Vivekanananda, an Indian monk credited with elevating Hinduism's status as a major world religion; he also founded the Sree Ramakrishna Mission. From Singapore's Hindi Society, I seem to remember we collected early letters. In her comprehensive essay on the foundation of the centre, the director of the IHC, Dr. Gauri Parimoo Krishnan, lists such illustrious items as bronze bust statues of Indian nationalist leaders as well as a copy of the Proclamation of Azad Hind made in Singapore on October 21st, 1943.[21] S. R. Nathan, from his own possessions, donated several wartime documents including an issue of *The Orient Weekly*, with a front cover illustration of Subhas Chandra Bose — proof that the regional Indian community had participated in the Indian National Army.[22]

Sadly, the person who had conceptualised and pushed the IHC through to its fruition with depth and sincerity was not there to witness its opening in 2015. Following a battle with cancer, Dr. Balaji passed away in September 2010. S. Iswaran, then Second Minister for Home Affairs and Trade and Industry, took over from Dr. Balaji as Chairman of the Steering Committee in 2010 and subsequently guided the rest of the construction. He is the centre's head today. The wife of the late Dr. Balaji, Dr. Ma Swan Hoo, who assisted Dr. Balaji with his book on Indian history, *The Dancing Girl*, also serves on the IHC board.

The New Building

The IHC has become a national monument operating under the aegis of the National Heritage Board (NHB), which oversees all the country's museums and art galleries. In 2009, a Memoranda of Understanding was signed with the NHB, which, as Dr. Gauri Krishnan cites in her essay, is there to "provide its management and professional expertise ... in such areas as operations, curatorial support, programming and marketing."[23] This is excellent because the NHB holds a high standard for all the heritage organisations under it. For a small community like ours to be recognised in such a magnanimous manner by the political leadership, and to be allowed to examine the past and project it collectively and cohesively for times to come, is really quite significant.

The IHC, although still a modest institution, is housed in a striking building whose architectural motifs span diverse and culturally resonant facets of India's rich heritage. The façade mural, illuminated in Little India at night by colour-changing LED lights, draws inspiration from the stepped *Baori* wells, a community gathering space in such Indian states as Rajasthan and Gujarat. The architects similarly designed the mural walls to reflect the community's vibrancy and continuing evolution.[24] The IHC attracts footfall from across the world and hopes to keep growing.

All the sub-committees made a whole-hearted effort to make the centre a reality — this is the hallmark to the project. We envisioned that every Indian organisation which had its own building would set up up its own mini heritage centre to create a hub-and-spokes system. The idea was that if someone visits the Indian Heritage Centre curious about, for example, the Bengalis, with an interest in studying their culture in greater detail, they would be able to find a link at the IHC to direct them to the Bengali Association so that they themselves can explain their heritage. Visitors could then follow this path if they wanted depth on any of the Indian communities in Singapore. The hub-and-spokes system is still a work in progress; however, various programmes have been organised to actively engage the Indian communities.

In line with Dr. Balaji's far-sighted guidance, we meticulously preserved what was given to us by the Indian organisations. And when the NHB later crystallised what it wanted to go into the stalls, my committee again met with the community to record their feedback. The government required the Indian community to fund a substantial portion of the cost of building the centre, while they funded the majority; the total cost was around $21,000,000.[25] I stepped down as chairman of the IHC's Advisory Board on December 31st, 2021.

24

ISAS and the South Asian Diaspora in Singapore

"I was the chairman of ISAS for more than fifteen years, and have had a wise Board and dedicated colleagues to guide me... I wish the university and ISAS the very best... The university had equipped me with the skills needed to lead a good, honest life; it even assisted me in finding my life partner. Doing the last lap with ISAS has been the crowning glory."

The Origin of ISAS

Some fifteen years ago, I received a call from then Permanent Secretary of the Ministry of Trade and Industry Heng Swee Kiat, asking if I would like to drop in and meet him at a coffee shop near his office in High Street. This is a small cafe, where government officers meet for a quick, informal chat. After some pleasantries, he came around to the topic he wanted to discuss.

His ministry, together with the Ministry of Foreign Affairs, planned to set up a think tank to study South Asia. His minister, George Yeo, had recommended my name to chair the institute, which would be called South Asian Institute, or SAI, for short. I noted that SAI was perhaps not the best acronym, as it has different meanings in different Asian contexts. Mr. Heng was surprised by my response and suggested that we put the name aside for the time being.

I suspect ISAS emanated from a discussion held between then Prime Minister Goh Chok Tong and certain other ministers. After a series of meetings and discussions, they concluded (as referenced in Mr. Goh Chok Tong's 'Foreword') that there was a need of such an institute. Another relevant issue for the establishment of the Institute would be its funding and logistics — how it was to be operated and launched as expeditiously as possible to Singapore's full benefit.

As regards the recommendation of my name, I felt that while I knew South Asia from an economic and political perspective, I was no scholar of the ilk of Professor Wang Gungwu or my friend Tommy Koh. But ISAS spoke to my interest in foreign affairs, and my approach to looking at the world has always been global. ISAS gave me the opportunity to examine South Asia while framing it within the broader context of important questions Singaporeans had about current affairs and developments in the region. South Asia has recently risen in prominence, thanks to an acceleration of the region's economic growth and a shifting in the world's strategic architecture eastwards.

Mr. Heng detailed his and Mr. George Yeo's expectations for ISAS. Although India is often the first country people think of when reference is made to "South Asia", ISAS was never meant to be an India-specific organisation. It was made clear that ISAS should cover all the South Asian countries. My impression from Mr. Heng was that they were not just looking for a scholar to share his knowledge of India but to look at the entirety of South Asian geography from the end of colonial rule onwards, and to generate insights about this important corner of the world coming into its own.

South Asia has a unique civilisational landscape, spanning diverse cultures, languages and customs. Our job was to weave the threads connecting them together and stitch them into a coherent narrative, while spotlighting those trends most relevant to the Singaporean community. We could interpret the region's past, but what was most important was to offer predictions on its future, according to research focus areas deemed worthwhile by our stakeholders. Examples might include politics, society and governance, with analyses on national or state elections or structural political changes; the government's approach to relevant industries, such as FinTech; or emerging technological trends, such as in artificial intelligence or social media.

Historically, one significant thread that passes through South Asia is the legacy of colonialism; and there are also religious ties, such as Hinduism and Islam, that form the countries' warp and weft. We were also to examine economic interlinkages, which manifest today as hard and digital connectivity in the region, especially as China's entry into South Asia expands the ambit of the Belt and Road Initiative. ISAS was envisioned to be a multi-faceted organisation that would pinpoint salient interconnections and offer views on how South Asian states and leaders might navigate new challenges and prospects.

~

Many dire predictions have been cast about South Asia over time. For instance, South Asia was viewed as a nuclear "hot spot" during the Cold War. Some British scholars speculated that India, with is abundant diversity, would splinter at the seams. But since 1947, it has stayed united. While the effects of post-colonialism and the subcontinent's partition linger in the region's collective memory, some serious problems show signs of being gradually cemented over. Bangladesh, once a poor country, has become second only to India in terms of wealth in all South Asia.

Official launch of ISAS in 2004 with former Prime Minister Goh Chok Tong (right), current Deputy Prime Minister Heng Swee Keat (second from left) and current chairman of ISAS, Professor Tan Tai Yong (left).

I believe that South Asian countries, similar to Iran, possess age-old, time tested and civilisational virtues which are bound to reveal their worth. I found the research and policy prospects of the Institute fascinating, and felt fortunate to have been asked to chair it.

Building the Team

My first major task was to recruit strong management and staff to the Institute. Indeed, following my conversation with Mr. Heng, my first challenge was to find a director. I spoke with the university, which assured me that they could assist with interviewing the candidates. Grateful for the help, I nevertheless thought, "My God, this will take time," and asked if there was any way to expedite this. I wanted a director of the Institute with a background on India; and preferred, at least as we learned to walk, for him or her to be Singaporean with a sense of Singapore's interests.

By chance, I came across a young man who had done his PhD on India in the United Kingdom. Mr. Heng had suggested I meet the university's then president, Professor Tan Chorh Chuan. The President had hosted a lunch whereupon I met Professor Tan Tai Yong, who had studied Indian history at Cambridge. I asked Chorh Chuan whether I might borrow Professor Tan Tai Yong for six months while we waited to recruit the new director. Both Chorh Chuan and Tai Yong agreed. But it so happened — either through my charm or his generosity — that Tai Yong stayed on for six years as ISAS' very first acting director. When I stepped down from ISAS on July 31st, 2021, Tai Yong was appointed as ISAS' new chairman.

These "temporary" arrangements put ISAS on the fast track. Our next major appointment was for head of research. I had been following the writings of several writers in the Indian newspapers and decided to zero in on Dr. S. Narayan, a former revenue secretary who had served as economic adviser to former Indian Prime Minister Atal Bihari Vajpayee. I then hand-picked a few other practitioner-scholars equipped to share their practical and theoretical insights on the region.

These stalwarts, in no particular order, included former Foreign Minister of Bangladesh, Iftekhar Chowdhury; former Governor of the Reserve Bank of India, Dr. Duvurri Subbarao; former Foreign Secretary and National Security Advisor, Shivshankar Menon; former 11th Comptroller and Auditor General of India, Vinod Rai; D. S. Jaishankar, then India's former Foreign Secretary; Shahid Javed Burki, Pakistan's former Finance Minister and Vice President of the World Bank as well as other accomplished figures. The appointment of well-known journalist and scholar C. Raja Mohan, who stepped down as director of ISAS in 2021, significantly boosted ISAS's profile. For a scholar of Professor Raja Mohan's calibre to agree to build ISAS signalled to me the potential of the Institute. All scholars and administrative staff contributed to making ISAS a success in their own distinct ways.

We quickly built up a good team, and my knowing India and having travelled there made it easier to identify people to fill research roles. I mentioned South Asia's diversity. This diversity becomes even more mind-boggling once you get to know the views and experiences of all the scholars: one challenge, therefore, became channelling this abundance of knowledge into a workable format for the priorities of our stakeholders. Along with recruiting sharp writers and thinkers, we organised an array of programmes. These might be as private as closed-door sessions; public lectures on general and specialised topics; international conferences or symposiums; and workshops and roundtables that culminate in publications.

I was fortunate to have the backing of the university and political leadership throughout my tenure. If I invited a minister to inaugurate a lecture, he usually made the time to do it. Similarly, when I wanted to bounce the idea for a new programme off someone, they consistently stepped forward with their views. ISAS was the first organisation, for example, to arrange a programme around the South Asian Diaspora, whose inspiration came from our former President S. R. Nathan. "The diaspora is a far flung group of South Asians," he told me. "You should look at organising them into a more cohesive grouping and draw out discussions amongst them. Many people would find this useful." So I have gone around trying to do this. We held four conventions, which I hazard to say have been moderately successful.

The South Asia Diaspora Convention

Our South Asia Diaspora Convention (SADC) functions according to two major relevant themes: the importance of the South Asia diaspora community in Singapore as well as, broadly, business and the skilling of labour. I separate the business side from — for lack of a better term — the humanitarian dimension. South Asians have an interest in one another irrespective of their business. The convention also serves as a bridge between Singapore and the wider South Asian region. As I mentioned in my chapters on India, those from outside the region often find entering South Asia for business to be a challenge. But South Asian businessmen have shown their acumen in creating new opportunities. The SADC is one forum for building bridges — both between Singaporean and South Asian businesses as well as the distinct diasporic communities.

Overarching all this, however, is the desire amongst South Asians to be part of and belong to a forum that allows them to chat amongst themselves and pursue activities that transcend policy, such as in art, drama or sport. At the last SADC, for instance, we audaciously hosted a three-nation cricket tournament. The cricket match was expensive to organise, because many South Asian cricketers have become multi-millionaires; they won't agree to just a small fee! This is unfortunate, because once they get to be that rich they are in great demand in countries like Australia and England, and might later demur, saying, "What does Singapore know about cricket?"

We managed, however, to pull it off. We extended the second "Outstanding Member of the South Asia Diaspora Award" in 2019 to Sir Fazle Hasan Abed, the founder chair of the Bangladesh Rural Advancement Committee (BRAC), one of the largest NGOs in the world. Before this, the award was conferred on S. R. Nathan, the first recipient of the award, in 2016.

As the Institute grows, it must not only maintain but also improve upon its level of research. I was the chairman of ISAS for more than fifteen years, and have had a wise Board and dedicated colleagues to guide me. I wish the university and ISAS the very best. NUS President Tan Eng Chye has showed me unstinting support; after I stepped down, he played an instrumental role in appointing me for three years as "senior advisor" to ISAS. I also wish to thank MFA, MTI and the Tote Board, and to encourage our younger scholars, on the cusp of bright careers, to be well read about the world, discussant on varying topics and sufficiently prolific to strengthen their profiles.

The university has equipped me with the skills needed to lead a good, honest life; it even assisted me in finding my life partner. Doing the last lap with ISAS has been the crowning glory.

Receiving an award at the Faculty of Arts and Social Sciences (FASS) Star Awards 2016 (with President of NUS, Prof. Tan Eng Chye, and my wife, Shyamala).

Part IV

Conclusion

At my eightieth birthday with my family and Tan Guan Heng.

25

A "Medical Diary"

I would like to mention a good friend, a former university classmate who was very active in the USC: Mr. Tan Guan Heng. After graduating and while working in a publishing firm, he developed some problems with his eyes.[1] He later lost his vision completely. Despite losing his eyesight at an early age, he has kept busy doing many things, such as running a bookshop. He also became the first blind president of the Singapore Association of the Blind. Until the pandemic hit Singapore, we would talk regularly and meet from time to time. He enjoys discussing world affairs, and I often find the insights he offers more illuminating than those who look at the world through regular vision.

He has authored four books, several of which were launched by former President Nathan and Professor Tommy Koh, also with us at university. His first book, published in 1995, was called *My Love is Blind*. It is a semi-autobiographical work that meditates on some of the challenges faced by blind people. It features a love story involving a girl the narrator was keen on, but who decided that living with a blind person might have been too difficult to handle.

Tan Guan Heng never tires of telling me, "Gopi, you are a very lucky man — the luckiest I have ever known." He came to this conclusion because, despite a spate of accidents and illnesses, I have come out, for the most part, quite well. Given my tendency to over-do things and stress test the universe whenever I get the chance, one might consider my luck twice as good.

But now that I am older, I find my time increasingly tied down by health concerns. Although my ears remain sharp, my eyesight is not as

Singapore's Association of the Visually Handicapped 2013
(Tan Guan Heng seated in the middle).

keen as it once was. And reading the daily news, once a source of joy, now requires assistance from Shyamala. I have had a few bad falls in the last year, and now have to go for regular checkups with the doctors — for blood tests, scans and that sort of thing. On the whole, I suppose I am in no position to complain.

One's accomplishments feature most strongly in autobiographical works of this sort; but they do not provide life's full picture. Life as we know it habitually throws up obstacles, including in the way of health, that force us to slow down and think. Amidst this historic pandemic period, many undergoing lockdown have been encouraged to write and reflect on their day-to-day and how their habits have changed. For me, being socially active and a person who enjoys regular lunches with friends, staying at home has taken some getting used to. However, I have taken this idea of a journal and modified it to record some humorous and more serious incidents, which readers might perhaps find relatable too. They also help to get at that life lived outside the public eye.

~

As I related in 'Chapter 1', the first most serious accident of my childhood was when, at around the age of three, I had broken my thumb after I lifted my father's office counter door at the Adelphi Hotel. The retractable door hammered down on top of it — what I recount as one of the most painful experiences of my life.

Later, when I was five years old, I suffered another accident: this time I fell and cut my tongue. The cut was so severe that my family members claimed that I could not even talk! No doctor was available in the village of Engandiyoor where I grew up, so we travelled — by multiple means of conveyance — to the nearby town of Thrissur, where a medical practitioner could be found.

Thrissur had a touch of arrogance because it was considered one of Kerala's major cultural centres, where some of the great Malayalam poets resided. Visiting the town was an adventure, as we had to travel first by boat, and then (depending on the traffic) by car or bus. Those days, hiring a cab required more work than now; one had to send a telegram far in advance if you wanted to book a car. (No road ran up to the house.) To cut a long story short, the doctor treated me; my tongue was cured; and, for better or worse, my elocutive abilities were restored!

The third accident occurred around one year later when I seriously injured my right arm. I had been trying to narrate a story I had heard to a cousin about two goats that were trying to cross a river along a narrow bridge. Neither was willing to give way, so they started to fight, and both fell into the river together. I have always been an enthusiastic storyteller, and demonstrated to my cousin the manner in which the goats fell. I must have become so excited in my re-enactment of the drama that I myself tumbled off the parapet wall I was sitting on!

The goats maybe swam to shore; but my condition was more alarming in that I had fractured and dislocated my right arm. It too needed treatment from a Western trained doctor. I was ferried by boat and then ushered by car. I recall my arm tingling with pain as it hung in a sling along the way. An ocean away from home, my accidents caused my father and my mother's two brothers in Singapore no end of worry and invited a barrage of questions about how I was being raised.

After that, a period of calm descended without any major accidents or terrible calamities to speak of — nothing, for instance, from my carefree days at university. Earlier on, I had narrated the story of starting an IT Co-operative, for the purpose of putting a computer in lower-income Singaporean Indian homes. One Saturday afternoon in 1999, I had gone for a committee meeting, but not long afterwards, upon entering the building, felt a severe pain stabbing my chest.

"It must be indigestion," I thought, and asked to be excused, deciding to drive back home: Shyamala would know what to do (I had a greater faith in her than myself). I am not sure why I did not think to just go to Tan Tock Seng Hospital, which in any case was quite close, just there on Balestier Road.

What I did was stupid, because, while driving, I started to vomit. Nevertheless, I kept on driving, passing Tan Tock Seng Hospital even, but determined to reach home.

I was right that Shyamala would know what to do: no sooner did she see me than she recognised the severity of the problem and dialled for an ambulance. The young registrar at the National University Hospital (NUH), where the ambulance had taken me, also had only to cast one look at me to diagnose that I had just had a serious heart attack and should be admitted to the hospital. The delay had caused a significant loss of heart function.

A young friend of ours in the medical profession rang up a well-reputed heart specialist for a consultation. However, the specialist would be leaving the country the very next day. Our friend said that my condition needed to be attended to at a fairly senior level. As none of the senior doctors at NUH were around, arrangements were made to transfer me to the Singapore General Hospital (SGH) under the care of Associate Professor Koh Tian Hai.

I was fortunate to have been put under Dr. Koh's charge. After some time at the hospital, he decided no major operation was needed. However, he said treatment would help. He recommended inserting a stent, not a very serious procedure — I went through with the angioplasty not long after that, which seemed to do the trick. Prof Koh sees me roughly every six months for regular check-ups. On the whole, it was a trouble free experience.

~

But a bill of good health is not a blank cheque. In 2009, another serious problem emerged, which was this time an "atrial fibrillation", or irregular heart rhythm. Professor Koh brought in another specialist, Dr. Teo Wee Siong, who said I might need to insert a pacemaker to regulate the irregular heartbeats. To prepare for its insertion, I underwent a routine examination which involved an X-ray of the chest. Dr. Teo dismissed it as a general procedure — nothing to be too concerned about. But on glancing at my X-ray, he observed, "There is a shadow on your left lung."

"Probably nothing sinister. Could just be a blip on the radar," he said. "But for now, we would like to do a biopsy, to make sure it is nothing more serious."

To my dismay, he discovered that the shadow was actually a tumour. "We have to clear this before we do anything else." He arranged for another excellent surgeon at SGH, Dr. Agastian, to see me. The hospital staff assured me that I would be quite safe in his hands.

"Agasthya", I knew, refers to an ancient Hindu saint and scholar of Sanskrit legend who supposedly authored the Rig Veda and meditated on the entire history of the world, gaining insights into events that could happen at any time. In Tamil Nadu he is called "Agastiyar" and appears across South and Southeast Asia in Hindu temple reliefs, inscriptions and artworks. It was an appropriate name for a person dealing with a scenario that could have had such uncertain results.

When I met with Dr. Agastian, I told him that his father must have been a very learned man to bestow him such a name. He was a little taken aback by this comment at first, but was pleased to meet a Singaporean well acquainted with the Indian classics, and affirmed that his father had been an avid reader. He did the operation, removing every last bit of the growth. Since 2009, I have continued to visit the National Cancer Centre annually for an X-ray and check-up.

~

This next entry, though also involving heartache, deviates from the pattern of stories shared thus far. We had a dear family friend, Dr. Narayanan Unni, who stood by our side through several frightful scenarios. Born in India, he had done his postgraduate studies in England and became a surgeon. When he came to Singapore, he stayed at my parents' house until he could secure a place of his own.

A major tragedy unfolded during his stay — the untimely death of my sister who was living in New York at the time with her husband. I had mentioned in 'Chapter 6' that he was Fiji's representative to the UN. Just shy of forty, she had a baby and contracted hepatitis. The hepatitis was not detected during pregnancy, and she did not recover. She passed away in 1971, leaving behind a son, Sree Kumar Nandan. Amidst the ensuing panic, Dr. Unni guided my parents through this horrendous period and lent them his strength. Once, a doctor called from New York to update my parents on how she was doing.

My parents anxiously pressed the doctor with several questions over the phone. Dr. Unni waited until my parents had left the room. Once they had done so, he approached me privately. "It doesn't look good." He confided that her chances of recovery were less than 10 percent. He never mentioned this to my parents: I found the delicacy with which he handled the situation touching.

Then came my own parents' passing: my father in February 1981 and my mother in December 1990. Both had always been my pillars of strength. What the astrologers predicted after my birth was true: I did care for them right up to the end. Dr. Unni, who today also is no more, was literally an angel sent from heaven during my time of grief. He has grandchildren and other relatives in Singapore whom I keep in touch with. Sometimes a friend like him is more valuable than a medical doctor, as he looks after your health in the broader sense.

I am standing next to my sister; my sister is next to our cousin Balan. Seated are my parents. The couple next to my mother are our close family friends, Dr. P.N. Unni and his wife, Radha, 1955–1957.

~

I had thought the incident of my atrial fibrillation would be my last entry into my "Medical Diary". However, on May 31st, 2021, another unforeseen accident occurred. The day was rainy and the ground was wet. I was walking up the stairs to my office on Robinson Road. A lady was walking up too. The day is a blur, but I remember turning to her to allow her to pass. In doing so, I lost my balance and fell down the steps. For some time I lay flat on the ground. My friends tell me they rushed over to talk to me, to see if I was all right — but I do not remember this part at all. They said I told them that I was fine and tried to get up. The next thing I knew I was lying in a hospital bed in critical condition. I had hit my head and suffered a brain haemorrhage and stroke. A second fall a few months later led to another brain haemorrhage and stroke.

Nowadays, I am mostly confined to the house and only go out on occasional walks. The brain surgeon tells me that things are looking good and that I am recovering, as far as such injuries are concerned. But he also says not to expect miracles. Recovery has its own pace; I must learn to be patient. Meanwhile, I have been instructed to rest and am subjected to a regimen of near daily physiotherapy. Everything I usually did in the office I now do from home. I am employing various strategies to get my alertness back.

In spite of the falls and, before those, some touch-and-go situations, my old friend Guan Heng was right to say that I have indeed been quite blessed. This is not least because, when I have needed them most, my close ones have rallied around me. Through their support, I have overcome many vexing trials. Whether it be in lending a hand during difficult job transitions, joining me for a lunch at the Guild House or simply calling to check up on me during this new "transition" towards a sedentary life at home, my family and friends have been my critical lifeline keeping my head above water — their names and kindnesses are too numerous to count. They have strengthened my character and furnished life with many fond memories and joyous laughter.

With V. Krishna, S. Rajendran, Patrick Yeoh, Sat Pal Khattar, and Charlie Phua, August 25th, 1988.

26

Parting Observations

At the age of 84, I might be expected to share a few words on my philosophy of life. I have mentioned that I am, like my grandfather, a fatalist; I believe certain things are destined to happen and that things will often resolve themselves. Else, they will remain a nagging pain for some time. The solution or "truth" that one ultimately arrives at may not be the solution that you or your loved ones had originally sought: but the answer that emerges will be *concrete* and will actually happen. Maybe you think such generalities are not overly profound. But this is more or less what I believe. Seldom do I cry my eyes out when events do not go as planned, or light up with gleeful smiles when things go my way.

I have referenced astrology several times in this book. Some might be wondering, given my penchant for fatalism, whether astrology is something I actually hold faith in. Not quite. It leaves plenty of room for speculation, and for me is mostly a subject to be wondered at. As time has passed, my faith in the stars has dimmed. As Shakespeare's character Cassius put it in *Julius Caesar*, "The fault, dear Brutus, is not in our stars."

As a teenager, I placed greater stock in what the astrologers told me than my father: he had neither the desire nor the guts to confront or challenge them. His stance was agnostic: he said that if you believe it helps you, take their advice. Otherwise, leave it be. The same might be said for many religions. Positively inclined towards astrology in my youth, as an adult I have dabbled in some amateur research recreationally.

There was an Irish scholar, William John Warner (who went by the name of Cheiro), who had written many books on astrology, numerology and palmistry. I have read them, but find, from his writings and the quality time I have spent with Indian astrologers, that they offer no finality: rarely are their answers satisfying. More often than not, I go home disappointed. The supporting evidence for astrology is lacking — it has never been studied in recent times, to my knowledge, seriously as a science. Still, whenever I hear a new astrologer is in town, this does not stop me from making a bee-line to see him.

My family asks me with exasperation, "Why do you waste your time on this business?", to which I have no reply: curiosity, I suppose. Just like the counter door at the Adelphi. There are certain things about this life that we do not catch right away, which are beyond our field of view, whose allure comes from the very fact that it withholds its mysteries.

I am certain what is destined to take place will take place, whether healthwise or otherwise. Little can be done to change that. I recognise that my life has been paradoxical in this respect, as my personality has tended to buck the limiters placed on me. My readers might not be unwarranted in challenging, "Well, what then is destiny? Who decides on destiny?" This is a complicated question, and I find few answers convincing: one might say God, one might say the Self. But I find that sometimes the way things turn out provides the answer one was long looking for.

"Gosh!" a person might exclaim, "This has got something to it, and is too strange to be ignored!" If there is one thing that I might definitely assert about life, it is that it carries on.

~

Singapore too will carry on. The purpose of this book has not been to make an ultra-patriotic story out of Singapore. Rather, it has been about how a person of relatively modest means was able to build himself up, according to his circumstances, and to string together the successes and failures he met along the way. My story does not fully mirror all the ongoing events in the past century, but it does pose interesting questions in my mind that might be explored in greater detail.

Many years ago, to motivate myself to write this book, I began giving interviews to various people. I am grateful to all who listened to my stories. My tale, for the greater part of it, unfolded in the 20th century. For many others, theirs will play out in the 21st.

With my nephew, Sree Kumar Nandan.

Several important pioneers came before me. Nearly a century has passed since my father, K. S. Pillai, arrived in Singapore in the mid-1920s. Singapore has also changed dramatically in this time. Examining the man I have become, I owe much to my parents and to that early community of settlers — M. R. Menon, C. G. Menon, K. P. Menon and others from the Malayalee community — as well as my primary school teachers such as B. R. Atherton, Seow Cheng Fong and Tan Keng Kang, who taught me what was relevant.

My father left me the gifts of civic consciousness and cautious circumspection; he also instilled in me an interest in the written word. I am unsure if, without his influence, I would have had the interest to write this book. Even today, one of the first things I do in the morning is to ask for my wife to read me the daily newspaper — my small way of remaining engaged with the world.

As far as politics and world affairs are concerned, I must of course honour the memory of Kochapamama for igniting my passion for the subjects. Ultimately, I did not choose the political life, instead opting for another type of risk-filled road as an entrepreneur. But I believe that, in my capacity as a diplomat and on the sidelines through organisations such as ISAS, I have been useful to my country.

My mother remains my greatest influence. Without her intervention when I had wanted to quit my studies to support my father after secondary school, my life could have taken a profoundly different turn.

S. R. Nathan had also once commented at a dinner after an awards presentation, "Gopi takes after his mother", referring to the many activities that I have been involved in. She was an exemplar of social service and education. Finally, there is my sister, Sree Kumari, who for me as a boy was the image of bravery. Even now, her legacy inspires me.

~

I opened in the 'Preface' of the book with the worry of whether my life made me a "jack of all trades or a master of none". I suppose the reader will be left to judge whether, as our friend David Copperfield astutely said, "I have proven to be the hero of my own life." Looking back, I feel fortunate to have adapted to new experiences, lands and occupations. Adjustments were not easy, but fate was on my side and I took the bull by the horns. I am grateful for my travels, the calculated and less calculated risks that I took and the fascinating people I met along the way.

Singapore too has weathered many storms. Some crucibles were of an economic sort, such as the industrial review undertaken while I was at Raya Mills, while others entailed unexpected political transitions — for instance, when the left-wing members were expelled from the PAP and formed Barisan Sosialis in 1961; the government's launching of Operation Coldstore in 1963; and Barisan Sosialis boycotting the General Elections in 1968, which deprived Singapore of a powerful opposition party.

After the very tough manner with which certain left-wing activists were dealt (some of whom were my friends), I too privately wondered whether the buoyancy and liveliness so readily apparent in Singapore's economic activity would reflect as vibrantly in her politics. However, following the 1969 race riots in Malaysia, and then living and working in Singapore in subsequent decades, I saw the unique virtues of the new system and its relevance for a complex, multi-racial society like our own, where merit and hard work as well as minority protections and cultural heritage are prioritised.

Our leaders, despite the doubts cast in the 1960s, have acted with integrity, and decisions have been buttressed by an honest and robust legal system. Moreover, I see political vivacity of the sort that surrounded me in my youth in social media exchanges and a burgeoning culture of open debate. Our political system in Singapore is unique: parallel to freedom of self-expression, we have developed mature laws to steer us away from the occasional acts of wantonness towards more sophisticated dialogue; they exist to ensure that the civil, rational elements of our democracy remain robust. Singapore, at the confluence of East and West, respects the rights of citizens while also refusing to shy away from hard and sometimes unpopular challenges of governance.

Singapore continues to refine her politics and is well poised to face the 21st century. We remain open to new ideas and technologies. We are at the forefront of global business, while our citizenry is confidently advocating for our perceived needs, such as through the desire amongst the young for greater consultation and collaboration. We have passed through heady times and have progressed well.

Much now depends on our younger generation. The world is becoming more turbulent. As I finish this book, the U.S. has withdrawn from Afghanistan, ending a 20-year war — what some have compared to the British withdrawal from the Suez Canal in 1956, which catalysed the withdrawal some fifty years earlier of the Malayalees from the British naval base in Seletar. A so-called systematic rivalry is emerging between China and the United States.

If there is one thing I have learned, it is that very rarely do we see the full picture. New experiences, insights and travails — for us as individuals and as a community — wait around the bend, for which we must be prepared. Two questions are pertinent to my mind as we move forward:

> *Firstly, how do we proceed on the basis of our self-interest, without upsetting those whom we might find it difficult to accommodate? That is, accepting others' place in the world while finding space to compromise?*
>
> *And secondly, how do we retain our dynamism — our ability to react to and solve the problems that come our way?*

We are not out of the woods. But I believe welcoming adversity will strengthen our resolve. My family, through many turbulent junctures, has always kept me steady. I continue to view my decision to migrate from Malaysia to Singapore as the second best decision of my life: marrying Shyamala was the first! I live with my wife and two daughters in a full, happy household. My son, Prakash, lives not too far away from us. I am also a grandfather blessed with two grandsons — Arjuna and Aditya — both of whom bring me tremendous joy.

In my time, I have been a teacher, a journalist, a businessman and a diplomat. I have participated and invested in my cultural community. Just as there are more stories I could tell, so too do our explanations lack definitive finality; there are always more angles for looking at life. Life — with family, friends, struggle, accomplishment and community — is more than the eye can see. And it is this vastness, which we struggle to comprehend, that keeps us optimistic, humble and enterprising.

My family and I at Shyamala's birthday dinner on March 10th, 2021. Back row (from the left): my son, Prakash, with his wife, Vidhya; my grandsons, Aditya and Arjuna; and my daughter, Preetha. Front row: Shyamala and my younger daughter, Priya.

Notes

(in order of appearance in the chapters)

Chapter 1

[1] Information from "Onapaharam 2009", a publication of the Singapore Malayalee Association.

[2] Ted Green, "The Fall of Singapore 1942", Historical Association, 1 February 2013, https://www.history.org.uk/publications/resource/6192/the-fall-of-singapore-1942. Accessed on 30 September 2021. Also see LCDR Alan C. Headrick, UNSR, "Bicycle Blitzkrieg: The Malayan Campaign and the Fall of Singapore," 8 February 1994, pp. 7–9, https://www.ibiblio.org/hyperwar/PTO/RisingSun/BicycleBlitz/index.html#III. Accessed on 30 September 2021. Paper directed by Commander Mark Hess, USN Faculty, Department of Strategy and Policy.

Chapter 2

[1] "The Guilty", *Collier's Magazine*, 30 September 1944. Excerpted in "Profile of Chandra Bose", The National Archives, United Kingdom, https://www.nationalarchives.gov.uk/education/resources/the-road-to-partition/profile-chandra-bose/.

[2] Thomas Johnson Nossiter, *Communism in Kerala: A Study in Political Adaptation* (London: C. Hurst & Company, 1982), p. 38.

[3] For more on the relationship between private landlords and tenants, see for example Suma Scaria, "Changes in Land Relations: The Political Economy of Land Reforms in a Kerala Village", Review of Agriculture, *Economic & Political Weekly*, Vol. XLV, Nos. 26 & 27, 26 June 2010, pp. 193-194, http://indiaenvironmentportal.org.in/files/Changes%20in%20Land%20Relations.pdf. Accessed on 30 September 2021.

[4] V. K. Ramachandran, "On Kerala's Development Achievements", in *Indian Development: Selected Regional Perspectives*, ed. Jean Dreze and Amartya Sen (Oxford Scholarship Online, September 2011), pp. 211–212, https://oxford.universitypressscholarship.com/view/10.1093/acprof:oso/9780198292043.001.0001/acprof-9780198292043-chapter-4. Accessed on 30 September 2021.

[5] Please see "Shri C. Janardhanan Member of Parliament (MP) from Trichur (Kerala) Biodata", *Entranceindia*, https://entranceindia.com/election-and-politics/shri-c-janardhanan-member-of-parliament-mp-from-trichur-kerala-biodata/. Accessed on 30 September 2021. My uncle's

Wikipedia entry states he was MP from 1967 to 1977. However, the term provided in the first source is more likely, as the first elected communist government served from 1967 to 1969. "C. Janardhanan", *Wikipedia*, https://en.wikipedia.org/wiki/C._Janardhanan. Accessed on 30 September 2021.

Chapter 3

[1] The Editors of Encyclopedia Brittanica, "Subhas Chandra Bose: Activity in Exile", *Encyclopedia Brittanica*, https://www.britannica.com/biography/Subhas-Chandra-Bose. Accessed on 12 November 2021.

[2] From the placard "World War II Experiences" at the Indian Heritage Centre in Singapore. Date of centre visit: 25 September 2021.

[3] The Wire Staff, "'The Light Has Gone Out of Our Lives': Nehru's Words on Gandhi's Assassination", *The Wire*, 30 January 2018, https://thewire.in/history/light-gone-lives-nehrus-words-gandhis-assassination. Accessed on 30 September 2021.

[4] Lee Kuan Yew, *From Third World to First, The Singapore Story: 1965–2000* (Singapore, Times Media, 2000), p. 191. For context on early Chinese involvement in the political process, see Yeo Kim Wah, "A Study of Three Early Political Parties in Singapore, 1945–1955", pp. 115–116, 140–141; and Pang Cheng Lian, "The People's Action Party, 1954–1963", *Journal of Southeast Asian History*, Vol. 10, No. 1., Singapore Commemorative Issue 1819–1969, March 1969, p. 143.

[5] The Citizenship Ordinance in 1957 offered foreign-born Chinese a pathway to naturalisation if they had "lived in Singapore for at least 10 years and were prepared to swear an oath of loyalty to Singapore and renounce allegiance to any foreign state." See C. M. Turnbull, *A History of Modern Singapore* (Singapore: NUS Press), p. 268 as referenced in Mervin Ang, "Singapore Citizenship Ordinance of 1957", Singapore Infopedia, https://eresources.nlb.sog.sg/infopedia/articles/SIP_2020-08-17_202903.html. Accessed on 26 October 2021.

[6] See Lim Tin Seng, "1959 Legislative Assembly General Election", Singapore Infopedia, September 2018, https://eresources.nlb.gov.sg/infopedia/articles/SIP_2019-04-08_145822.html.

[7] "Legislative Council General Election 1948: Rural West", Singapore Elections Archive, http://www.singapore-elections.com/general-election/1948/rural-west.html. Accessed on 30 September 2021.

[8] The date regarding the newspaper's print-run was obtained in Shobha Tsering Bhalla, "Gopinath Pillai: An all-rounder, this seasoned diplomat

and administrator has helped shape the progress of Singapore in more ways than one", *Diaspora Dialogues* (Extra-ordinary Indians), November 2013, p. 20. However, details of the paper's editors during this period are not provided.

Chapter 4

[1] "Presbyterian Boys' School, circa 1982", BookSG, National Library Board, https://eresources.nlb.gov.sg/printheritage/image.aspx?id=04ae5c59-c09a-4d1a-8f4f-0c5523c802b1. Accessed on 30 September 2021.

[2] See, for example, "Protests by Chinese Middle School Students: 10th October 1956", HistorySG, https://eresources.nlb.gov.sg/history/events/376486b7-a68b-4a2b-acad-97e0b678a8e7. Accessed on 30 September 2021.

[3] "Discover ten key public policies that made us who we are", Singapore Chinese Cultural Centre, https://singaporeccc.org.sg/discover-ten-key-public-policies-that-made-us-who-we-are/. Accessed on 16 November 2021.

[4] For more on Chinese language policy, see Charlene Tan, "Change and Continuity: Chinese Language Policy in Singapore", *Language Policy*, 5(1), January 2006: pp. 41–62, https://www.researchgate.net/publication/226842776_Change_and_Continuity_Chinese_Language_Policy_in_Singapore. Accessed on 16 November 2021.

[5] Rajesh Rai, "'Rising from the Ashes': The Development of Hindi in Independent Singapore", *50 Years of Indian Community in Singapore*, eds. Gopinath Pillai and K. Kesavapany (Singapore: World Scientific, 2016), p. 61. Accessed on 15 November 2021.

[6] For more information on Netaji Hindi High School, see Rajesh Rai, "The attrition and survival of minor South Asian languages in Singapore", in R. Rai, P. Reeves (eds.), *The South Asian Diaspora: Transnational Networks and Changing Identities*, London, p. 149, as cited in Rai, "'Rising from the Ashes': The Development of Hindi in Independent Singapore", op. cit., p. 60.

[7] The Government of India, "The Dakshina Bharat Hindi Prachar Sabha Act, 1964", https://legislative.gov.in/sites/default/files/A1964-14_1.pdf. Accessed on 16 November 2021.

[8] "National Registration for Singapore Identity Cards Begins: 9th May 1966", HistorySG, 30 September 2021, https://eresources.nlb.gov.sg/history/events/07ffb260-e535-4dbb-a946-fa3403f47e72#2. Accessed on 16 November 2021.

Chapter 5

[1] S. R. Nathan and Tim Auguer, *50 Stories from My Life* (Editions Didier Millet Pte Ltd, 2013), p. 80. Also see, "23rd to 25th August 1954: Acquittal at the Fajar Trials", The Life of J. J. Putucheary, https://www.jamesputhucheary.org/may-1954/. Accessed 16 November 2021.

[2] "Ex-PAP leader Woodhull dies at 71", *The Star*, 29 November 2003, https://www.thestar.com.my/news/nation/2003/11/29/expap-leader-woodhull-dies-at-71. Accessed 15 November 2021. Also see Soo K Poh, Jing Quee Tan and Kay Yew Koh, *The Fajar Generation: The University Socialist Club and the Politics of Postwar Malaya and Singapore* (Petaling Jaya: SIRD, 2010), p. 36.

[3] "Dominic Puthucheary: How do History and Philosophy Reveal Insights into Human Nature?" The Wisdom Archiver, https://thewisdomarchiver.com/dominic-puthucheary-how-do-history-and-philosophy-reveal-insights-into-human-nature/. Accessed on 16 November 2021.

[4] Tien Mui Mun, "Lee Siew Choh", Singapore Infopedia, https://eresources.nlb.gov.sg/infopedia/articles/SIP_706_2005-01-12.html. Accessed on 30 September 2021.

[5] Daljit Singh and Lye Liong Fook, "30 Years On: A Reflection on Southeast Asia's Fight Against Communism During the Cold War Years", *Trends in Southeast Asia*, Issue No. 14, (Singapore: ISEAS Yusof Ishak Institute, 2021), p. 2, https://bookshop.iseas.edu.sg/publication/2504. Accessed on 16 November 2021.

[6] Yeo Kim Wah, "A Study of Three Early Political Parties in Singapore, 1945–1955", op. cit., p. 127.

[7] Daljit Singh and Lye Liong Fook, "Executive Summary", op. cit.

[8] Daljit Singh and Lye Liong Fook, op. cit., p. 3.

[9] "Legislative Assembly By-Election 1961: Hong Lim", Singapore Elections, http://www.singapore-elections.com/by-election/1961-4/hong-lim.html. Accessed on 30 September 2021.

Chapter 6

[1] Tullio Treves, "United Nations Convention on the Law of the Sea: Montego Bay, 10 December 1982", Audiovisual Library of International Law, https://legal.un.org/avl/ha/uncls.html. Accessed on 30 September 2021.

[2] International Seabed Authority, "Satya N. Nandan", Press Release, Biographical Note, Tenth Session, Kingston Jamaica, 24 May–4 June 2004,

https://isa.org.jm/files/documents/EN/Press/Press2004/sb_10_14.pdf. Accessed on 16 November 2021.

[3] Satya N. Nandan and Kristine E. Dalaker, *Reflections on the Making of the Modern Law of the Sea: The Search for a New Legal Order* (Ridge Books: July 2021), https://www.amazon.in/Chaos-Sea-Search-Legal-Order/dp/9813251379. Accessed on 16 November 2021.

Chapter 7

[1] Reuters Staff, "Former Reuters editor David Chipp dies", *Reuters*, 11 September 2008, https://www.reuters.com/article/uk-chipp-idUKLB63337520080911. Accessed on 19 November 2021.

[2] This quotation is from memory. We were unable to find it in secondary sources.

[3] Rajesh C. Bali, "Dr Kotnis Ki Amar Kahani", *Spectrum*, 17 December 2006, https://www.tribuneindia.com/2006/20061217/spectrum/main6.htm. Accessed on 18 November 2021.

[4] Ibid.

[5] Sandeep Dikshit, "Wife of Dwarkanath Kotnis is no more", *The Hindu*, 29 June 2012, https://www.thehindu.com/news/national/wife-of-dwarkanath-kotnis-is-no-more/article3582261.ece. Accessed on 19 November 2021.

[6] V. V. Paranjpe, "Zhou Enlai: The Man and His Work — Jawaharlal Nehru & Zhou Enlai: Contrasting Personalities", *World Affairs: The Journal of International Issues*, Vol. 2, No. 2 (April–June 1998), pp. 53–54, https://www-jstor-org.libproxy1.nus.edu.sg/stable/45064520?seq=4#metadata_info_tab_contents. Accessed on 16 November 2021.

[7] FPJ Bureau, "When Jawaharlal Nehru chaperoned China", *The Free Press Journal*, 1 June 2019, https://www.freepressjournal.in/analysis/when-jawaharlal-nehru-chaperoned-china. Accessed on 16 November 2021.

Chapter 8

[1] Hermann Kulke, "Srivijaya Revisited: Reflections on State Formation of a Southeast Asian Thalassocracy", *Bulletin de l'Ecole francaise d'Extreme-Orient*, Annee 2016, 102, pp. 45–95, https://www.semanticscholar.org/paper/%C5%9Ar%C4%ABvijaya-Revisited%3A-Reflections-on-State-Formation-Kulke/75d8c8b0612c6c8ab5aeb3bafab7b5926377c409. Accessed on 19 November 2021.

[2] Aditya Iyengar, "How fake news may have shaped the future of a Tamil empire in medieval India", *Scroll.in*, 11 November 2018, https://scroll.in/article/901102/how-fake-news-may-have-shaped-the-future-of-a-tamil-empire-in-medieval-india. Accessed on 19 November 2021.

[3] Sanjeev Sanyai, "There's a Dragon in the Sea", *The Economic Times*, 27 April 2016, https://economictimes.indiatimes.com/blogs/et-commentary/theres-a-dragon-in-the-sea/. Accessed on 19 November 2021.

[4] Hermann Kulke, op. cit.

[5] Sanjeev Sanyai, op. cit.

Chapter 9

[1] The article states he was the Former Registrar of Vehicles. However, he may have been demoted to the position as Registrar. The article signals confusion about the reasons behind his resignation. See "Call to Clarify Resignation", *The Straits Times*, 20 September 1967, page 13, https://eresources.nlb.gov.sg/newspapers/Digitised/Article/straitstimes19670920-1.2.85. Accessed on 19 November 2021.

Chapter 10

[1] Grace Ho, "Former top civil servant Ngiam Tong Dow dies, aged 83", *The Straits Times*, 20 August 2020, https://www.straitstimes.com/politics/former-top-civil-servant-ngiam-tong-dow-dies-aged-83. Accessed on 19 November 2021.

Chapter 12

[1] "Portrait of Mr. Michael Yeo Chee Wee, Chairman of Singapore Manufacturers' Association", Book SG, National Library Board, https://eresources.nlb.gov.sg/printheritage/image.aspx?id=2aa7ccc1-088e-4737-b7ac-ea7882d31c00. Accessed on 19 November 2021.

Chapter 13

[1] Ministry of Education, Government of Singapore, "For O: Level Students: Where do I want to go?", Polytechnics, https://www.moe.gov.sg/microsites/whats-next/for-gce-o-level-students/where-do-i-want-to-go/i-want-to-further-my-studies/polytechnics/index.html. Accessed on 21 November 2021.

Chapter 14

[1] Faizal bin Yahya, "Chapter 1: INTRACO and its Role in Economic Development in Singapore", in *INTRACO: Blazing a Trail Oversees for Singapore?* (World Scientific, 2015), pp. 1 and 6, https://www.worldscientific.com/doi/suppl/10.1142/9328/suppl_file/9328_chap01.pdf. Accessed on 23 November 2021.

[2] Faizal bin Yahya, "Lessons form Intraco, Singapore's original trail blazer", *Today*, 28 April 2015, https://lkyspp.nus.edu.sg/docs/default-source/ips/pa_faizal_td_lessons-from-intraco-singapore-s-original-trailblazer_2804151-pdf.pdf?sfvrsn=9b0c9f0b_0. Accessed on 23 November 2021.

[3] Faizal bin Yahya, "Chapter 1: INTRACO and its Role in Economic Development in Singapore", op. cit., p. 2.

[4] Ibid., pp. 3, 12 and 14.

[5] Ibid., p. 9.

[6] Roger Mann, "Amin Buys Loyalty of Soldiers", *The Washington Post*, 6 April 1977, https://www.washingtonpost.com/archive/politics/1977/04/06/amin-buys-loyalty-of-soldiers/92db022c-dc34-4a6a-af97-56eae2ccf728/. Accessed on 23 November 2021.

[7] Pervez Daruwala, "Shifting of the Parsee Fire Temple from Aden to India (Aden 1886–1976), *The Flames of Faith: A Historical Saga*, in *Jam-e-Jamshed Weekly*, Parsi New Year Special, published originally on 16 August 1998, https://parsikhabar.net/heritage/aden-to-india-shifting-of-the-parsee-fire-temple/566/. Accessed on 23 November 2021.

[8] Ibid.

[9] Ibid.

[10] The CESS tax at that time "required local companies proposing to trade with socialist economies like China to pay a tax of about 1 percent of total value of good traded". See Faizal bin Yahya, "Divesting State Owned Enterprises", *International Review of Business Research Papers*, Vol. 8., No. 4, May 2012, pp. 196 and 204, https://www.academia.edu/6109668/Divesting_State_Owned_Enterprises. Accessed on 23 November 2021.

[11] See, for example, Nora Cheng, "More Senior Intraco Executives May Join Exodus", *Straits Times,* 26 August 1986, https://eresources.nlb.gov.sg/newspapers/Digitised/Article/straitstimes19860826-1.2.35.4. Accessed on 23 November 2021.

[12] Faizal bin Yahya, "Divesting State Owned Enterprises", op. cit.

[13] See Intraco Limited, "Overview", Official Website, https://www.intraco.com.sg/overview.html; and also "Intraco Limited: Reset — 2020 Annual Report", https://investor.intraco.com.sg/ar.html. Accessed on 23 November 2021.

Chapter 15

[1] Alan Lee and Elaine Koh, "Taking up the Pizza Challenge", *Business Times*, 12 April 1989, https://eresources.nlb.gov.sg/newspapers/Digitised/Article/biztimes19890412-1.2.25.2. Accessed on 23 November 2021.

[2] Ibid. According to Magdalene Ng in "Inno-Pacific acquires Shakey's franchise", *Straits Times*, 1 October 1988, https://eresources.nlb.gov.sg/newspapers/Digitised/Article/biztimes19881001-1.2.31.6, "Inno-Pacific (had) budgeted about US$2 million as start-up cost for the Shakey chain in the various countries, or about US$500,000 per outlet, for the first year". Accessed on 23 November 2021.

[3] An account of the case and the court's ruling may be found in Yang Ing Loong, "The Mens Rea of Dishonesty in Property Offences", https://v1.lawgazette.com.sg/2000-8/Aug00-focus.htm. Accessed on 23 November 2021.

[4] See other references to the learned judge's remarks on the case in Desmond Chye & Russell Vaz, "Director's Duties: Re-Examining the Bona Fide Test", *Singapore Law Review*, https://www.singaporelawreview.com/juris-illuminae-entries/2021/directors-duties-re-examining-the-bona-fide-test. Accessed on 23 November 2021.

[5] Yang Ing Loong, op. cit. Also see "No costs for those acquitted of crime", *The Straits Times*, 13 March 1996, https://eresources.nlb.gov.sg/newspapers/digitised/issue/straitstimes19960313-1. Accessed on 23 November 2021.

Chapter 16

[1] Gopinath Pillai, "The Genesis" in *Gateway Distriparks: The Story of a Successful Singapore–India Joint Venture*, A GDL Publication to Commemorate the Visit of Singapore Prime Minister Mr. Lee Hsien Loong, July 2012, p. 6.

[2] Ravi Velloor, "Singapore, India to take bilateral ties up a notch", *The Straits Times*, 23 November 2015, https://www.straitstimes.com/singapore/singapore-india-to-take-bilateral-ties-up-a-notch. Accessed 23 November 2021.

[3] I offer similar views in Fern Yu, "IPS Corporate Associates' Lunch Dialogue: Doing Business in India", IPS Update, September 2017, https://lkyspp.nus.edu.sg/docs/default-source/ips/enews_cal-doing-business-in-india_140917.pdf. Accessed on 24 November 2021.

[4] Krishnadas Rajagopal, "Kesavananda Bharti — the petitioner who saved democracy, but lost his case in Supreme Court", *The Hindu*, 6 September 2020, https://www.thehindu.com/news/national/kesavananda-bharati-the-petitioner-who-saved-democracy-but-lost-his-case-in-sc/article32535243.ece. Accessed on 6 June 2022.

[5] *Nani Palkhivala: A Role Model*, ed. Maj Gen Nilendra Kumar, 3rd Ed. (New Delhi: Universal Law Publishing Co. Pvt. Ltd., 2009), p. 222.

Chapter 17

[1] Much of my account in this chapter of GDL's expansion has been adapted from my chapters "Introduction" and "Genesis" in the book *Gateway Distriparks: The Story of a Successful Singapore–India Joint Venture*. See Gopinath Pillai, "The Genesis", op. cit., p. 7.

[2] Gopinath Pillai, "The Genesis", ibid., p. 5.

[3] Gopinath Pillai, "The Genesis", ibid.

[4] Ibid.

[5] Ibid., pp. 3 and 5.

[6] Kirpa Ram Vij, "The Start Up", *Gateway Distriparks: The Story of a Successful Singapore-India Joint Venture*, p. 25.

[7] Gopinath Pillai, "The Genesis", op. cit., pp. 6–7.

[8] Kirpa Ram Vij, "The Start Up", op. cit., p. 24.

[9] Gopinath Pillai, "The Genesis", op. cit., p. 8.

[10] Ibid., p. 10.

[11] Ibid., pp. 10 and 11.

[12] Ibid., p. 12.

[13] *Gateway Distriparks Annual Report 2014–15*, "About the Group", https://www.bseindia.com/bseplus/annualreport/532622/5326220315.pdf. Accessed on 23 November 2021.

[14] Gopinath Pillai, "The Genesis", op. cit., p. 12.

[15] See *Gateway Distriparks Annual Report 2014–15*, and Gopinath Pillai, Oral History Interview, interviewed by Santanu Gupta, Oral History Centre, pp. 153 and 154.

[16] I voiced similar opinions in "ISAS Chairman: We Need to Understand India Better" for *India and Singapore: 50 years of strategic partnership*, Commemorative Issue of High Commission of India on the State Visit of Prime Minister Narendra Modi, 23–24 November 2015, p. 43.

Chapter 18

[1] Faizal bin Yahya, "Chapter 1: INTRACO and its Role in Economic Development in Singapore", op. cit., p. 8.

[2] Stephanie Ho, "Wong Kan Seng", Singapore Infopedia, https://eresources.nlb.gov.sg/infopedia/articles/SIP_2013-11-26_174343.html. Accessed on 30 November 2021.

[3] Alvin Chua, "Herman Ronald Hochstadt", Singapore Infopedia, 2015, https://eresources.nlb.gov.sg/infopedia/articles/SIP_1557_2009-08-28.html. Accessed on 30 November 2021.

[4] "Kok Swee Foo", Prabook, https://prabook.com/web/kok_swee.foo/1038702. Accessed on 29 November 2021.

[5] "Overview: Sohrab and Rustum", Oxford Reference, https://www.oxfordreference.com/view/10.1093/oi/authority.20110810105902816. Accessed on 30 November 2021.

[6] John Darwin, "Britain, the Commonwealth and the End of Empire", British History, BBC, last updated 3 March 2011, https://www.bbc.co.uk/history/british/modern/endofempire_overview_01.shtml. Accessed on 30 November 2021.

[7] William Wallace, "British Foreign Policy after the Cold War", *International Affairs*, Vol. 68, No. 3 (July 1992), p. 424, https://www.jstor.org/stable/2622964. Accessed on 30 November 2021.

[8] Malcolm Byrne, "CIA Admits It Was Behind Iran's Coup", *Foreign Policy*, 19 August 2013, https://foreignpolicy.com/2013/08/19/cia-admits-it-was-behind-irans-coup/. Accessed on 30 November 2021.

[9] Mark J. Gasiorowski and Malcolm Byrne, eds., Abstract of *Mohammad Mosaddeq and the 1953 Coup in Iran* (Syracuse University Press, 2017), https://www.amazon.com/Mohammad-Mosaddeq-Intellectual-Political-History/dp/081563529X. Accessed on 30 November 2021.

[10] Welles Hangen, "Mossadegh Gets 3-Year Jail Term", *The New York Times*, 22 December 1953. https://archive.nytimes.com/www.nytimes.com/library/world/mideast/122253iran-jail.html. Accessed on 30 November 2021.

[11] Reza Aslan, "The Epic of Iran", *The New York Times*, 30 April 2006, https://www.nytimes.com/2006/04/30/books/review/the-epic-of-iran.html. Accessed on 30 November 2021.

[12] The embassy, which was suspected by some of being an American spy centre, has since been converted into a museum called the "Den of Espionage". See Syed Zafar Mehdi, "Inside America's former embassy

in Iran", *Anatolia Agency*, 5 August 2019, https://www.aa.com.tr/en/middle-east/inside-america-s-former-embassy-in-iran-/1549710. Accessed on 30 November 2021.

13 CRF.org Editors, "The Islamic Republic's Power Centers", Council on Foreign Relations, 25 February 2020, https://www.cfr.org/article/islamic-republics-power-centers. Accessed on 30 November 2021.

14 "Iran: How Ayatollah Khamenei became its most powerful man", *BBC News*, 9 March 2020, https://www.bbc.com/news/world-middle-east-29115464. Accessed on 30 November 2021.

15 Singapore Trade Mission: Iran, Turkmenistan, 8–13 December 1995. Brochure. Hard copy.

16 Irfan Parviz, "Pillai Says Iran-Singapore Relations Problem-Free", *Iran News*, 29 January 2002. Hard copy.

17 The Editors of Encyclopedia Brittanica, "Kerman: Introduction & Quick Facts", https://www.britannica.com/place/Kerman-Iran. Accessed on 30 November 2021.

Chapter 19

1 "The Islamic Republic's Power Centers", op. cit.

2 "Umar Khayyam", *Stanford Encyclopedia of Philosophy*, last updated 10 February 2017, https://plato.stanford.edu/entries/umar-khayyam/. Accessed on 30 November 2021.

3 Djavad Salehi-Isfahani, "Iran's economy 40 years after the Islamic Revolution", 14 March 2019, https://www.brookings.edu/blog/order-from-chaos/2019/03/14/irans-economy-40-years-after-the-islamic-revolution/. Accessed on 30 November 2021.

4 Henry Rome, "The Iran Primer", United States Institute of Peace, 10 February 2021, https://iranprimer.usip.org/blog/2021/feb/10/iran-struggles-under-oil-sanctions. Accessed on 6 June 2022.

5 "The Islamic Republic's Power Centers", op. cit.

6 Keith Crane, Rollie Lal and Jeffrey Martini, "Chapter Two: Domestic Politics" in *Iran's Political, Demographic, and Economic Vulnerabilities* (RAND Corporation, 2008), p. 10. Accessed through JSTOR, https://www.jstor.org/stable/10.7249/mg693af.10?seq=1#metadata_info_tab_contents, on 30 November 2021.

[7] Kersten Knipp, "Ali al-Sistani: Spiritual leader and stabilizing factor", trans. Charlotte Collins, DW Made for Minds, 6 March 2021, https://www.dw.com/en/ali-al-sistani-spiritual-leader-and-stabilizing-factor/a-56766421. Accessed on 30 November 2021.

[8] Keith Crane, Rollie Lal and Jeffrey Martini, "Chapter Two: Domestic Politics", op. cit.

[9] "The People's Mujahedin: Iran's exiled opposition", *France24*, 10 August 2021, https://www.france24.com/en/live-news/20210810-the-people-s-mujahedin-iran-s-exiled-opposition. Also see "Iran: How Ayatollah Khamenei became its most powerful man", op. cit.

[10] Shobha John, "Temples & Taboos", *The Times of India*, 24 July 2011, https://timesofindia.indiatimes.com/home/sunday-times/deep-focus/temples-taboos/articleshow/9342277.cms. Accessed on 29 November 2021.

[11] K. V. Lakshmana, "Atheist CM Karunanidhi sidesteps jinxed temple entrance", *Hindustan Times*, 28 September 2010, https://www.hindustantimes.com/india/atheist-cm-karunanidhi-sidesteps-jinxed-temple-entrance/story-G2vGWA2vRi2j5sVGHez6wK.html. Accessed on 29 November 2021.

[12] This anecdote has been integrated with modifications from Gopinath Pillai, "Letters to a Young Public Officer", www.challenge.gov.sg, November/December 2015, Public Service Division of the Prime Minister's Office, p. 25. Hard copy.

[13] Gopinath Pillai, "Dealing with Iran: Without Iran, M-E peace can't take flight", *The Straits Times*, 12 March 2009. Hard copy.

[14] For other views on the significance of the speech, see David Frum *et al.*, "Analysis: The Long Reach of a Speech", *Frontline*, PBS, https://www.pbs.org/wgbh/pages/frontline/shows/tehran/axis/axis.html. Accessed on 29 November 2021.

[15] I was personally unhappy with some aspects of Ahmadinejad's way of doing things. See also Robin Wright and William Branigin, "Ahmadinejad Met With Protests, Criticism at Columbia University", *The Washington Post*, 24 September 2007, https://www.washingtonpost.com/archive/business/technology/2007/09/24/ahmadinejad-met-with-protests-criticism-at-columbia-university/14f8dd1e-096a-4dbf-9fde-fd79ecdf46a3/. Accessed on 30 November 2021.

Chapter 20

[1] Lee Kuan Yew, *From Third World to First, The Singapore Story: 1965–2000* (Singapore, Times Media Private Ltd., 2000), op. cit., p. 466.

[2] Huma Nawa Syal, "Pakistan and Malaysia: Economic and Trade Relations", *Strategic Studies*, Vol. 27, No. 1 (Spring 2007), pp. 40–41, 43, https://www.jstor.org/stable/45242380. Accessed on 30 November 2021. For more recent data, See "Pakistan GDP Annual Growth Rate" Trading Economics, https://tradingeconomics.com/pakistan/gdp-growth-annual and "GDP Growth (annual %) – Pakistan, the World Bank, data, https://data.worldbank.org/indicator/NY.GDP.MKTP.KD.ZG?locations=PK. Accessed on 30 November 2021.

[3] S. Akbar Zaidi, "Special Report: Darkness Descends 1977–1988", *Dawn*, 1 November 2017, https://www.dawn.com/news/1364410. Accessed on 30 November 2021.

[4] See William Claiborne, "Pakistani Parties Rally, Defying Martial Law", *The Washington Post*, 15 August 1983, https://www.washingtonpost.com/archive/politics/1983/08/15/pakistani-parties-rally-defying-martial-law/73335e8f-b777-4c72-85b2-137b0f8250e9/; and also Reuters, "Foes of Pakistani Chief Reject Election Plan", reprinted in *The New York Times*, 14 August 1983, https://www.nytimes.com/1983/08/14/world/foes-of-pakistani-chief-reject-election-plan.html. Accessed on 30 November 2021.

[5] A similar full itinerary can be found in Department of Foreign Affairs, Republic of the Philippines, "PHL Ambassador Presents Credentials to President of Pakistan", 23 November 2015, https://dfa.gov.ph/dfa-news/news-from-our-foreign-service-postsupdate/7986-phl-ambassador-presents-credentials-to-president-of-pakistan. Accessed on 30 November 2020.

[6] Association of Southeast Asian Nations, "Overview", https://asean.org/our-communities/economic-community/integration-with-global-economy/asean-india-economic-relations/overview/. Accessed on 30 November 2021.

[7] Nithya Subramanian, "Ertugrul: A Turkish delight for Pakistan", ISAS Insights No. 650, https://www.isas.nus.edu.sg/wp-content/uploads/2020/11/650.pdf. Accessed on 30 November 2021.

[8] "Singapore delegation visits Pakistan to look for investment avenues", *The Express Tribune*, 1 March 2019, https://tribune.com.pk/story/1920566/2-singapore-delegation-visits-pakistan-look-investment-avenues. Accessed on 30 November 2021.

[9] "PM Imran, Singapore's Loong discuss boosting bilateral ties at Davos", *The Express Tribune*, 22 January 2020, https://tribune.com.pk/story/2142203/pm-imran-singapores-loong-discuss-boosting-bilateral-ties-davos. Accessed on 30 November 2021.

[10] Narendra Aggarwal, "Pakistan to step up ties with Singapore", *The Business Times*, 23 March 2020, https://www.businesstimes.com.sg/hub/pakistan-national-day/pakistan-to-step-up-ties-with-singapore. Accessed on 30 November 2021.

[11] "Zia ul-Haq", Encyclopedia Brittanica. Also see Shamil Shams, "Pakistan's Islamization — before and after Zia-ul Haq", DW Made for Minds, 17 August 2016, https://www.dw.com/en/pakistans-islamization-before-and-after-dictator-zia-ul-haq/a-19480315. Accessed on 30 November 2021.

[12] S. Akbar Zaidi, op. cit.

[13] Lee Kuan Yew, op. cit., pp. 467–468.

[14] Ibid., p. 469.

[15] Khaled Ahmed, "Who killed Murtaza Bhutto?", *The Indian Express*, 3 October 2015, https://indianexpress.com/article/opinion/columns/who-killed-murtaza-bhutto/. Accessed on 30 November 2021.

Chapter 21

[1] Pattarin Kusolpalin, "National University of Singapore", 29 February 2016, https://eresources.nlb.gov.sg/infopedia/articles/SIP_50_2005-01-17.html. Accessed on 1 December 2021.

[2] Peter H. L. Lim and Dana Lam, "Gopinath Pillai", *The Heart Is Where It Is: The NUSS Story*, Ed. Maurice Baker (National University of Singapore Society, 1994), p. 134.

[3] Peter H. L. Lim and Dana Lam, "Ernest Wong Thian Yow", op. cit., p. 130.

[4] Christine Chua, "Formation of University of Singapore", *True Passion: NUSS Fifty Years and On*: 1954–2004, p. 34.

[5] Peter H. L. Lim and Dana Lam, "Dr Maurice Baker", p. 126.

[6] Ibid.

[7] Ibid., p. 128.

[8] Peter H. L. Lim and Dana Lam, "Prof Kiang Ai Kim", p. 123.

[9] "Kent Ridge Campus" in *It's Yesterday Once More: NUS 1959–1964 Recollections*, p. 5.

[10] "Prof Kiang Ai Kim", op. cit., p. 123.

[11] Peter H. L. Lim and Dana Lam, "Ernest Wong Thian How", op. cit., p. 132.

[12] Facts taken from an interview I gave to Peter L. Lim and Dana Lam in "Gopinath Pillai", *The Heart is Where It Is: The NUSS Story*, op. cit., p. 135.

[13] Ibid.

[14] Christina Chua, "A Home on Campus: The Alumni Complex Project", op. cit., p. 116.

[15] Ibid., p. 118.

[16] "NUS Society Donates $20m to centre for alumni", *The Straits Times*, 26 July 2003, reproduced in Christina Chua, op. cit., p. 119.

[17] "The Story of NTUC Fairprice: Singapore's Very Own", Citeman, 13 December 2009, https://www.citeman.com/8046-the-story-of-ntuc-fair-price-singapore%E2%80%99s-very-own.html. Accessed on 1 December 2021.

[18] Pang Eng Fong and Linda Seah, "The Singapore Economy in 1975: Stagnation and Recovery", *Southeast Asian Affairs* (1976), p. 339, https://www.jstor.org/stable/27908288. Accessed on 1 December 2021.

[19] Details can be found in a commemorative booklet provided by the NTUC Fairprice staff to me called *Mr Gopinath Pillai and NTUC Fairprice 1983–1993*. Hard copy.

Chapter 22

[1] "About Us" on Hindu Endowments Board Website, https://heb.org.sg/about-us/. Accessed on 1 December 2021.

[2] Gayathiri Chandramohan, "S. R. Nathan", *Roots*, https://www.roots.gov.sg/stories-landing/stories/sr-nathan/story.

[3] S. R. Nathan and Timothy Auger, *An Unexpected Journey: Path to the Presidency* (Editions Didier Millet, 2011), p. 444.

[4] S. R. Nathan, "Foreword", p. viii. Reproduced from *V. R. Nathan: Community Servant Extraordinary* by Bala Baskaran, Said Abdullah and Arun Senkuttuvan (Singapore: Institute of Southeast Asian Studies, 2012), https://bookshop.iseas.edu.sg/account/downloads/get/13950.

[5] Gopinath Pillai, "Oral History Interview," interview by Santanu Gupta, op. cit.

[6] Gopinath Pillai, "NUS-Chairman-Kerala", unpublished interview with Robin Jeffrey, 2017.

Chapter 23

[1] Malvika Agarwal, "Once Upon a Time — The People and Places of Singapore's Little India", *Once Upon a Time in Little India*, ed. Nalina Gopal (Indian Heritage Centre, 2019), p. 22.

[2] Ibid., 23.

[3] Ruchi Mittal, "Little India: A Cultural and Historical Precinct", publication date unknown, https://www.roots.gov.sg/stories-landing/stories/little-india-a-cultural-and-historical-precinct/story. Accessed on 2 December 2021.

[4] For more details on the conservation, see "Little India Arcade", *Roots*, https://www.roots.gov.sg/places/places-landing/Places/landmarks/little-india-heritage-trail-shop-till-you-drop/little-india-arcade. Accessed on 2 December 2021.

[5] Shobha Tsering Bhalla, op. cit., p. 20.

[6] Rajesh Rai, "Indians in the Modelling of the Global Metropolis", *50 Years of Indian Community in Singapore*, op. cit., p. 17.

[7] Rajesh Rai, as quoted in Radhika Dhawan Puri, "Cultural differences: Within Singapore's Indian community, a clash between the old and the new", *Scroll.in*, 12 August 2016, https://scroll.in/article/813428/cultural-differences-within-singapores-indian-community-a-clash-between-the-old-and-the-new. Accessed on 2 December 2021.

[8] Rajesh Rai, "Indians in the Modelling of the Global Metropolis", p. 15.

[9] Gopinath Pillai, "A Place in the Sun", *50 Years of Indian Community in Singapore*, op. cit., p. 3.

[10] Rajesh Rai, "Indians in the Modelling of the Global Metropolis", p. 16 and K. Kesavapany and Asad Latif, "The Singapore Indian Community towards SG100", *50 Years of Indian Community in Singapore*, op. cit., p. 132.

[11] Anitha Devi Pillai, "SMA is 100", *Tabla*, 1 September 2017, p. 12, https://www.tabla.com.sg/jrsrc/310817full/epage012013/TA20170901-TAB-012-00-013.html.

[12] Ibid.

[13] Prime Minister's Office, Singapore, "PM Lee Hsien Loong at the Singapore Malayalee Association 100th Anniversary Dinner", 29 September 2017,

https://www.pmo.gov.sg/Newsroom/pm-lee-hsien-loong-singapore-malayalee-association-100th-anniversary-dinner.

[14] Anitha Devi Pillai, op. cit.

[15] "Putting a PC In Every Indian Home: Giving The IT Advantage", brochure of the IT Services Cooperative. Hard copy.

[16] "Friend of IT: Gopinath Pillai", IT Leaders Awards, 24 February 2001, SCS Gala Dinner for IT Leader Awards 2001, Ritz Carlton. Hard copy.

[17] Gopinath Pillai, "A Place in the Sun", op. cit., p. 3.

[18] Gauri Parimoo Krishnan, "Singapore's Indian Heritage Centre: Curating and Negotiating Heritage, Diversity and Identity", *50 Years of Indian Community in Singapore*, op. cit., p. 19

[19] K. Satku, "Citation for Dr Balaji Sadasivan", *Feature*, https://news.sma.org.sg/4205/citation_smssadasivan.pdf. Accessed on 2 December 2021.

[20] Gauri Parimoo Krishnan, op. cit., pp. 20 and 28.

[21] Ibid., 29.

[22] Melody Zaccheus, "Five things to know about the new Indian Heritage Centre", *The Straits Times*, 8 May 2015, https://www.straitstimes.com/singapore/five-things-to-know-about-the-new-indian-heritage-centre. Accessed on 2 December 2021.

[23] Gauri Parimoo Krishnan, op. cit., p. 20.

[24] Janice Seow, "Indian Heritage Centre: A New Cultural Landmark", Indesignlive.sg, 13 May 2015, https://www.indesignlive.sg/projects/a-new-cultural-landmark. Accessed on 2 December 2021.

[25] Gauri Parimoo Krishnan, op. cit., p. 19.

Chapter 25

[1] Tommy Koh, "Foreword", *My Love is Blind* (Asiapac Books, 2017). Also see "Tan Guan Heng", profile on The Purple Parade website, https://www.purpleparade.sg/stories/tan-guan-heng. Accessed on 12 April 2022.

Index

A
Abdullah, V. P., 30, 39
Adelphi Hotel (Adelphi), 4, 6–8, 15, 25, 27, 29–30, 237, 269
Ambassador Holdings Ltd., 152
ambassador-at-large, 217
ASEAN, 214
Asian Seamen's Club, 54, 237
Atherton, Bernar R., 47–49

B
Baker, Maurice, 221–222
Balakrishnan, R. (Bala), 110–111, 152
Bandung Conference, 60, 80
Barisan Sosialis, 63, 124, 278
Bhutto, Benazir, 212–213, 216
Bhutto, Mir Murtaza, 216
bonyad (foundation), 201
Borujeradi, Alaeddin, 196
Boonchu Rajanastien, Khun, 88, 98
Bose, Subhas Chandra ('Netaji'), 28, 35, 37–38, 255
Britain (Great Britain, England, the United Kingdom), 10, 20, 74, 89, 95, 122–123, 143, 145, 188, 260, 272
British naval base (Seletar), 4, 30, 37, 39, 279
Bukit Timah Campus, 56

C
Chandra Das, S., 142–144, 147, 150–151, 164, 172, 185–186, 224–225, 230, 238, 254
Cheam Tat Pang, 109, 118, 152, 156–157
Chipp, David, 79
China, 4, 36, 41, 50, 79–81, 89, 97, 120, 142–143, 147–150, 162, 177–178, 202, 215–216, 259, 279
Chola Empire, 97
Choon Guan English School (Choon Guan), 41–42, 44–52, 96, 118, 183, 219, 233–234
Chuang Wen Lian, 135–136, 138
Cold War, 60, 89, 142, 164, 211, 214, 259
communism (communists, Karl Marx, Marxist), 20–22, 31, 33–34, 36, 48, 67, 76, 79, 142, 146, 233
Communist Youth Movement, 19, 31
Indian National Congress (Congress), 19, 21, 61
container freight stations, 170–172
Container Warehousing and Transport (CWT), 171–173

D
Darda, Jawahar, 171–172
DBS, 224, 244, 246
D'Costa, Francis, 236–237
democracy, 33, 37, 45–47, 49
Dhanabalan, S., 251
Dinshaw, Cowasjee, 146
Dinshaw, Saroosh, 146

E
E&O Hotel, 25
Export-Credit and Insurance Corporation of Singapore (ECICS), 186, 189, 200, 204
Economic Commission for Asia and the Far East (ECAFE), 89, 94
Economic Development Board (EDB), 118, 129, 142
Engandiyoor, 8–9, 21, 23, 241, 269
Esteghlal (Royal Tehran Hilton), 201
Europe Hotel, 7

F
Fajar, 58–62, 65, 76, 78
Far East Economic Review (FEER), 91–92, 112
Fiji, 74–75
Foo Kok Swee, 186–187

G
Ghandi, Indira, 165, 205, 245
Gateway Distriparks Limited (GDL), 146, 159, 168, 170–177
Goh Chok Tong, 134, 148, 160–162, 171, 181, 191, 207–208, 216, 218–219, 257, 259
Goh Keng Swee, 141, 148–149
Goho, S. C., 37–38

H
Haig Road, 25, 27, 39
Heng Swee Kiat, 257–260
Hertie, 126–127
Hindi, 43, 71–72, 212, 214, 231, 248, 254
Hinduism (tradition, beliefs and customs), 9, 18, 233–236, 239, 241–242
Hindu Advisory Board (HAB), 192, 236, 239–42, 247
Hindu Endowments Board (HEB), 236–239, 243, 246, 247
Ho, David, 159–160, 170
Hochstadt, Herman, 75, 186–187, 221
Hon Sui Sen, 115, 134, 148

I
India (childhood, international relations, business), 8–24, 79–81, 126, 147, 153, 159–179, 206–208, 211, 258–261
Indian Heritage Centre, 252–256
Indian Independence Movement (Independence), 21, 23, 28, 31, 35, 37–38, 43, 160
Indian National Army (INA), 28–30, 255
Inno-Pacific Holdings (Inno-Pac), 152–160
Institute of South Asian Studies (ISAS), 161, 231, 257–263
International Trading Company (Intraco), 141–151, 162–165, 172, 183
Iran, 19, 186–210, 216–217
Islamic Revolution, 187, 191, 199, 201, 204, 215
Isfahan, 207–208
IT Co-operative, 250–252, 270

J
Janardhanan, C. (youngest uncle, Kochapamama), 17, 19–23, 31, 33–34, 48, 57, 277
Japanese Occupation, 10–12, 24, 26, 28–30
Jayachandran, R., 254

K
Khamenei, Ali, 191, 193, 199, 202
Kesavapany, K., 254
Kent Ridge Guild House, 219–224
Kerala, 4–6, 8–9, 13, 15, 21–23, 31, 30, 52–53, 61, 72, 204, 206, 249, 269
Kerala Bandhu (printing business), 27, 30–31, 38–39
Kerman, 195–196
Khatami, Seyed Mohamad, 210
Khattar, Sat Pal, 158, 168, 170, 176, 222, 247, 274
Khayyam, Omar, 198, 206, 208
Khomeini, Sayyid Ruhollah Musavi, 187, 199, 204
Kiang Ai Kim, 78, 223
Kishan Gupta, Prem, 170–173
Koh, Tommy, 66, 74, 202, 258, 267
Kotnis, Dr. Dwarkanath Shantaram, 79–80
Kwan Sai Keong, 222

L
Lakhani, Amin, 212
Lee Hsien Loong, 215, 250–251
Lee Kim Yew, Dennis, 134, 136–139
Lee Kuan Yew, 36, 58–59, 66–68, 134, 160, 204, 212, 215–216, 222, 231–233, 253
Leembruggen, H. F. G., 103, 107
Lee Siew Choh, 62–63
Leghari, Farooq, 212–213, 216
1955 Legislative Assembly Election, 45
1959 Legislative Assembly Election, 36–37, 66
1948 Legislative Council Election, 35–38, 47
Libya, 144–145

Lim Jit Poh, 157, 181
Lim Yew Hock, 36
Little India, 178, 243
Little India Arcade, 243–247

M
Madras, 5, 9, 24, 39
Mahatma Gandhi ("Gandhi", Gandhian), 19–20, 29, 33, 35
Mahbubani, Kishore, 205, 216
Majlis, 193
Malayalee, Malayalam, 4–7, 8, 11–12, 19–20, 30–31, 35, 37, 39, 42, 51, 70, 248–249, 252, 277, 279
Malaysian Industrial Finance Bhd (MIDF), 99–105, 108, 111, 117, 127
1969 Malaysian Race Riots, 106–108, 110, 125, 221, 278
Mandarin, 42–44, 62
Mao Zedong, 36
Mathrubhumi, 11, 29
Menon, C. G., 6, 28, 277
Menon, K. P., 28–29, 277
Menon, M. R., 5–6, 28, 277
Menon, T. K. N., 94–95, 99, 101
Middle Road Union Headquarters, 62–63
Ministry of Education (MOE), 81
Ministry of Foreign Affairs (MFA), 191, 200, 205–206, 211, 217, 253, 257, 263
Modi, Narendra, 161–162, 176
Mosaddegh, Mohammad, 188–189

N
Nair, Devan, 30, 63
Nair, Narayana (grandfather), 9–11, 13–14, 16–23, 31, 236, 239, 275
Nandan, Satya, 74
Nandan, Sree Kumar, 272, 277
Nanyang University Political Science Society, 66, 69
Nathan, S. R., 237–239, 255, 261–262, 267, 278
Nathan, V. R., 239–241, 247
National Heritage Board, 255–256
National Trades Union Congress (NTUC, NTUC Fairprice), 63–64, 128, 150, 175, 181, 196, 224–230
National University of Singapore (NUS, NUSS), 219–220, 222–224, 249, 262–263
Nehru, Jawaharlal, 21, 31, 35, 61, 79–80, 89, 160, 245
Ngiam Tong Dow, 109, 118–123, 125, 141
non-resident ambassador (NRA), 147, 185–190, 195–196, 201, 206, 209, 216–217

O
Ong Eng Guan, 59–60, 69
Ong Teng Cheong, 181, 225, 230
Operation Coldstore, 86–87, 113, 124, 185, 237, 278
Oppenheim, Alexander, 63–65

P
Pakistan, 89, 145–147, 151, 211–217
Palkhivala, Nani, 165–167
Pang Tee Pow, 134–138
Parsee, 145–146
Parukuttyamma (grandmother), 16–17, 22, 24
People's Action Party (PAP), 36, 45–46, 59, 63, 66–69, 124–125, 184, 278
People's Mujahedin Organization of Iran (PMOI) 201–202
Pillai, K. S. (father), 4–7, 10–11, 13–15, 22, 24–35, 37–39, 41–44, 47–48, 52, 54, 78, 84, 86, 117, 184, 233–237, 272, 275, 277
Pillai, Malathi (mother), 1, 4–6, 8–14, 17, 19–22, 24–26, 34, 37–40, 44, 47, 50, 52, 56, 85, 105, 245, 272–273
Pillai, Prakash (son), 106–108, 131, 280
Pillai, Preetha (daughter), 105–106, 110, 131, 280
Pillai, Priya Kumari (daughter), 130–131, 280
Pillai, Sree Kumari (sister), 5–6, 8, 13–14, 17–18, 25–26, 38–39, 73–74, 108, 272–273, 278
Pillai, Shyamala Devi (wife), 70–73, 84–86, 93–96, 98, 100, 104–107, 110, 112, 220, 263, 268, 270, 280
Parimoo Krishnan, Gauri, 255
Puthucheary, Dominic, 62–63
Puthucheary, James, 65, 68

R

Raghavan, V. R., 93–94
Rajah, A. P., 37–38
Rajan, V. K., 191, 193
Raffles Institution (Raffles Players), 41, 82–83
Rafsanjani, Akbar Hashemi, 190–191, 194–196
Rameshan (younger uncle, Rameshamama), 14–15, 25, 27
Rao, Narasimha, 160, 208, 214
Raya Mills Corporation Ltd. (Raya Mills), 109–110, 112–113, 115, 117–130, 133, 141, 278
Reuters, 79, 81–82

S

Sadasivan, Balaji, 253–256
Sarawak and Sabah, 102–103
Sharif, Nawaz, 215–216
Stalin, Joseph, 22, 33–34
Sea View Hotel, 6, 29
Seow Cheng Fong, 49–51, 57–59, 184, 277
Shakey's Pizza, 153–155, 169
Singapore Indian Development Association (SINDA), 239, 249, 252
Singapore Malayalee Association, 249
Singapore Manufacturer's Association (SMA), 132, 144, 148
Singapore Polytechnic Political Society, 59, 66, 69
Singapore Teacher's Union (STU), 85
Singapore Trade Development Board (TDB), 147, 194–195
Sithawalla, Haider, 75, 157, 168, 170, 181, 233
Sithi-Amnuai, Paul, 83–84, 88, 90–92
Snowman Logistics (Snowman), 175–176
socialism, 33, 57–58, 76, 85, 113, 142–143
South Asia Disapora Convention (SADC), 262
Southeast Asia Treaty Organization (SEATO), 89
Soviet Union, 34, 57, 188, 215
Sri Vrijaya Empire (Sri Vijayas), 97
St. Andrew's Secondary School, 52–53, 55, 219, 234
St. Hilda's School, 40–41
St. Joseph's Institution, 35, 41
Stuchen, Philip, 99–101
Svoboda, Ladislav, 101–104
Syamal Gupta, 163–166

T

Tan Chorh Chuan, 260
Tan Eng Chye, 262–263
Tan Guan Heng, 66, 267–268, 274
Tan Keng Kang, 44, 51, 96, 277
Tan Tai Yong, 259–260
Tan, Tony, 226
Tata Consultancy Services (TCS, Tata), 147, 163–165
Technical College campus, 56–57, 71
Temasek, 134, 139, 174
Thailand (Bangkok Bank, Bangkok), 83–86, 88–96, 98–101, 124, 226
Thivy, John, 35–36
Thrissur, 8–9, 17, 241, 269
Toh Chin Chye, 45, 221–222
Tusi, Qasem Ferdowsi ("Ferdowsi"), 189, 206

U

ul-Haq, Zia, 211–212, 215
United Nations Convention on the Law of the Sea (UNCLOS), 74
Unni, Dr. Narayanan, 272–273
Unni (elder uncle, Unnimama), 14–15, 17, 25–27
UNESCO, 93–94, 99
United Industrial Corporation (UIC), 133–139
United States (U.S., America, Americans), 91, 94–95, 99–100, 104–105, 143, 153–155, 164, 187–188, 192–193, 195, 200, 203–204, 210–211, 246, 279
University of Malaya, 39, 52, 54, 56, 58, 66, 77, 85, 109, 111, 153, 219
University of Singapore Society (USS), 219–221
University Socialist Club (USC, The Socialist Club), 57–69, 75–76, 188

W

Windmill, 159–160, 170, 173
Winston Churchill, 10, 183

Wong, Ernest, 75–76, 133, 135, 137–138, 143, 145, 147, 220, 221–223
Wong Kan Seng, 186, 190
Woodhull, S., 60, 62–63, 65, 85
World Bank, 99, 101, 261
World War II, 4, 8, 10, 29, 48, 188

Y
Yemen, 145–146
Yeo, George, 176, 205–207, 257–258
Yeo Chee Wee, Michael, 132
Yong Pung How (chief justice), 156–157
Young Men's Christian Association (YMCA), 5–6, 28

About the Authors

Gopinath Pillai was Chairman of the Management Board of the Institute of South Asian Studies, Ambassador-at-Large in the Ministry of Foreign Affairs (2008–2021) and Chairman of the Indian Heritage Centre. He has had a varied career as journalist, teacher, entrepreneur and corporate leader. His business interests include education, logistics and information technology.

He is a distinguished diplomat with over 25 years' experience and was Singapore's longest serving Non-Resident Ambassador to Iran between 1989 and 2008, and also served as Singapore's High Commissioner to Pakistan. He has been involved in organisations connected to social development. He was the Founding Chairman of the NTUC FairPrice Co-operative Limited, Chairman of the Hindu Advisory Board and President of the National University of Singapore Society.

Mr. Pillai has received several awards, including the Friend of Labour and Meritorious Award from NTUC in 1987 and 1990, respectively; Friend of MCD from the Ministry of Community Development in 1998; Friend of IT from Singapore Computer Society in 2001, and Outstanding Service Award from the National University of Singapore in 2015. For his manifold contributions to public service, the Singapore government has awarded him the Public Service Star Award (BBM) in 1999, BBM (BAR) in 2009 and The Meritorious Service Medal in 2015. For his efforts in bridging and advancing Singapore-India relations, the Indian government conferred him with the Padma Shri at the 2012 Republic Day.

John Vater is a writer, literary translator and South Asian Studies scholar. He was a research associate and deputy editor at the Institute of South Asian Studies, Singapore (2019–2022). Mr. Vater was a Fulbright-Nehru Student Researcher in 2014, and was selected as the 'Emerging Translator' from the U.S. in 2018 for the residency at the Banff International Literary Translation Centre (BILTC) in Banff, Canada. He was an artist-in-residence at the North East India Company in 2019 in Assam, India. In 2020, he was selected to participate in the Kautilya Fellows Programme on foreign affairs and public policy hosted by the India Foundation, New Delhi.

As a researcher at ISAS, he wrote on Indian domestic politics, India-Pakistan relations, Nepal, Afghanistan and the wider Indo-Pacific and South Asian region. His essays and translations have appeared in *91st Meridian*, *Words Without Borders*, *Indian Literature Today*, *Ploughshares*, *The Quint*, *The Asian Literary Review*, *Exchanges* and others. He is co-translator of *The Play of Dolls* (Penguin Random House India, 2020), a collection of short stories by Hindi author Kunwar Narain.

Mr. Vater holds a Master of Fine Arts in Literary Translation from the University of Iowa and obtained a Bachelor of Arts with highest distinction in South Asian Studies from the University of Virginia. He received several scholarships and awards for his research and language study in Hindi and Urdu while at both universities.